PLANET PROPERTY

BY PETER BILL

After one look at this planet, any visitor from outer space would say, 'I want to see the manager'
William S Burroughs

ORDER VIA:
WWW.PLANET-PROPERTY.NET

Matador
9 Priory Business Park, Kibworth Beauchamp
Leicestershire LE8 0RX, UK
Tel: (+44) 116 279 2299
Fax: (+44) 116 279 2277
Email: books@troubador.co.uk
Web: www.troubador.co.uk/matador

ISBN
SB: 9781783061266
HB: 9781783061358

British Library Cataloguing in Publication Data.
A catalogue record for this book is available from the British Library.

Copy editing by Studio Ahira.

Printed and bound in the UK by TJ International, Padstow, Cornwall.

Matador is an imprint of Troubador Publishing Ltd.

For

Anna, Emilia, Elsa,
Tom, Kinsa
&
Elizabeth

FOREWORD

Between 1997 and 2012, the £385 billion UK commercial property market was remodelled by globalisation and reshaped by the biggest boom and bust in modern history. An eventful fifteen years, and a drama that I watched largely from the editor's chair at *Estates Gazette*, although latterly from a columnist's soapbox at the *London Evening Standard*.

Why write a book? The main driver was a desire to provide, from the viewpoint of someone with a front-row seat, a basic script of events, a simple plan of the stage, and a short cast list of some leading players – described in a way that would interest novices and experts alike. A concern for posterity and vanity also played their part, of course.

Two relevant books on the property industry have been previously published, the more recent of these in 1992. That was Alastair Ross Goobey's *Bricks and Mortals*, a forensic account of the Eighties property boom and bust. The earlier book was Oliver Marriott's authoritative *The Property Boom*, first published in 1967 and refreshed in 1989. I met Marriott in April 2010; he was encouraging.

A BOOK FELT DUE

Two books, two cycles: a third felt due. The ten-year up-cycle between 1997 and 2007 had been followed in 2007–2009 by the biggest collapse since the Thirties, and the market had just barely recovered by December 2012, when this book draws to a close. The most recent boom and bust cycle – and the scene in which it played out – showed some startling new features, as globalisation changed the market in ways that would have seemed fanciful during previous cycles of the Sixties, Seventies and Eighties. Cheap and plentiful debt provided the usual fuel for the boom. But an unparalleled influx of foreign equity set the market on fire in a way that had never been seen before.

Planet Property aims to provide a picture of this topsy-turvy world. This is a portrait with three purposes: first, to inform and entertain those working in the market; second, as an educative primer for real estate students; third, as a window on an ill-lit scene to help those who simply want to understand how things operate. The picture's frame is defined by what readers of *EG* do for a living: in the main, to fund, develop, hold, buy, sell, broker, value, manage, mend and give professional and legal advice on UK offices, shops, industrial property, tenanted homes and new-build apartments.

NEW BOY

I came fresh to the sector in 1997, joining *EG* after a year in the City and eleven years at *Building* magazine, the last half-dozen as editor. I wasn't especially charmed at first by the inhabitants of Planet Property. It seemed dominated by clubbable males, bound each to the other by old-school ties and/or mutual self-interest. The market still does not stand up terribly well to an outsider's gaze; it remains a male-dominated and semi-enclosed order, a place where who you know can matter as much as what you know. But editing *EG* turned out to be the best job ever.

Real estate is peopled with sharp, stimulating and gregarious folk. Those who reach middling-to-senior positions enjoy a better time than is openly admitted. This is a conclusion based on attending roughly three thousand breakfasts, lunches, cocktail parties and dinners between 1997 and 2012, first as editor of *EG* between May 1998 and February 2009, then as the writer of a weekly column for the magazine since that time and as property columnist for the *London Evening Standard* from 2007. To all those Planet Property dwellers I have met over the years: thank you, for being (mostly) approachable, honest (as possible) and (nearly always) friendly.

Peter Bill
London, June 2013

ACKNOWLEDGEMENTS

Inspiration *for Planet Property* has been drawn from reading the late Alastair Ross Goobey's *Bricks and Mortals* and Oliver Marriott's *The Property Boom*. Information has been drawn from Michael Brett's *Property and Money* and Richard Barkham's *Real Estate and Globalisation,* as well as *Property Auctions* by Clive Carpenter and Susan Harris. Wider intelligence comes from *Back from the Brink* by Alistair Darling, *Anglo Republic: Inside the Bank that Broke Ireland* by Simon Carswell; *The Big Short: Inside the Doomsday Machine* and *Boomerang: The Meltdown Tour* by Michael Lewis, and *Too Big to Fail* by Andrew Ross Sorkin, a matchless account of the events in America that triggered global meltdown.

Thank you to all who contributed to this book. First and foremost, to those who gave interviews – your thoughts greatly help illuminate the text: Louis Armstrong, Alan Carter, Ian Coull, Richard Cotton, James Darkins, Jeremy Helsby, Ian Henderson, Alastair Hughes, Sir George Iacobescu, Richard Lay, Sir Stuart Lipton, Ian Marcus, David Marks, Andy Martin, Neil Mitchenall, Martin Moore, Raymond Mould, Liz Peace, Robert Peto, Tony Pidgley, Sir John Ritblat, Gerald Ronson, Francis Salway, Lord (Wilf) Stevenson, Mike Strong, Nick Thomlinson, Patrick Vaughan and Ian Womack.

My thanks to those who have either checked text, provided information or helped with suggestions in the period since the idea for the book was born in 2007. Most contributed knowingly, some unknowingly, typically coming up with an idea worth pinching over lunch or a drink. These include: Lizzie Bill, Roger Bright, Sue Brown, John Burns, Julia Cahill, Christian Candy, Nick Candy, Alan Collett, Stuart Corbyn, Ian Cullen, Richard Donnell, Alistair Elliott, Sara Fox, Susan Freeman, Fenella Gentleman, Alison Henry, Tony Key, Bob Kidby, Roger Madelin, John Martin, Bill Maxted, Gary Murphy, Rupert Nabarro, Phillip Nelson, Greg Nicholson, Mark Preston, David Pretty, John Rigg, Melville Rodrigues, Jackie Sadek, Ian Selby, Irvine Sellar, Toby Shannon, Ken Shuttleworth, Kasia Sielewicz, Mike Slade, Michael Stancombe, Alistair Subba Row and Hans Vrensen.

Thanks to everyone at *EG* for making it easy for me to spend so much time out and about in the market. I was frequently asked "How do you do you manage to fill the pages every week?" The answer: I didn't. That was done by a team of forty self-motivated and talented journalists who needed little direction. What direction they took came from a team of four editors: deputy editor Julia Cahill and news editor Samantha McClary, who looked after "the front of the book", Stacey Meadwell, in charge of regional coverage, and legal editor Sarah Jackman. Thanks also to *EG* editor Damian Wild for his support and generous access to the archives.

Final thanks must go to Kate Ahira, the meticulous and matchless editor of *Planet Property*.

A STORY IN THREE-AND-A-BIT PARTS

THE PLAY
The first three chapters form a three-act drama, dealing firstly with the greatest crash in modern history, between 2007 and 2009, secondly with the long, slow boom that began in 1997 and ended in 2007, and thirdly with the primal force that drove the market up then down again – money.

THE STAGE
Another trio: chapters four and five provide a student guide to the structure of the market and to how money is made and lost; chapter six describes for students of government how the property world has handled the changing political and planning agenda over fifteen years.

THE PLAYERS
The actors are more important than either the stage or the play, and this section of the book contains six chapters. Chapter seven surveys big developers, while eight profiles those who dared think big. Nine reviews the complex history of the agent community; ten the residential development market; and eleven the close-knit auction community. The penultimate chapter covers the great estates of London.

ENCORE
A glance over the market as it stands in mid 2013, with some reflections on the 2009–2012 recovery, the scourging of the banks, and finally some parting words of wisdom from those who have seen it all before.

A STORY IN THREE-AND-A-BIT PARTS

CONTENTS

THE PLAY

THE PLAY

CHAPTER ONE
BANG

Dear God, just let there be one more property boom.
I promise I won't piss it all away this time
Harvey Soning, property veteran

Let's start with a yarn from John Rigg of Savills, a tale too good to check. Picture the scene: it's January 2007, and an American-born property financier employed by a global bank in London is lazing on a Caribbean beach. Let's call him Hank. His mobile tinkles, and a glance at the screen reveals it's his feckless brother Art calling from California. Hank answers, expecting to be dunned for another handout. Instead the out-of-work actor gives his sibling some "great news": he's bought a house. "How the hell did you manage to raise the money?" asks Hank. "Easy," Art explains: "The broker got me a hundred percent mortgage."

Passing over the obvious question – how you qualify for a mortgage without having a regular job – the puzzled banker moves on: "But you don't have a steady income to make the repayments." "Oh, that doesn't matter," answers Art insouciantly, "I'm not going to pay. The broker said it would take them at least nine months to evict me. Which is great – I get to live rent-free till fall!" he laughs, adding: "All of my friends are doing the same." At this, banker Hank jerks upright on his lounger, alarmed. "Why are you telling me this?" he asks. "Well, I thought you might like to know," says Art. "Your bank is providing the loans." The great property bang of 2007–2009 began with whispers such as these.

SUB-PRIME? WHAT'S SUB-PRIME?

ALASTAIR HUGHES, THEN CHIEF EXECUTIVE FOR EMEA AT JONES LANG LASALLE:

I did a TV interview with a US-based financial channel at MIPIM in March 2007. I was told the first question was going to invite me to canter round the European property markets, so I didn't feel particularly nervous. Instead the first question was: "No doubt you'll have noticed yesterday there was a meltdown in the sub-prime market in the US. What implication will that have for European property?" I had heard the word "sub" and I had heard the word "prime", but never in that order.

So I started drivelling on about the market, saying that as it stood it felt okay because there was quite a lot of demand and no supply. She said: "Yeah, but sub-prime: what impact?" I still hadn't worked out what the hell it was, so I answered a different question. She asked for the third time, by which time I had worked out sub-prime wasn't a good thing, and I could easily have said: "Ah, it will just wash away" – and would have been horrified to see that over and over again, given the fact that it kind of broke the world in half.

I think I managed to say: "Well, anything that affects America will eventually affect Europe. But here and now..." and went back to my script. So I just about got away with it, but it was a pretty alarming moment. I then spoke to a lot of people that day and evening to check I hadn't missed something. And I would say eighty percent of the people had never heard of "sub-prime". And the twenty percent who had heard of it thought it was something to do with lending too much money to Hicksville, America, to buy trailers and they probably shouldn't have been buying them. That was the first time I remember hearing little alarm bells.

2005–2006: COASTING ALONG IN DENIAL

Alarm bells had in fact been ringing since 2005, forewarning of what turned out to be the biggest property collapse in modern history. In May of that year, the Bank of England gently raised an eyebrow at the mounting level of commercial property debt. Outstanding loans had jumped from £76 billion in 2002 to reach £122 billion in 2005, amounting to ten percent of total lending – the same percentage it had been in 1973 and in 1990, as the Bank pointed out without actually saying "Stop". And that was only the official figure. The authoritative De Montfort survey of seventy or more UK and foreign lenders showed the real number in 2005 to be nearer £172 billion, up from £100 billion just three years earlier.

There was little that the Bank could do to control money flooding into property, especially from abroad. Irish banks were lending like there was no tomorrow. Other foreign banks were doing the same. British banks simply ignored the Old Lady in Threadneedle Street. De Montfort showed the level of new loans granted jumping from £25 billion in 2002, up to £44 billion in 2004, before leaping to almost £70 billion in 2005.

By then, incautious lenders had begun advancing cash on the "value" of the property, rather than the price paid. On 11th June 2005, a leader in *EG* – where I was then editor – took its lead from that raised eyebrow at the Bank of England as well as from a more explicit warning given by William Newsom, head of valuation at Savills.

Collective Madness

Clear and present dangers exist for banks and valuers: for banks, the danger is lending on value, rather than price paid... an issue that comes into focus this week because the head of valuation at Savills has criticised banks for incautious lending in a market where prices may have peaked. The practice is an old bull-market game. The over-friendly valuer calls the open market value of Fawlty Tower at £20m. The over-clever buyer will say to his bank, "I'm doing an off-market deal and only paying £18m." The overanxious lender will write a cheque for 90% of £20m – 100% of the £18m purchase price.

Last year, UK banks increased lending by 48% to £44bn, according to a study by De Montfort University. This year, 95% say they are "seeking to increase" the size of their loan books. Are they completely crazy?... There is a collective madness at work here: a madness driven by a desire for market share, a madness rooted in bankers' bonus systems that reward the volume of money lent rather than the performance of the loan. Will this madness evaporate? Eventually, yes. But the sheer weight of money bearing down on the sector, and the prospect of lower interest rates, mean sanity may return later rather than sooner...

The madness intensified in the second half of 2005, reaching a point where the entire market was engulfed in cash, pushing prices higher and higher. A November 2005 *EG* leader warned: "The current market is now a scramble with the cautious selling to the incautious – who then find the bet has paid off when they flip the deal, so leaving the cautious flummoxed."

Valuers were flummoxed as well: with prices rising so fast, they were struggling to ensure that year-end valuations reflected the current market. Richard Batten, who was then joint senior partner at King Sturge, warned: "The weight of money is still driving yields down. So valuers have to ensure that values issued in December are in line with deals being done at the time." Hermes property chief Rupert Clarke added: "Valuers can't do a valuation on December 1st as it will be out of date by the 31st."

Greg Nicholson, chair of capital markets at CB Richard Ellis, warned that the "unprecedented" market would make 2006 a year when "one will be able to measure how good valuers are". But that year, valuers could only follow the market upwards. The IPD capital values index for offices is a measure of how values move in the investment market, which is largely office-based. IPD collects data on around £150 billion worth of UK property from major companies and institutions. In 2006, the index jumped up by seventeen percent, after a much steadier rise of ten percent in 2005.

In 2006, the warnings intensified but continued to be ignored – even one from Hank Paulson, then boss of Goldman Sachs and later to become, as US treasury secretary, the man charged with cleaning up the mess. In April 2006, he warned Goldman bankers to curb their enthusiasm for property. Conversations with agents and developers during the spring of 2006 took on a darker tone; worry over escalating prices began to be expressed by many, but not in public. This *EG* leader published on 22nd April 2006 reflects that private mood:

Darker and Scarier

The accelerating rise in capital values, as tracked by the Investment Property Databank indices, has seen sentiment shift from bemused but grateful acceptance last autumn to a darker and scarier feel of an investment market now detached from the reasonable view that markets go down as well as up.

IPD judged in the month of March that capital values rose by 1.6% across its £40bn balanced universe of commercial property. Compound that up for the next nine months and you get a 15.5% rise on top of the 3.1% in the first quarter. In other words, capital values could rise by nearly 19% in 2006.... Now, that 19% figure is not a forecast – simply an extrapolation.

But the rise does look likely to again confound the 37 forecasters from the Investment Property Forum who, on 18 February, had a consensus forecast for capital growth in 2006 of 5.7%.... But it is not hard to hope that the IPF forecasters turn out to be right. If only because continued yield compression is also becoming a source of fear rather than wonderment.

The Jones Lang LaSalle prime yield figures published on 8 April showed the all-property yield at a record low of 4.71%. The office prime yield has fallen from just under 6% to around 4.75% in 12 months; sheds are down from 6.5% to

5.5%; and retail from 5% to just under 4.5%... there is talk in the retail sector of parks being offered at yields of 3%.

Is the world going crackers?... Yields have fallen so low it is more profitable to stick the money into an Abbey e-saver account, which currently yields 5.05%. Will capital values continue to rise? Nobody, frankly, has a clue. But it does not require much detective work to discover the prime driver: the lending banks. Only when they curb their enthusiasm for property will the acceleration of values slow. Right now, there is not a sign of that happening.

Despite some worries, bankers were desperately competing to lend. Even Rothschild was keen to promote its services: in June 2006, this most discreet of banks went so far as to advertise its real estate services in *EG*. "It takes a great deal of boldness and a great deal of caution to make a great fortune," opined the bank in the advert, quoting the wisdom of founder Nathan Mayer Rothschild (1777–1836). "And when you have got it, it requires ten times more wit to keep it."

Few showed much wit over the coming year, with the exception of DTZ's head of research, Joe Valente. Each year, the agent assembles statistics tracking the flows of money into and out of real estate. On 28th June 2006, its annual *Money into Property* research was presented to three hundred clients over lunch at the Dorchester hotel. Valente revealed that UK purchases in 2005 had outstripped sales by £70 billion, triple the gap in the previous year – meaning that £70 billion of additional debt and equity had been raised to buy property in a single year. "Is this a bubble?" asked Valente rhetorically of a startled audience. "No," he concluded. "But it's the top of the market." The DTZ researcher, who later went on to work at JP Morgan, rather spoiled the moment by adding, "At the moment, we believe investing in property is risk-free."

But the words were out: someone with credence had called the top of the market, even though it was twelve months early. I mentioned Valente's presentation in *EG*, then added as an afterthought: "This week two young men, unscarred by memories of a downturn, persuaded an Icelandic bank to put up much of the £175 million needed to buy the Middlesex Hospital site in the West End – three acres that more experienced bidders felt was worth no more than £150 million. The fortunes of Nick and Christian Candy will be followed with a mixture of admiration and trepidation..."

Why did I say that? Because I'd just met a stunned under-bidder at the DTZ lunch. He could not get over the price paid – or the wonderful job the brothers has done in presenting their bid. The deal would collapse in late 2008 along with the Candys' backer, Icelandic bank Kaupthing. But back in 2006, wise heads were beginning to think of drawing in their horns.

FRANCIS SALWAY, CHIEF EXECUTIVE OF LAND SECURITIES 2004–2012:

I think the danger signs came in 2006. There were one or two instances where people failed to sell high-profile assets, and then re-financed them at very high loan-to-value ratios. That to me was quite a warning sign. What that tells you is that the market has shown there wasn't a buyer at that price. But the banks still advanced even higher loans, as though there would be. So owners were able to take out an awful lot of capital through refinancing, even though they didn't deliver a true sale.

During 2006 we were aware that we were finding it increasingly hard to find value in the market. We couldn't find many properties that would generate a return above our cost of capital. We began to sell a bit. But we were holding back on a number of sales until the REIT legislation came in in January 2007, which would remove capital gains tax liabilities. In the first quarter of 2007, we started selling some secondary retail warehouse assets.

What came over was that investor demand was weakening and pricing was already falling away. So we sold at ten to twelve percent below book valuation, when the indices were saying the market was still rising. We also sold Devonshire House in Mayfair, which used to be Land Secs' headquarters. That went for a yield of under four percent. And we sold a shopping centre we had just completed in Canterbury for a yield of just over four percent. We certainly made some good sales.

LOUIS ARMSTRONG, RICS CHIEF EXECUTIVE 1998–2010:

I was at a conference in America in early 2006, where I was speaking, and the speaker before me warned of the dangers of securitising loans: "Gentleman, we have learned nothing in five hundred years. The current financial engineering is the same as the medieval alchemists claiming they have turned base metal into gold. I have been in this business thirty-five years. But the incredibly ingenious, opaque, complex instruments invented by the smartest blokes on Wall Street are so opaque that I can't understand them. If I don't, there is no hope. This will all end in tears."

A mood of caution appeared within weeks of Valente's pronouncement that the market had peaked. At meeting after meeting between late June and late August of 2006, off-the-record comments from the agent community were becoming gloomier. Oddly enough, during that time *EG* was invited to lunch in the private dining rooms of both Goldman Sachs and Lehman Brothers to meet with their European real estate bosses. Lovely wine, and butler service – both organisations had previously tended to treat journalists as outcasts.

Why the hospitality? In hindsight, I can think of only three explanations. One, the marketing departments at both banks pressed the reluctant real estate chiefs to meet with the press to generate more publicity, in order to generate more work. Two, the real estate bosses were getting twitchy and wanted to know what others were telling us – which seems unlikely. Three, neither of the above; it was just a coincidence.

"The party is not over, but ending" summed up the mood in the autumn of 2006 among those with experience of the Nineties crash. Not a single figure wanted to be seen publicly spitting in the punchbowl. But the mood shift can be sensed by comparing the forward-looking statements uttered by Land Securities in November 2005 and then in November 2006.

Land Securities presented its interim results for the six months to September 2005 in November. The talk was of "exceptional activity" and "exploiting scale" and the "forward pipeline". Twelve months on, the presentation contained no such boasts, despite glowing figures. A profit of £1.2 billion was reported, even after swallowing a £293 million loss on the sale of property management company Trillium.

Chairman Peter Birch and chief executive Francis Salway struck a more cautious note in a joint statement accompanying the 2006 interims: "After an extended period when buyers of commercial property investments significantly outnumbered sellers, we are moving closer to equilibrium conditions, with less parties bidding for investments and an increasing number of properties being marketed for sale. This is likely to herald an end to yield compression." This was code for "It's over".

But it can be hard to spot the warnings, can't it? Nevertheless, there were signs back in 2006, as Francis Salway noted (see page five). And it was not just the chief executive of Britain's largest property firm who was getting concerned. In July and August, the mood among his peer group during off-the-record lunches and on-the-record results meetings was becoming cautious. But how to capture the change of sentiment? This jokey *EG* leader from early September 2006 fails to show how serious things were becoming:

Some Harassed Talk at the Top Table

There is a cautious subtext to the pronouncements of the chief executives of the businesses that have announced their results in recent weeks. But perhaps the best way to get a fix on the current odd mood is to imagine a conversation with a financial PR adviser tasked with putting together a public statement for one of the companies.

Property Boss: "We've had another stonking six months. Current trading is fine. But, for heaven's sake, this has been going on for 10 years. It has got to stop soon."

Financial PR: "Why is that, sir? You're still steaming along. I can do a really good spin on these numbers!"

Property Boss: "Well, don't. I can feel it in my water. The party is ending. I've been around a long time, you know!"

Financial PR (sighing): "As you wish. What do you want the headlines to say?"

Property Boss: "Well, let's forget all the usual 'poised to exploit growth' guff. And, for heaven's sake, bury the stuff on the ditched plans to move into the US market. What I want to convey is that we are an utterly sound and focused

business, not given to wild adventures, with sensible and realistic plans to con-
serve shareholder value."

Financial PR: "This doesn't sound very exciting, sir. The City doesn't like dull."

Property Boss: "It's not bloody well meant to sound exciting, you fool. I'm sick
and tired of excitement. For 10 years this business has done nothing but grow.
I've given the City my blood and all it ever wants is more. Stuff 'em. All the
chaps at the dining club think we've seen the best of the market. So it must be
true. Mustn't it?"

Yet on went the party. The cautious chaps in the dining clubs feared
the end was near, but those drunk on debt roared on regardless. The final *EG*
leader of the year was headlined "2006: Stubbornly Refusing to Go Wrong".
Those looking for a barometer of the market were asked to weigh that week's
EG. The magazine and its attendant supplements totalled four hundred and
sixty-six pages. This was not the biggest-ever *EG*; that honour went to the
pre-MIPIM issue in early spring of 2006, a monster that totalled five hundred and twelve pages and weighed a kilogram.

The Estates Gazette Group, which included EGi and *EuroProperty*,
turned over £27 million in 2006 – and made £12 million profit. Revenues
had more than doubled since 1997. Each month the advertising and subscription departments dazedly reported better and better figures. What could
go wrong?

JANUARY 2007–AUGUST 2008: DOWN A STEEP'NING SLOPE

The ten-year boom ended in July 2007. This was a year of two halves: not bad, then quite bad. The IPD capital values index for offices rose five percent in six months to reach a crest of 180 in July. Between July 2007 and September 2008, values dropped by twenty-four percent – an average of 1.7 percent per month. The hope, all the while, was that the bottom would turn out to be a not-that-far-away Happy Valley.

The first real distress signal had come in May 2007, with a sign that showed trouble had been quietly brewing throughout the previous year. Bill Maxted of De Montfort University published a survey of bank lending showing that the value of loans in breach or default had more than tripled between 2005 and 2006, ballooning from £1.2 billion to £4.2 billion.

Sentiment began to turn bearish. In July 2007, RBS chose to market the Grosvenor House hotel in Park Lane for £650 million. (The bank had taken possession of the property in 2003, when the previous owners had gone bust.) But no one wanted to know: a clear signal that the market had peaked. It would take RBS until 31st December 2010 to get the hotel off its books – sold to the Indian Sahara Group for £470 million.

As the market began to slide, there was a dangerous reluctance of valuers to mark down prices. IPD figures showed a reduction in values of just 2.2 percent between June and September 2007, a reading that many considered an underestimate, caused by owners putting pressure on valuers to maintain values. Property companies were fearful that marking down assets would put them in breach of loan-to-value covenants.

Nevertheless, buyers soon started smelling a rat: on 11th August 2007, it was reported in *EG* that institutions had begun to "lose faith" in the values put on properties being offered for sale. The FTSE 100 index plunged seven hundred points that month, before recovering. Pension and life funds started to withdraw from the market. Frustrated agents reported that the UK's largest property fund, Prupim, was "stalling, chipping or pulling out of deals and bids".

The sale of the three-hundred-thousand-square-foot Palestra office block in Southwark by Royal London and Mallory Clifford for £210 million fell through after the US buyer pulled out. Rows over values kept breaking out; deals were collapsing everywhere. In early November, DTZ director Robert Peto decided to speak out. The occasion was the Royal Institution of Chartered Surveyors valuation faculty annual conference at the Royal Society of Medicine, north of Oxford Street.

ROBERT PETO, DIRECTOR OF DTZ:

The defining moment of my career was in November 2007 at the annual RICS valuation conference in London. As head of the RICS valuation faculty, my job was to tell valuers what I thought we were facing. I unloaded both barrels and said, "Guys, you are bringing us into disrepute. If you go on ignoring what's actually happening in the marketplace, everybody will be the loser."

I said values had fallen by at least ten percent since the summer and not the 2.5 percent being reported by the Investment Property Data-bank. I said it has to be at least ten percent. Did I believe it was ten percent? No, more. But there was a degree of politics involved. If I'd said the fall from the summer was twenty percent – which it proba-bly was... You will lose your credibility if you take an extreme posi-tion; people will just think you are a bit of a loony.

By November 2007, it was clear that the numbers of transactions were falling and prices were being chipped. It had actually started before August 2007. In certain areas – like secondary retail ware-housing – the slide began in January 2007. But at the time, if you wanted to sell, you just phoned New Star: because they had lots of money and they just kept buying stuff.

But people were beginning to sell. And you can't have what was go-ing on in the marketplace not being reflected in the values. You have to mark prices to the current market values; you don't mark them to some airy-fairy number. But part of the problem was that as deals slowed to a halt, valuers were saying they didn't have transaction evidence to mark to market. That was the moment when the word "sentiment" became a dominant feature. It is permissible to value in accordance with sentiment. There is nothing in the Red Book that stops you doing it. People think the Red Book is all about compara-bles – mostly, yes, but it's not the driving force.

EARLY 2008: NOT A PROPER RECESSION

The mood was strangely benign in early 2008. Property stocks were still holding up. Land Securities' share price opened the year at around £14.50 and was still over £14 in early September. The mood was thus: "Well, we've grown fat over the past decade. The downturn will make us leaner, healthier and more cautious. This correction will be good for the industry. By spring or summer, it will have bottomed out."

That was the tenor of many a conversation I had between January and March 2008. A business confidence survey published by the CBI and GVA Grimley in January that year suggested that half of all occupiers intend-ed to increase the amount of space they rented. The feeling was the "correc-tion" had maybe another ten percent to go, at most.

So this was a good time for "opportunity" funds to buy distressed as-sets, wasn't it? Well, no, as it turned out, but at the time many did think so: American vulture funds darkened the sky that spring. Even the very respect-able fund manager Fidelity said that now was the time to invest.

Even so, in early 2008, everyone was nervously looking at everyone else, trying to determine what would happen next. On 31st January, some six hundred and fifty anxious seekers after truth crowded into the TUC head-quarters in Holborn for the annual presentation by property data specialist

IPD. The audience was twice that in any normal year. What did they hear? That values would plunge until spring, level out, then rise gently until December, leaving them roughly where they had been in January. That was the conclusion of IPD.

"When I were a lad, we had proper recessions," joked Dennis Turner, chief economist of HSBC, in a brilliant speech. "This is a correction, not a crash." The audience left, vaguely reassured. The following week I had lunch with Martin Moore, the levelheaded boss of Prupim, the biggest real estate fund of them all. Afterwards, as we walked up Chancery Lane, I asked him as an afterthought if he thought it was time to start buying.

He said yes. Would he mind saying so in print, I asked. Fine. Moore told *EG* that he saw "green shoots in the UK market. We certainly think the worst is behind us. As a whole, property is now at fair value." The man running funds containing £18 billion of real estate was not some outlier. Far from it: he was just retailing what was at that time the view of even the most cautious of fund managers.

What happened to Bear Stearns jolted that confidence. The eighty-five-year-old US investment bank unravelled and collapsed between Monday 10th March and Friday 14th March – coincidentally the week of the MIPIM property jamboree in Cannes. Each year at the fair, Harvey Soning of James Andrew International holds a jammed party at the Majestic Hotel. That year, the property veteran gave me a mug emblazoned with the following prayer: *Dear God, just let there be one more property boom. I promise I won't piss it all away this time.*

For Ian Marcus, the collapse of the American investment bank was his "Oh, shit!" moment. The head of real estate banking at Credit Suisse at the time says that "the writing was on the wall when Bear Stearns went in March 2008. Because there were enough organisations run in a similar style that you sort of think: unless they were complete crooks or completely stupid, neither of which is the case, then why should this just be a one-off?"

ALASTAIR HUGHES, THEN CHIEF EXECUTIVE FOR EMEA AT JONES LANG LASALLE:

We started out 2008 with reasonable optimism; by the end we were very pessimistic. For me the big turning point was MIPIM in March 2008. All the European property industry went there thinking it was one of these things that we just shrug off. We came back from that really worried, because MIPIM was full of bankers and Bear Stearns visibly shook them. Several bankers told me that this was really serious. I'm a member of an investment agents club; we invited some top investment banking people along and we just sat there in stunned silence as this very senior guy just quietly explained what the implications were.

The mood darkened. The best-known Irish investor admitted something was amiss. Derek Quinlan had built up an €11 billion property empire serviced by two hundred and fifty employees in Quinlan Private. The King Midas of Irish property later lost his golden touch, then his empire. But at the time his spokesman said: "There has been a bit of restructuring and eight or nine people are being let go. However, we have two hundred and fifty people in the group and we will be hiring in specialised areas. The company is continuing to raise funds and to invest."

An observer was more frank. "They are making the cuts because of the state of the financial markets. The excesses of the last few years are now coming back to haunt a lot of people." May saw a series of darker turns. De Montfort reported at the end of 2007 that the total amount of loans in danger of default stood at around £20 billion, while the level of outstanding debt was £250 billion, up from £200 billion in 2006.

Martin Gudgeon, head of restructuring at private equity giant Blackstone, said: "There are early signs of distress coming into the real estate market." The banks began to get tough. More and more loans were falling into default as prices declined and loan-to-value covenants were breached. The wholesale transfer of well over £100 billion of land and property into the hands of the banks commenced in earnest in May 2008.

Developers began firing staff. On 5th July 2008, *EG* reported: "The commercial development world is bracing itself for a level of job losses not witnessed since the early 1990s crash." Scottish Miller Developments, Irish Ballymore and English Rok Development all announced plans for office closures and redundancies.

Schemes started to be shelved. In August, British Land announced that the seven-hundred-and-forty-foot Cheesegrater skyscraper at 20 Leadenhall in the City of London would be put on hold until 2012 – an accurate forecast by chief executive Stephen Hester, as it turned out. Right next door, the owners of the site of what was intended to become the City's tallest tower – at nine hundred and forty-five feet – admitted they couldn't persuade anyone to lend them the necessary £600 million: consequently the Pinnacle remained stalled until late 2012.

SIR PHILIP GR**N

It's September 2008, the week before Lehman Brothers collapses. The phone rings in my office: "Can you take a call from Sir Philip Green?" Er... yes, okay. "'Oooo the f***ing 'ell do you think you are?" roars the Croydon-born king of the rag trade. "You know the square root of f*** all!" I recall at the moment he shouted it thinking momentarily that this was a very good line from an expert in vilification. I'd written an article in the *Evening Standard* on 5th September that had clearly failed to amuse.

The head of the Arcadia Group, which operated brands like Bhs, Topshop and Dorothy Perkins from some two thousand, three hundred retail outlets, had just returned from cruising round the Med on his £32 million boat, *Lionheart*, where he had been snapped with Kate Moss and Sylvester Stallone. The tirade continued for a few minutes.

I reverted to a technique I'd learned the hard way: stay silent. Eventually, the person delivering the tirade begins to wonder if you have hung up. They gradually slow down, leaving you room to interject. Don't. In the end, they trail to a halt, leaving the abused smiling (well, in theory). He stopped.

I thanked him for his views in a shaky voice and gently put the phone down. But I was not smiling; I was shaking. It was a horrible experience, not lessened by later learning that I'd shared it with many others.

What Sir Philip had objected to was the larky and landlord-friendly tone I'd taken in the *Evening Standard* article, which discussed a letter he had sent to the British Property Federation in August. Retailers were under huge pressure as the retail market slid into steep decline, and Sir Philip was taking up the cudgel on behalf of the British Retail Consortium. He wrote to British Property Federation president and Land Securities chief executive Francis Salway, complaining of high service charges and rip-off building insurance commissions.

But what had caught the headlines was his demand that landlords accept just one month's rent in advance, in place of the usual ninety days'. Salway deflected Sir Philip's arguments with the expertise of *Yes, Minister's* Sir Humphrey Appleby: "A small number of retailers have raised the monthly rents issue on new lettings," he said. "A number of owners have been prepared to allow tenants in real financial difficulty to move to monthly rents to ease cash flow. However, it is a different story when you are talking about a successful retailer that is making hundreds of millions of pounds of profit," added Salway, pointing unmistakably at Sir Philip. "Why should you transfer value from one set of shareholders to another when you have an existing contract?" This was a view that had informed an *EG* leader on 30th August 2008, written a week before the *Evening Standard* article:

Green Envy Undermines Rent Debate

The weighty name of Sir Philip Green of Arcadia Group was used in late July by the British Retail Consortium to fan the embers of an old campaign to persuade landlords to abandon quarterly in advance rental payments in favour of a once a month cheque. Since then, the man who owns Bhs and Topshop – and is landlord of a few properties himself – has enjoyed a holiday on his £32m yacht Lionheart in the Med, keeping company with Kate Moss and Sylvester Stallone, and, understandably otherwise occupied, has said little. But on 20 August, Green weighed in on the topic with a letter sent to leading retail landlords.

Sir Philip says he wants an "open and honest conversation" with regard to the "existing archaic leasing and rent review structure". Not just on the practice of payments being made on the ancient quarter days, but also on "rental evidence, service charges and insurance charges". The fight is clearly going to be about more than paying rents 90 days in advance. So, retailers should expect mud to be flung back – how long do you take to pay your suppliers, for instance? None of his landlords will say it to his face, but lying just below the surface is a fierce personal resentment against a billionaire leading a campaign to screw down retailers' costs. If there really were an "open and honest" conversation it would include the phrase: "Why on earth should I subsidise the gaudy lifestyle of this particular billionaire?"

Actually, maybe it was that which annoyed Sir Philip, rather than the *Evening Standard* article (not that I had him down as an *EG* reader). Anyway, he had timed his assault to perfection, had he but known. The collapse of Lehman Brothers came just sixteen days later, plunging a precariously poised retail sector into deeper trouble, unnerving landlords still further. The web was taking more and more traffic from the high street.

Retailer after retailer began to choose the path of company voluntary administration, a legal way of tearing up lease agreements and getting lower rents which infuriated helpless landlords. Sir Philip Green's intervention was a tipping point: before, landlords had been able to hold the line; afterwards, they were forced slowly back from their defensive positions. Sir Philip seemed to back out of the fray as fast as he had entered. So I was surprised to receive a call sometime in 2009 (I can't quite remember when), with the usual preface of "Would you take a call from Sir Philip Green?"

I had already decided to tape the next call from him and keep it for general amusement. I took a few steadying breaths and said: "Hello?" Sir Philip was sweetness itself, presenting merely a mild complaint about some minor point in a story we'd written on Arcadia's search for new offices. He ended by giving me his mobile number and the invitation to call any time. I never did switch the recorder on. Nor call him again, any time.

SEPTEMBER 2008–JUNE 2009: OVER THE CLIFF

The real "Holy shit, we're doomed" period began with the fall of Lehman Brothers in September 2008, ending when the market finally touched bottom in June 2009. During those nine scary months, values fell a further twenty-six percent on top of the twenty-four percent fall between July 2007 and September 2008. That's a monthly average decline of 2.9 percent – the fastest and steepest collapse in living memory, and almost double the monthly fall of 1.7 percent over the preceding fifteen months.

GERALD RONSON, CHIEF EXECUTIVE OF HERON INTERNATIONAL:

We were looking at Armageddon in the last quarter of 2008. If you were sitting on cash, you were scratching your head and saying: what bank is safe? So there was a rush here to open lots of new accounts – with Deutsche Bank, with JP Morgan, and with a whole range of banks. We're not a big company, but Heron had something like £140 million of cash, and I suppose my family office had not too dissimilar a sum.

At that point, I was thinking to myself: we don't want more than £5 million and a maximum of £10 million with any one bank. Then of course you've got the people who owed the banks hundreds of millions of pounds. Some of them thought that that was the bank's problem, not theirs. I spoke to some of them, saying, "You don't seem to be particularly worried" – to which their answer was: "Let the f***ing bank worry."

Lehman Brothers filed for bankruptcy protection at 1.45am on the morning of Monday 15th September in a New York court. Less than twenty-four hours earlier, Bank of America had rescued Merrill Lynch when the latter was teetering close to bankruptcy – a situation for which the drop in value of Merrill's real estate mortgage portfolio was blamed. That same evening, the US government was forced to bail out insurance giant AIG, by providing an $85 billion overdraft in exchange for eighty percent of the company.

The AIG rescue had been made necessary by a disastrous foray into insuring almost $450 billion of credit default swaps. Exactly what these might be eludes wiser men than me, but the underlying value of such credit derivatives lay in these two sets of initials: RMBSs, or residential mortgage backed securities, and their siblings CMBSs, or commercial mortgage backed securities. In other words, plummeting property values had nearly destroyed one of the largest companies in the world.

America's two largest mortgage lenders, Freddie Mac and Fannie Mae, had been rescued two months earlier. The pair either owned or guaranteed almost half the mortgages in America, and the US government had been forced to take responsibility for more than $5 trillion of debt set against property on which prices were plunging. The price of an average home in the US fell by a third between 2007 and 2008. The US Moody's/REAL commercial property price index dropped ten percent between its peak in July 2007 and the edge of the Lehman Brothers cliff in September 2008. Prices then collapsed, halving over the next nine months, before hitting bottom in June 2009, simultaneously with UK values.

IAN COULL, THEN CHIEF EXECUTIVE OF SEGRO:

The week of 15th September 2008 was the most extraordinary week of my life; I happened to be in New York at a property conference organised by Merrill Lynch. Lehman's had gone bust; Merrill was taken over by Bank of America; AIG very nearly went bust. The financial world felt it was in meltdown.

Until that week, I was in the camp of thinking of June 2007 to August 2008 as being pretty tough. We had seen values falling probably more than I expected. But it looked like it was stabilising, it looked like we had got through the worst of it. The general feeling until then was: this isn't as bad as we feared, so our occupiers are still going to be there.

There were fifty or so property company chiefs at Merrill's offices over two days, along with a hundred or so investors. The mood was one of total amazement at the speed of events. I came down for breakfast and saw an American real estate guy I knew and said: "Have you seen the FT this morning?" He said: "No, I'm not interested in that; it's yesterday's news."

Every hour there was a new revelation that just shocked us. People were feeling suicidal. Everybody had travelled to the New York conference feeling we were through the worst – then suddenly these cataclysmic changes were occurring. I sat on a couple of panels; I talked to a lot of investors who were also shocked at what was going on. People were shell-shocked that week.

The position in the UK was equally precarious. The government a year earlier had rescued Northern Rock, after the former building society's incautious lending to the buy-to-let sector turned sour. Now it was the turn of Bradford & Bingley, another traditionally cautious former building society tempted by the booming buy-to-let market to grant mortgages on precariously high loan-to-value ratios. On 29th September 2008, the government announced its rescue of the Bradford & Bingley. The bank's hundred and ninety-seven branches were sold for £612 million to Abbey (later Santander), while the mortgage book remained in government hands.

But this was only a sideshow. Two days after Lehman Brothers collapsed, HBOS warned the government it was experiencing much higher levels of withdrawals than was usual. The bank had seen thirty-five percent of its stock market value wiped out on 16th September, the day after Lehman went. Chancellor Alistair Darling says in his memoirs: "HBOS had the look of Northern Rock about it. There was a grave risk we would end up having to take on another, much larger and more complex wreck of a bank."

Lloyds TSB was already mulling a takeover of HBOS, so Darling and his prime minister, Gordon Brown, gave it a push. A deal was announced on 17th September. Eight days later, the chancellor took a call from RBS chief executive (then Sir) Fred Goodwin saying that conditions were "very bad". Three weeks after that, on 13th October, Brown announced a bailout for both banks: £20 billion for RBS and £17 billion for Lloyds, in return for shares. Hey, presto! The taxpayer owned eighty-two percent of RBS and forty-three percent of the combined Lloyds/HBOS business, Lloyds Banking Group.

NICK THOMLINSON, SENIOR PARTNER AT KNIGHT FRANK SINCE 2004:

I can remember being on summer holiday in August 2008, worrying this was the year it was going to slow down. We had already begun to reduce costs: it wasn't just people, but all the marketing side of things that runs away with you in the good years. We put a clamp on opening new offices. I think by then we probably thought a slowdown was inevitable. Then I went on my wedding anniversary break to St Tropez in September. We were in a hotel, totally oblivious to what was going on in the rest of the world – until I saw a paper on the breakfast table, probably the International Herald Tribune, *with a headline saying: "Lehman's Collapses". And the rest, as they say, is well-documented history...*

Everywhere, the world just stopped. September, October, November, December: no one did anything. "If we've any money left in the bank, we're certainly not going to go and spend it" was the view. So we moved very quickly to cut costs: in the end we cut just under twenty percent. Yes, it was mainly people, sadly, but it was also a frightening amount of waste which had crept in, and things that were jolly nice to have and nice to do. Frankly, you suddenly realised you didn't need to do them. If you were making people redundant, it would have been positively obscene to take clients out for expensive meals. Even if you wanted to, which we didn't, it would have looked utterly wrong – and it's frightening how much money you can save by not doing so.

The prime driver of the destructive fear that swept round the globe that autumn was of course property: more precisely, over-leveraged property. Those who had borrowed £80 to buy something worth £100 found themselves with something worth £60. The financial world cracked on its sinking real estate foundations. The impact on the UK and continental European real estate markets was immediate and catastrophic.

Property venture after property venture collapsed. More and more land, half-built developments and over-leveraged investment stock fell into the hands of the banks. A fresh and larger wave of layoffs swept through the major agents and property companies. By then, the rot had spread around the globe. "After September 2008, all the EMEA markets became seriously affected," says Jones Lang LaSalle's Alastair Hughes, "apart from Dubai and Russia. Russia was big business for us – then Russia just went. All international investment capital headed for the hills; all international occupiers stalled all decisions. Very shortly after that, Dubai went."

The global losses are impossible to calculate. Hundreds of billions of dollars' worth of equity was extinguished. A single Morgan Stanley global property fund with assets once worth $8.8 billion was facing a $5.4 billion loss by 2010. Barry Gilbertson, former president of the Royal Institution of Chartered Surveyors, was part of the PricewaterhouseCoopers administration team that entered Lehman Brothers' European headquarters in Canary Wharf the day the bank collapsed. He gave an initial estimate of Lehman Brothers' property assets: the fifty-strong property team was supposedly tending £8.3 billion of real estate in the UK and southern Europe. This figure included the £833 million Northern Rock commercial loan book, acquired when the former building society collapsed in 2007. "We bought that on the basis that we could sell it on," said a former Lehman banker. "But we just couldn't. We didn't get any of it away."

The administrators discovered the bank had taken majority equity stakes in more than a hundred property deals, including large stakes in the Spanish residential market, between November 2006 and September 2008. Two months after making that initial estimate of £8.3 billion, Pricewater-houseCoopers in effect marked Lehman's property assets down to zero. "On a property investment geared with a debt of eighty percent a twenty percent fall in asset values might reduce the equity to nil," it reported, adding that values had fallen twenty-five percent.

Even bigger problems emerged in Iceland. In 2006–2007, the rocky island was rumoured to be "the biggest washing machine for Russian money in the world". Not that this turned out to be true – the rumours flew simply because no one could figure out the prime source of the cash. Some of it turned out to be British. In early October 2008, Kaupthing bank collapsed, shortly followed by the rest of the Icelandic economy.

The immediate fallout in the UK was the call-in of a £175 million loan granted to Nick and Christian Candy for the development of the Middlesex Hospital site in London. The bank also lost millions on a $500 million development of two hundred and fifty-two luxury flats on Wilshire Boulevard in Beverley Hills, being developed in partnership with the Candys.

Kaupthing's administrators kept the rump of the UK operations going. Much later, around the middle of 2012, I had a pleasant chat over dinner with one of its representatives. The meal was to celebrate the start of building work on the Middlesex Hospital redevelopment, on which the bank had done a deal with insurer Aviva and a newish developer run by two more up-and-coming young men, Dan Van Gelder and Clive Bush of Exemplar.

HOW FAR AND HOW FAST?

On 5th November 2008, I chaired a session at the Royal Institution of Chartered Surveyors' annual conference of valuers at the Royal Society of Medicine, the very place where, a year earlier, Robert Peto of DTZ had warned the audience that values needed cutting hard and fast. Nearly two months on from the near-collapse of the banking system, there was more inclination to take a pessimistic view. Prices were in freefall. That week it had emerged that Kaupthing was hoping for only fifty pence in the pound from its assets, and I asked for a show of hands among the two hundred valuers: "How many think values will fall five to ten percent next year?" A few hands. "How about ten to fifteen percent?" More hands. "What about fifteen to twenty percent?" A sea of hands rose.

The consensus in the room was that the bottom of the market was roughly twelve months away, in November 2009, with values halving from the 2007 peak by late 2009. Close: the floor turned out to be seven months away, in June 2009, and the overall drop in values forty-five percent. Deep cuts in interest rates played their part: they fell from 4.5 percent in October 2008 to just 0.5 percent in March 2009.

The mood of the valuers was curious: resigned acceptance of a steep fall, yes, but a consequent confidence that this meant it would be over all the sooner. This glimmer prompted an *EG* leader in November 2008 containing a small spark of optimism, three days after the Royal Institution of Chartered Surveyors' conference and just after the first deep cut in interest rates:

Is a 1.5% Cut Enough to Break the Fall?

... the consensus forecast from a group of valuers is that the peak-to-trough drop in values will be between 45% and 50%. This alarming number relies on the already known fall of almost 25% between the summer of 2007 and this September. It factors in a forecast 5% fall in the last quarter of 2008 – and a further 15-20% fall in 2009 suggested by a deeply unscientific show of hands at the RICS valuation conference on Wednesday.

In one very bleak sense this is good news. This grim prospect is what is stopping banks with loans already submerged by the 25% fall from forcing lenders into liquidation. Best to write down the value of the loan, extend the terms and hang on in there and hope.

After all, there is no shame now. Every single bank is "kitchen sinking" down the price of their real estate loans. The welcome 1.5% drop in interest rates on Thursday may break the fall. The stock market feels less jittery. The distressed debt funds are rubbing their hands. The odd brave buyer can be spotted bargain hunting.

Early 2009 turned out to be the right time to snap up bargains. The year opened with the news that veteran investors Raymond Mould and Patrick Vaughan had bought a block of a hundred and seventy thousand square feet at One Fleet Place in the City for £74 million – at a yield of 7.75 percent. Legal & General had been trying to sell the offices at a reported £100 million for twelve months.

Santander spent £115 million buying the freehold of its own headquarters, two hundred thousand square feet on the Marylebone Road, from British Land. King Sturge partner James Beckham said at the time: "With yields now at historic highs and rents falling steeply... there is now great potential for tenants to buy into ownership at economic levels."

Morrisons felt the same. The supermarket chain spent £120 million purchasing property that it had previously been renting. In March, agent Atis Real (which became BNP Paribas Real Estate) called the bottom of the market, with its investment head Paul Griffiths declaring that yields had stabilised. Of an Atis Real survey suggesting that two-thirds of investors saw the market bottoming out in the next six to nine months, Griffiths said: "The research indicates real optimism within the market and that investors are now seeing opportunities for real estate investment again."

In late January 2009, Helical Bar raised £27 million; chief executive Mike Slade explained why: "We believe that the exceptional market conditions we are currently witnessing will present buying opportunities that arise only once or twice in a property career." But the most compelling evidence of a change of mood came from the auction rooms, when Allsop held a two-day event in London's Cumberland hotel around the middle of February.

The Ocean Suite was overflowing with prospective bidders, and nine-tenths of the four hundred and twenty-eight lots were sold, raising £56 million. Auctioneer Gary Murphy declared: "Property is back. I have only seen a room like this in extreme boom conditions. It is clear buyers perceive that, for the time being, the market has stabilised."

Even so, these were just sunbeams shining through the thunder-clouds. I spent three days in Paris in early February 2009, chairing the Urban Land Institute's annual European conference at the InterContinental hotel. The forty-thousand-strong institute is a US-based organisation filled with WASP-ish American developers and European bankers. Four hundred of them turned up in Paris.

The legendary Gerald Hines was on one panel, while on another was an extraordinarily rude banker from RBS whom I'd been forced to ask to leave my office ten years earlier. An erudite American developer by the name of J Byrne Murphy, formerly of retail outlet specialist McArthur Glenn, also turned up – along with his book, *Le Deal* (published by St Martin's Press). This beautifully written account of McArthur Glenn's struggles in getting a retail centre built in Troyes, to the south-west of Paris, should be required reading for any outsider who might dare to develop in France.

But the main publication of the conference came courtesy of John Forbes, real estate funds partner at PricewaterhouseCoopers. The cycling fanatic had overseen the interviewing of five hundred property bankers and fund managers in the period up to Christmas 2008. Their mood was captured by the title of the resulting research, which was named: *Hunkering Down: Debt Has Vanished, Value Has Been Destroyed and Equity Is Playing a Waiting Game.*

Falling values had by then wrecked the balance sheets of most of the large property companies. The top four saw billions wiped from the credit side of their balance sheets in just a single year. Land Securities' investment properties had been valued at £12.3 billion at the end of March 2008; a year later, largely the same portfolio was valued at just £7.9 billion. After writing off another £800 million, a record loss of £5.2 billion was declared for 2009. Over at British Land, gross assets shrank over the same period from some

£13.5 billion to £8.6 billion, forcing the declaration of a £1.6 billion loss. Hammerson meanwhile took a £1.6 billion hit, and Segro (formerly known as Slough Estates) suffered a £1 billion loss.

The quartet moved fast to repair their balance sheets in 2009. Each created more shares, then sold them at a huge discount to the price of the existing shares. "All the majors were forced into raising capital to prop up their balance sheets," says City analyst Alan Carter. "Hammerson were the first to see it, hotly pursued by Land Securities and British Land and Segro. But they all raised equity at prices which gave away years of value creation. They were forced to sell shares very cheaply. Existing shareholders were furious at the dilution of the value of their holdings."

One PLC failed to do so – Brixton. The industrial property firm paid the price, as Segro swallowed it up for a song that summer. But first, Segro boss Ian Coull had a rights issue to deal with, as he explains: "At Segro, we knew we would come under some pressure if values fell. We had been tracking our debt-to-equity ratio very carefully since the beginning of 2008. Before Lehman's, we felt that we probably would want to have a rights issue in the second half of 2009. We would pick the time we went to the market. When we came back from New York the week of the Lehman collapse, David Sleath and I realised – he was the finance director then – that we were facing a much more serious issue. We started work on the rights issue right away."

By early 2009, industrial property values had fallen thirty-five percent from their July 2007 peak. At the time of the £500 million rights issue by Segro on 4th March 2009, the firm's liabilities stood at a hundred and nineteen percent of asset value. The share price at the time was 75p, but the new shares went on sale at just 10p – the offer was fully subscribed. Gearing fell to seventy-seven percent, and Segro was safe.

As it turned out, Segro was the last to market among the big four property firms. First out of the gate was Hammerson, on 9th February. With its gearing having almost doubled to a hundred and eighteen percent, the office and retail specialist raised £584 million by offering shares at a sixty-two percent discount. Then came British Land on 12th February. The UK's second-biggest property company raised £740 million by selling shares at 225p against the most recent closing price of 468p – close to a fifty percent discount. One week later, Land Securities offered shares at almost exactly the same discount as British Land, raising £755 million. With Segro's new shares also sold, the biggest giveaway sale in property history was over. These rights issues raised altogether over £2.5 billion; the undiscounted value of those shares was over £8 billion.

While this was going on, Hammerson chief executive John Richards organised a dinner for a handful of chief executives from the listed property companies. It was in my honour, because a few weeks earlier I'd announced my intention to retire from *EG* at the end of February 2009. Ian Coull of Segro was among the diners, still working on his rights issue. John Richards was more relaxed, having got his away. As we stood around having drinks, a call came through from Francis Salway of Land Securities. Always the gentleman, he had sent his apologies.

We all knew what was keeping him away, even though his rights issue was supposed to be a secret: the lawyers were clearly keeping him late. My memory of the night is of a mood of hesitant optimism: an odd, unidentifiable feeling among the group that this was its darkest hour and that the worst would soon be over. The next day was cloudy for me; John Richards and I had shared a final bottle of red after the other guests had left. But the earlier mood and the good news from the Allsop auction coloured my penultimate *EG* leader that week:

When the Darkest Clouds Are in the Sky

Fidelity is making cautious noises about buying real estate. That would be nice. But perhaps the brightest little sunbeam emanates from the auction room. Allsop has just experienced packed rooms and high success rates in both commercial and residential sales... but best not get overexcited, for there are plenty of thunderclouds still around.

The stack of property companies announcing rights issues has depressed property stock prices to ridiculously low levels. You could buy Land Securities, Hammerson, British Land and SEGRO for £5.8bn at this week's share prices. These four companies have net assets of £10.8bn, for heaven's sake. In two years' time, those buying the discounted shares may well have a bargain. But, for now, all the City can see is clouds.

The clouds soon began to clear. Office values still had another six percent to fall, through the first six months of 2009, before they finally hit bottom in July. At that point in 2009, the IPD index of office capital values stood at 100 – the figure at which the index first commenced in 1986. In other words, you could buy an office block for the same price as you could have done some twenty-three years earlier. The FTSE reached its nadir slightly sooner, bottoming out at 3,530 on 6th March 2009. Then the stock market began to recover.

This proved too late for mid-sized industrial property company Brixton, run by Tim Wheeler. His share price had fallen from 230p in the summer of 2008 to 43p by February 2009. The City had no appetite for further rights issues. The last sentence of the last leader I ever wrote for *EG*, on 28th February 2009, read: "There are several ways out for Wheeler, none of them pleasant." I packed up and went off to enjoy a pleasant "retirement" writing a weekly column for *EG* and continuing with another for the *Evening Standard*. This departure was marked by a retirement party held on 4th March 2009 in the library of the Reform Club.

Earlier that day, Wheeler had resigned. A takeover fight ensued. The obvious winner all along was Segro, which had long coveted the nineteen million square feet of sheds in west London owned by Brixton. In early July, it bought the company for £110 million; twelve months earlier, Brixton's net assets had been valued at £1 billion. Ian Coull recalls the purchase:

IAN COULL, THEN CHIEF EXECUTIVE OF SEGRO:

Every time I looked at the possibility of buying Brixton, it proved just too difficult because valuations were too high; share prices were too high. When Tim Wheeler was in charge it was almost certainly going to be a hostile bid, and that meant a premium on top of what was already a high share price.

So it was never really on, but it was always there on the radar screen. We had a successful rights issue. Brixton tried to do the same thing and failed. They were then in real financial distress.

Everyone knew that they were probably going to breach their covenants at the half year. Private equity houses like Blackstone and Apollo took a look. But we were clearly able to put these two portfolios together better than anyone else. Once we announced our intent, pretty well everyone disappeared and we were able to get to an agreed position with their board by the early part of July. So it was a bit of a no-brainer once the scale of their financial affairs became obvious.

The FTSE had moved up from 3,500 in February to 4,400 by July 2009. The index went on to gain another 1,100 points to reach 5,500 by the end of the year. The summer of 2009 turned out to be the turning point in the worst downturn in property history. All that was left to do was clear up the terrible, terrible mess. That was still under way in late 2012.

GERALD RONSON... A FINAL WORD:

Unless we get a dose of inflation it will take the banks ten years to work through their losses. Even if you dump everything in the toxic bin, it's still going to have to be sorted out. When it comes to sorting out big, complicated, problematical deals, there aren't hundreds of people in the business who are capable of doing that.

There are people who have survived. But a lot of people have been very severely burnt. Anybody who had leverage is bombed out altogether. The school that I came out of is that you had a responsibility, and if – God forbid – you did have a problem with the banks like we did in the Nineties, you sit down with the banks and work it out, eat a lot of humble pie and work together to maximise the value.

These people didn't want to do that. Not having given personal guarantees, I suppose they felt they didn't have to. They felt that the bank should be privileged for giving them the money. The degree of arrogance in the property business is higher than in any other industry I know.

CHAPTER TWO
BOOM

Bull markets are born on pessimism, grow on scepticism,
mature on optimism, and die on euphoria
Sir John Templeton

Sir John Templeton, who died in 2008, was hailed as the greatest stock pick-er of the twentieth century. The American-born fund manager could pick an apposite aphorism too. The property bull market between 1997 and 2007, described in this chapter, can be roughly divided into the four phases he so illuminatingly described:

- **Pessimism: 1997 to 2000**, while the clouds from the early Nine-ties recession cleared only slowly.
- **Scepticism: 2001 to 2003**, when the stock market fell sharply, but then so did interest rates.
- **Optimism: 2004 to 2005**, which brought a gush of cheap money into the market from a rush of new players.
- **Euphoria: 2006 to 2007**, during which the market surfed happily along on a mounting wave of debt.

There was overlap, of course, and the stages could be framed this way only with hindsight. No one says, "Hey! The boom starts today." Lucy Preb-ble, writer of the 2009 play *Enron*, puts it well: "There's a strange thing goes on inside a bubble. It's hard to describe. People who are in it can't see out-side of it; they also don't believe there is an outside."

Fellow playwright Sir David Hare also talked of this powerful effect when discussing his 2009 production, *The Power of Yes*, a forensic examination of the financial crisis. "Once you're in a bubble, it needs nerves of steel to stay out. Can you imagine the pressure? Everyone around you is making money – and you're the one who says 'I don't believe'?"

GERALD RONSON, CHIEF EXECUTIVE OF HERON INTERNATIONAL:

From 1997 onwards, there were ten golden years for the property business, where anybody with one arm, one eye and one leg could actually make money because you had the banks offering you money, you had institutions buying the market, the yields were being driven down. Most people did well. It didn't matter whether you were a retailer, a wholesaler or whether you were manufacturing cars, or whether you were making washing machines or in the property business. Everybody had a good time. Everybody was making a lot of money.

Tony Blair became prime minister on 2nd May 1997, which is my designated start date for the decade-long commercial property boom. Why? Because values had scarcely moved during the previous five years, after the early Nineties crash, but in the month Blair took over from John Major values began to rise. Their eventual fall started in the month after Blair left office on 27th June 2007 – precisely ten years, one month and twenty-five days after his prime ministership began.

The clearest track left by the Blair boom is again the IPD capital values index for offices. Values in 1986, the year that property data specialist IPD began operations, were indexed at 100. The office index rose sixty-four percent during the four-year Thatcher boom, peaking at 164 in January 1990. The crash that followed sent it to a low of 101 by May 1993, during John Major's time in office.

The offices capital values index barely moved during the next four years, so that in May 1997 it stood at 107 – just six points higher than in May 1993. Enter Blair, and the long upward climb began, dipping only in 2003 and 2004. The index reached 179 in June 2007. In other words, the capital value of offices rose by sixty-seven percent in a decade. Retail values rose even higher – gaining ninety-five percent. Industrial values rose by seventy-three percent. Then Tony Blair was replaced by Gordon Brown, and in July the offices index started to fall. By June 2009, it was back down to 100 – which is exactly where it had stood in 1986, and even lower than at the start of Blair's term in office.

The rise and fall in real estate values shows a similar pattern for the Thatcher/Major and Blair/Brown cycles, but the big difference is timing. The Thatcher/Major cycle obeyed the seven-year rule, running from 1986 to 1993; the Blair/Brown cycle played out over twelve years. That was because the actual boom lasted ten years rather than four, and the crash took two years rather than three, thanks to the precipitous rate of fall. The similarity is that in both cases capital values pretty much returned to 1986 levels.

RENT AND CAPITAL VALUES INDICES FOR OFFICES IN 1997–2007, THE BLAIR YEARS

Office values increased by sixty-seven percent in the Blair boom, falling gently only in 2003–2004. Rents grew just thirty-two percent – not much at all, considering inflation

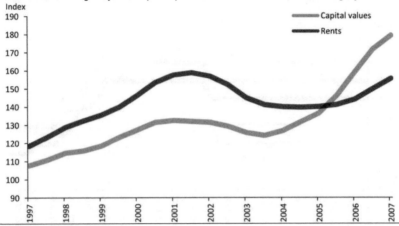

Source: IPD (1986 = 100)

Capital values are generally calculated as a multiple of the annual rent a buyer is prepared to pay, so it follows that rents should rise in parallel. Not during Blair's time in office. The office rental index produced by IPD stood at 118 in June 1997 and had grown to 156 ten years later, representing a rise of thirty-two percent – just under half the increase in capital values. Rental growth was, however, much smaller in real terms, given that there was a twenty-two percent rise in the rate of inflation over the same period. A study produced by CB Richard Ellis in 2010 found that, measured against inflation, office rents were forty-one percent below where they stood in 1975.

The Blair boom was all about "yield compression" – a willingness to pay higher and higher multiples of the annual rent. Yields have always been low in central London, hovering in the region of five to six percent historically. That's where they were in 1997. By the end of 2006, prime yields ranged between 3.5 percent and five percent.

A drop from five percent to 3.5 percent may not seem much. But look at it in terms of the multiple of the annual office rent that investors are prepared to pay: twenty times the rent in the case of a five percent yield; twenty-eight times the rent at 3.5 percent. That's a whacking forty percent more. Why were investors willing to pay so much more? Because money was costing less and less.

Interest rates more than halved during the first half of the long boom, from 7.25 percent in 1998 to 3.5 percent in 2003. This drop brought with it something not seen in living memory, the "positive yield gap": in other words, rental income (the yield) on all but prime property more than covered the interest charges on the mortgage.

PRIME YIELDS FOR LONDON OFFICES IN 1997–2007, THE BLAIR YEARS

A rising tide of money drove down yields, but only from the spring of 2004

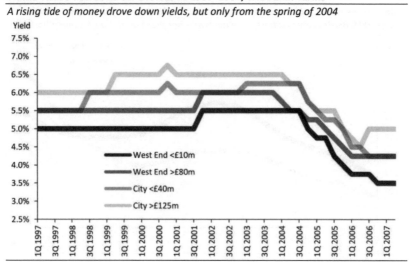

Source: Jones Lang LaSalle

1997–2000: PESSIMISM

A scramble for space in the Square Mile was getting under way in 1997, with bankers and lawyers competing for what accommodation was available. In September 1997, deals totalling half a million square feet were announced within five days. Colin Hargreaves, then of Healey & Baker, is not the sort of City agent to exaggerate. He told *EG* at the time that "the week's activity is reminiscent of the mood of the late Eighties. But, unlike then, today's lack of speculative buildings has helped create a prelet market that has occupiers fighting for space."

Between May 1997 and December 2000, the stock market rose steadily, with the FTSE 100 index climbing fifty-one percent, from 4,500 to almost 6,800. But property values remained relatively subdued. The IPD capital values index for offices rose by twenty-two percent. Not bad. But office rents grew thirty percent during that time. Lack of supply and rising rents are exactly the environment in which to grow towers. They appear, like beanstalks in the spring, at the start of every new cycle. The trick is to get them built before the next downturn, but this is a feat rarely performed. Take four London towers, three dreamed up during the last years of last century – just one of them managed to get built before the crash of 2007.

TOWERING AMBITIONS

1. The Gherkin: Swiss Re had a problem in 1997: the Zurich-based insurer was searching for office accommodation in the City of London, but nothing could be found. It eventually bought the ruined Baltic Exchange buildings in January 1998 for £85 million. Bombed by the IRA in April 1992, the site was owned by Trafalgar House, which had commissioned Foster+Partners to design a Millennium Tower one thousand, two hundred and sixty-four feet tall. Planning permission was refused in 1996. Trafalgar House then entered talks with now defunct German state bank WestLB, which was looking for a signature building in the City.

Architect Ken Shuttleworth of Foster+Partners had worked on the plans, which were adopted by Swiss Re after it bought the site. The lead partner on the project showed me a folder of more than two dozen of his early A4 sketches. They depict a mid-rise haystack gradually pulling up into a cigar shape. "We thought it might get called the Cigar," recalls Shuttleworth, who left Foster+Partners in 2004, when construction on the tower was largely complete, in order to set up his own practice, Make. In July 1999, the first pictures of the new Swiss Re building appeared, and the forty-storey tower quickly became known as the Gherkin.

Redoubtable American Sara Fox of Swiss Re ran the project from September 2000. Builder Skanska began work in January 2001. The five-hundred-and-ninety-foot pickle, officially called 30 St Mary Axe, opened in May 2004. Swiss Re took half the space, and the rest was rather slowly let over the next couple of years. The cost of the Gherkin was £350 million, says Fox – an all-in figure that included land, professional fees and construction costs. Valuers estimated that the fully let tower would be worth £385 million – not much higher than the cost of building it.

Happily, capital values were soaring. The fully let tower was sold in February 2007 for £600 million to a joint-venture vehicle owned fifty-fifty by German fund IVG and a UK investment fund managed by Evans Randall. They paid £30 million in transaction fees on top. In March 2012, the fully let Gherkin was valued at £530 million, some £70 million less than Swiss Re's selling price two years earlier. Swiss Re had pulled off the sole successful entrance and exit from the tall tower stage in the City of London during a boom more than twice as long as usual. That's how hard it is to develop a tower successfully. By accident.

2. The Shard: In the spring of 2000, Irvine Sellar unveiled designs for what was to become the Shard. The saga (see pages 166–168) lasted a dozen years. The development had to be rescued by the government of Qatar in 2008, and the thousand-foot tower was eventually finished in 2012. Not a single floor of office space was let by December 2012.

3. The Heron Tower: On 1st September 2000, Gerald Ronson submitted plans for a tower of thirty-seven storeys on Bishopsgate (see pages 136–138). Permission was granted for the Heron Tower in July 2002 after an acrimonious public inquiry. But work did not begin until April 2008, nearly six years later, when £500 million of financing was finally put in place.

The tower was eventually finished in 2011. By late 2012, only half the four hundred and forty thousand square feet of office space was let. Opposite the Heron Tower a cleared site for an eight-hundred-thousand-square-foot tower at 100 Bishopsgate stood empty at the end of 2012. Developer Brookfield was searching for a prelet.

4. The Pinnacle: A little later came the tower that suffered arrested development. This was the Pinnacle – or the Helter-Skelter, as the thousand-foot City skyscraper was described upon its launch in June 2005 by German fund manager Difa. The furled top of the Kohn Pederson Fox tower and the bell-bottom base made it vaguely resemble a fairground ride, and towers attract nicknames like flypaper attracts flies.

The Germans sold the site in early 2007 for £200 million to an Arab consortium led by Khalid Affara. He kindly gave *EG* the first chance to publish pictures of the newly tweaked design, which did not yet have a name. We put the name "Pinnacle" in the headline: my only claim on posterity. The Pinnacle it became, for a while at least. But by the end of 2012, all there was to see was a £140 million stump – and no money to build the rest. Kohn Pederson Fox was busy downscaling the plans into a Pinnacle-ette.

WEB MANIA STRIKES
The rumbling beginnings of an office boom could clearly be heard in the City at the turn of the millennium: Knight Frank reported a forty percent rise in lettings during 2000. But the newfangled worldwide web seemed much more

interesting to all. With worries about computers crashing as the new millennium arrived, IT departments gloried in their newfound importance.

There commenced a period of what might be called "portal pottiness". Sane business folk felt that if only they could funnel those looking for the BBC news through their own website first, a fortune could somehow be made. *EG* glued a CD on the front of thirty thousand magazines one week, offering readers the delights of an Estates Gazette portal. When the website closed a few years later, just one reader complained.

Web mania drove some formerly sensible companies quite loopy, among them IT hardware supplier Cisco. On 26th July 2000, I was invited to breakfast at Claridge's by Alistair Elliott of Knight Frank. The man due to become senior partner in 2013 was then in charge of letting offices in the hundred-and-eighty-acre GreenPark development on the M4 near Reading, being funded by Prudential. By him sat Mike Rolls, the man from the Pru in charge of GreenPark. They had a story, and here it is, as told in *EG*:

Pru Nabs Mega-Prelet at GreenPark

The largest-ever prelet outside London was sealed last week by Prudential. Cisco Systems will take more than 116,125m^2 (1.25m sq ft) at GreenPark south of Reading on 25-year leases at rents of £28-£32 per sq ft. The US network supplier has committed to 607,000 sq ft in five separate buildings on the Prudential-owned park adjacent to the M4. Options that need to be exercised by March 2003 on a further 57,319m^2 (617,000 sq ft) have been agreed.

When the dot-com bubble burst soon afterwards, Cisco discovered it needed only a tenth of the space. Five buildings alongside the M4 lay empty for years, with Cisco paying the rent. In late 2011, Prudential sold GreenPark for £400 million to Oxford Properties, a subsidiary of a Canadian pension fund. By the end of 2012, much of the space still stood empty.

A more serious attempt to capture the elusive value of web-accessible information was made in July 2000 by a group that included *EG*'s parent company, Reed Business Information. Project Pathway was an attempt to set up a "pan-European property portal" through which paying customers could access property news, research and (most important of all) sales and investment data on individual properties.

A joint venture between DTZ, CB Richard Ellis, Jones Lang LaSalle and Reed was formed to manage Pathway. I knew nothing, until called by Mark Kelsey, former publisher and by then managing director of *EG*. Kelsey set up EGi in 1996, as one of the first-ever magazine websites, and had the wisdom to charge for access in an era when everyone else was giving it away for free – a brilliant decision, which enabled EGi to flourish while others wilted. Project Pathway, however, never got to the point of charging: it wilted and died as companies set up their own websites.

But 1999 saw the birth of a web shopping revolution that slowly and inexorably squeezed bricks-and-mortar retail, reducing high-street values to the point of sparking a "save our high streets" campaign ten years later. This *EG* leader from June 1999 passed on the warnings being sounded even then in both the City and the property community:

The E-tail Revolution Will Reshape Retail...

Forget retail, start investigating e-tail. The ballooning growth of internet purchasing has got a first tranche of retailers rethinking their supply-chain requirements. This could result in demand for an extra 13m sq ft of warehouse space over the next five years. That is the conclusion of a timely and well-argued report from FPDSavills, which has spoken to the top 250 retailers.

Now, there is a tendency at the start of any trend for expectations to exceed eventual reality. But there is no doubt that the IT revolution, which has already hit demand for secondary office space, will boost requirements for home-delivery depots. This is because retailers' supply networks will start to be respun to cope with shoppers who surf. New entrants to the market, like bookseller Amazon, will add an extra fillip. That is the good news. The bad news is the cloudy fate of the high streets and shopping centres when an appreciable slice of their trade migrates to virtual reality in, say, 10 years' time.

E-fever continued to burn, causing delirium in one case. In November 1999, two well-known property figures joined forces with a well-known retailer and floated a shell company to buy retail property. Nick Leslau and Nigel Wray, along with ex-Asda boss Archie Norman, floated Knutsford at 2p a share. That was an appropriate name, as it turned out; nutty investors piled in and *whoosh* – the price climbed to 250p before collapsing.

This fever raged right through 2000. Agents, developers, occupiers – just about everyone – announced e-initiatives. Most were barmy, based on lunatic business models that involved all-too-certain expenditure and very uncertain income. But this was not the case for PrimeLocation, a residential website launched in January 2001 by a collaboration of top-end agents, led by Knight Frank and Savills.

More than two hundred firms clubbed together to raise £11 million and, critically, promised not to advertise their details on other websites. It worked: by 2003, PrimeLocation was in profit. In December 2005, the site was sold to the Daily Mail group for £48 million, netting Savills £6 million and Knight Frank £4 million. By early 2001, the fever had begun to subside. This from *EG* on 27th January:

No Longer in a Spin over Wonders of the Web

"Everyone thought if they were not part of that year's steamroller they would become part of that year's road." This phrase, borrowed from Business 2.0, sums up how most businesses felt about the web. Note the past tense. We are now well down the hype curve and sliding into a trough of disillusionment.

Web initiatives seem risky, naive or oddly dated, like last year's pink pashmina.... Little blood has been spilt – beyond consultants' fees and interminable amounts of management time. But business plans are being examined in a far more realistic light.... This does not mean the internet can now be ignored. Far from it: to borrow from Business 2.0 again: "The internet is going away like the phone went away, permeating everything and, in the process, becoming invisible."

2001–2003: SCEPTICISM

MIKE STRONG, CHAIRMAN FOR EMEA AT CBRE:

This was a boom that was fuelled by non-real-estate people. In 2000, there was quite an overhang of space, rents were down and leasing volumes were down. Yet against that backdrop, volumes in the capital markets were ramping up. What you had coming in was new entrants. You had financial engineers, not real estate people: those who saw the power of a line of income from a given covenant, with the real estate being largely immaterial.

Industry folk were saying: "Hang on a minute, rents are static, and demand for space isn't very strong." Real estate people weren't rushing to join the party. But thanks to the low cost of debt and high levels of leverage, new entrants drove prices up.

The "pessimistic" phase of the Blair boom was over by December 2000. Some pessimism: the IPD capital values index for offices had risen by a fifth since May 1997 – an improvement almost drowned out by the buzz of the internet. What happened over the next four years appears odd, until you set it against the slump in the stock market.

As 2001 opened, the FTSE 100 index stood at 6,220. By the eve of the Iraq war, in March 2003, it had slumped forty-three percent to 3,500, before recovering to 4,500 by December 2003. This fall and rise was almost exactly matched by what was later to happen between the summers of 2007 and 2009. But the effect on property in 2001–2003 was minimal, thanks to the plummeting cost of money. Interest rates were cut from six to four percent during 2001, while bank lending began to climb steeply in response. The level of outstanding commercial property loans nearly doubled over the three years to the end of 2003, from £56 billion to £100 billion.

Retail property values rose by fifteen percent on the back of strong consumer spending, despite fears that the web would cut trade, while the price of sheds rose by about half that amount, partly on increased demand from "e-tailers". Office values, however, languished. The IPD index for offices stood at 131 at the start of 2001 and barely moved through 2001 and 2002, before dipping to 124 at the end of 2003.

"Offices were hit hard by the fallout from the disastrous dot-com bust in 2000, and poor performance was then hurt by 9/11," explains Greg Nicholson, who specialised as a retail investment agent at CB Richard Ellis. "Low interest rates triggered consumer and development booms and a surge in public spending." Okay, but why did retail property values rise in the face of the online threat? "There were not the same occupancy problems then," says Nicholson. "Retail was not affected by the dot-com bust, and branch growth was very strong. At this time, the internet had not had any measurable impact on retail property demand."

More than £20 billion of real estate disappeared into private property vehicles during those three years, most of it office stock. Quoted property companies disposed of £6 billion of assets between 2001 and 2003. Institutions sold down £5 billion, while corporates sold £10 billion of their own property, according to DTZ.

Saudi Arabian investors led by Prince Alwaleed bought Berkeley Square from the BP Pension Fund in April 2001 for £335 million – including the actual square, as I remember checking in disbelief. It turned out that when BP paid £12 million for the freeholds of a hundred or so buildings surrounding the square in 1967, the grass and trees in the middle were included.

CANNED IN CANNES

The mood at the MIPIM property fair in March 2001 was mildly upbeat, a fact I mentioned in a leader that took a sideswipe at the "efficient fleecing machine" that is Cannes. Delegates have a love/hate relationship with the world's most successful property show, which is run with brutal efficiency by Reed Midem, a sister company of the Estates Gazette Group.

Fifteen to twenty-five thousand property folk from around the world turn up. They love to come, despite resenting the high prices of food and drink in the restaurants and bars of Cannes. Organiser Reed Midem asks those who come to pay around €1,000 for the privilege of wandering around the maze of stands inside the Palais des Festivals et des Congrès and the surrounding tent city.

The organisers hate those who come to Cannes without buying tickets and just hang around the town hawking for business. Special ire was once reserved for Knight Frank and Drivers Jonas, both of which came to Cannes, hired hotels and restaurants for events, but did not take stands at the show. One year Knight Frank tried to hang a banner on the balcony of a flat it was renting right opposite the Palais. "We got a call to take it down almost before the string was tied," recalled the company's Alistair Elliott. This sort of activity was condemned each year by Reed Midem, with increasing anger, as "commercial piracy".

My "fleecing" remark went unchallenged. A year later, in 2002, I repeated the taunt, in a leader in an early March edition of *EG*. The comment came after suggesting that if MIPIM in 2001 was *Saturday Night Fever*, then Cannes in 2002 would be more like the dark gangster film *The Long Good Friday*. With 9/11 still fresh in everyone's minds, the mood was sombre. Fifteen thousand copies of *EG* containing those remarks were ferried to Cannes, ready to be popped into the bag of each and every delegate. I'd completely forgotten that was going to happen.

That cut no ice with Reed Midem, which went completely crazy, dumping every copy of *EG* into a French skip. A complaint zoomed its way up the many-layered management chain to someone important at holding company Reed Elsevier, and then all the way back down to my publisher, Jim Muttram, a quiet, thoughtful character, who shaped *EG*'s successful web business. He was charged with asking me if I could possibly publish a nice story about MIPIM by way of apology. He wasn't really expecting a yes – and didn't get one.

The tension between the "commercial pirates" and Reed Midem went on for years. Access to the harbour full of yachts became restricted to ticket holders during the day. Reed Midem barred those without badges from entering the bars of the Majestic and Carlton hotels.

Happily, this edict came too late to prevent my introduction in the bar of the Carlton to the madam of a group of earthy Northern women who described themselves as "Cheshire's finest for discerning gentlemen". The introduction was effected by Allsop auctioneer Gary Murphy, who, it should be stressed, did not avail himself of their services, which were priced at "£250 an hour, or part thereof". We had a few beers costing £8 per bottle (or part thereof) instead. That's Cannes: parties on the boats of more louche developers tended to have women on board who were clearly not there to discuss yield compression. It could get very embarrassing: six poor girls sitting together while all around yammered on, pretending not to notice them. All very sleazy. But get a client or banker in a compromising position, and his (always a his) heart and mind will follow the procurer's will.

The piracy issue came to a head in 2009, when Reed Midem sued Drivers Jonas for €350,000 in the French courts. Rather than pay for a stand in the Palais des Festivals, the agent held court every year in a café just up the street. Reed Midem won the case in March 2010, much to the shock and amazement of the UK agent fraternity. At almost the same moment, Drivers Jonas was taken over by Deloitte, auditors to Reed Midem's parent, Reed Elsevier. There was no appeal.

11TH SEPTEMBER 2001

My wife Lizzie and I were lolling around on loungers in a thatched villa in Bali when the planes crashed into the twin towers in New York. By the time we got back to England, the blind panic was already dying down. This *EG* leader is from 29th September 2001:

Disregard the Squawks of Headless Chickens

"If you can keep your head..." – Kipling's sage advice comes to mind as the economic aftershocks of 11 September reverberate still. But the outpourings on the economic consequences contain great doses of drivel. Normally continent forecasters have been spewing predictions that seem based on little more than the state of their entrails. Swallowing the facile business reporting of events may be to blame.

Happily, more measured views are now being expressed. UK property is still groping for an indication of how individual firms will be affected. So it may help to summarise the views garnered over the past week from those who actually operate in the business. For this, thanks to the members of *EG*'s advisory board, which met on Monday, and to John Carrafiell, MD of European real estate at Morgan Stanley, for his Wednesday speech to the British Council for Offices.

The bad news: Demand for space will fall; allow for rental growth to halt and in some sectors to decline. Transaction business is being hit. Development will slow; a number of projects that have yet to leave the drawing board are being quietly postponed. Finance on deals will cost more: spooked banks will up charges and take less risk. Insurance costs will generally rise; and, if you own a tall building, the price could rise threefold.

The good news: Property's value as a "safe financial haven" is soaring; few funds are divesting. Many are holding steady even though the fall in equities means they are overweight. Some funds are thinking of increasing allocations and others have halted sales. The latest fall in interest rates will help; it is 50 years since borrowing rates were this far below rental income.

Firms large and small have held "blimey, what shall we do" meetings. But re-member, pre-11 September, caution was already in the air. The tragedy has simply put the issues into sharper relief. The consensus seems to be business as usual with a dash of further caution. Oh, and ignore the incontinent com-mentators – be guided by what is really happening in the business – good and bad.

VALUELESS VALUATION ADVICE
Early 2002 brought a perfect example of how not to fashion a stable door. In the autumn of 2000, a survey of thirty firms by Reading and Trent universi-ties found that valuers were being pressured in all sorts of ways by clients to alter their valuations – upwards, obviously. The Royal Institution of Char-tered Surveyors reacted by asking the former director general of the Office of Fair Trading, Sir Bryan Carsberg, to recommend what might be done.

In January 2002, Sir Bryan reported back. His recommendations in-cluded audit trails and the recording of discussions and changes made to valuations at client meetings; rotation of staff on recurring assignments; and a requirement to disclose total fee-earning relationships with clients. The ideas that Carsberg did come up with – to the extent that they were imple-mented – completely failed to prevent the system being abused as the boom gathered pace.

HERE COMES THE SUN
November 2002 brought pleasant news from *The Times* economic commen-tator Anatole Kaletsky, who came to speak at an *EG* conference held at Claridge's. Organising events is a complete pain in the backside for editors, because it throws up conflicts of interest: do you now have to be nice in print to that crowd-puller who was kind enough to accept your invitation to speak? It can be the start of an insidious process.

The next thing you know, conference programmes are being "shaped" by the wishes of sponsors. After that comes wholly sponsored mock "events", faithfully recorded in print under the watchful eye of the sponsor. Next fol-lows advertising masquerading as sponsored "editorial". There's a whole sto-ry about the pollution of editorial freedom by publishers happy to pressure their editors in order to made a fast buck. But happily, this was never an is-sue at *EG*.

Anyway, Kaletsky was a crowd-puller. He was brilliant. "The recession is clearly over," he said to an audience who had watched the FTSE index crash by over a thousand points during the previous ten months. "The UK economy has enjoyed its longest period of economic growth in history – and that growth is still going pretty strong." I was sitting in the audience. "It doesn't feel much like that from here," muttered my neighbour. Events, however, proved Kaletsky right. He helped brighten my *EG* round-up of 2002:

A Year That Turned Out Better than Feared

Better than feared: that is the consensus on the health of the UK commercial property market at the end of a troubled year. Thus the general mood now is as it was in January: calm and mildly optimistic. But optimistic that things won't get much worse. That in itself may be optimistic. Rents have stagnated, and in some places are diving. Capital values are starting to stall. But thus far lenders and investors still mad to buy bricks and mortar have supported prices.

Developers are leaving plans rolled up. Big-ticket office lettings have died. The M4 from junction 1 to 14 is Death Valley. Occupiers all over the UK are hibernating. As many property firms are quietly shedding staff as are boasting about taking people on. But the property investment market steams on, fuelled by cheap debt, low interest rates – and a lack of alternatives. Buoyant consumer spending supports retail property.

A hundred pounds invested in the FTSE 100 in January is now worth £80. The same amount invested in commercial property is worth £109: that is 36% more. The Great Missed Trick of 2002 was (yet again) the reluctance of pension and life funds to increase significantly the weighting of property in their portfolios.... Most funds waited in cash for a rise in shares that never came. Fortunately it hasn't mattered – except to pensioners, because 2002 has been the year when lending banks and private investors kept the market afloat. That, unsurprisingly, is why the year has turned out better than feared.

THE FTSE BEGINS TO CLIMB

In early 2003, the FTSE 100 began its four-and-a-half-year climb from 3,500 towards the high of 6,700 it would eventually achieve in the summer of 2007. But the "optimistic" phase of boom had not yet begun. What did begin that year was a flood of cheap money that would water the ground. So-called "debt buyers" were starting to flourish under the lower interest-rate regime in early 2003. Libor had fallen from 5.75 percent in January 2001 to 3.5 percent in July 2003.

Lenders were beginning to compete fiercely, with margins dropping ever closer to Libor and arrangement fees falling too. The deputy governor of the Bank of England, David Clementi, had warned in September 2002 of "potential upsets" caused by rising levels of commercial property debt, which had soared by £10 billion to reach £81 billion in the first nine months of 2002. By the end of 2003, outstanding debt touched £100 billion. Clearly, no one was taking a blind bit of notice of the Old Lady of Threadneedle Street.

There was cheap debt – buckets full of the stuff. That changed the language of the industry. Instead of looking really carefully at the fundamentals of a property investment, everybody started talking about the swap rate you could borrow at being lower than the rental yield. The cheapness of money and the bountiful nature of it was just palpable.

I remember we received ten bids from investors on a small portfolio, and eight of them said they had either debt or equity financing from a certain Scottish bank. I wonder if the bank realised they had backed eight different bidders? Or whether their equity team knew their debt team?

I remember speaking to one young finance guy. He was twenty-eight and was retiring to Switzerland. I asked him: "What did you do?" He said "mezzanine finance". I asked: "Why are you retiring?" He replied, "Well, I've got a lot of money, but even I can't do this any more. I've just done a deal with two guys I've never met before in my life; they had a shopping centre under offer in a place I've never heard of somewhere in eastern Europe."

He said he did it for two reasons: one, that was the basis upon which he got paid (the more he lent, the bigger his bonus) and, two, he handed over the mezzanine finance loan to the guy sitting next to him. That guy stapled the loan together with another batch of debt and sold it on again. So he didn't ever have to sit and watch the thing unravel. Nobody ever held him to account for it.

There was all that sort of stuff going on. We weren't really aware of that. Not many of us were exposed to the whacky financial products loosely derived from the hard assets we were dealing with. What we did understand was that the level of leverage was getting really, really serious.

Desperate-to-lend banks were also directing borrowers towards "friendly" valuers: those who would make sure that amicable agreement could be reached on what the property supporting the loan was worth. And if it wasn't quite enough, well, the value could surely be nudged up a bit, couldn't it? After all, we both want the fees, don't we? And the market is rising anyway, isn't it? I kept hearing of one firm of valuers in particular which banks deemed "friendly" – and cheap. The laws of libel prevent me from naming them to this day. The only point to make is this: in a real estate boom, it is in everyone's interest for prices to rise. It is in no one's interest to check that rise, including that of put-upon valuers.

"One thing that was going on – but not at JLL," remembers Alastair Hughes, who went on to run the European and then the Asian business of Jones Lang LaSalle, "was to get somebody to value the property at a higher price than the buyer was actually paying in order to achieve a hundred percent debt financing. So you're buying it for £80, you get a valuation at £100. Then you borrow eighty percent of £100 and get to pay a hundred percent of the purchase price with borrowed money. Wonderful! People were dressing it up, saying, 'We've agreed to pay £80, but it's a great deal, it was off-market and well worth £100.'" The wheeze worked even better for owners who wanted to refinance at lower interest rates. This appeared in *EG* on the topic of dodgy valuations in the spring of 2003:

'Friendly' Valuers Need to Come under Fire

There is disturbing anecdotal evidence that lenders are pushing prospective borrowers in front of "friendly" agents who give optimistic valuations. These are then used to tempt the said borrower to refinance with the said bank. And how tempting it must be. Imagine owning a property worth £1m – or so your last lender thought a year or so back.

You personally invested £200,000 and have a loan from Bank A of £800,000. Bank B says go and see valuer X. Valuer X says the property is now worth £1.2m. So, Bank B says, let us lend you £1m. Bingo. Debt paid off and the £200,000 equity paid back. A building worth, well, who cares, and an even lower-interest loan that is more than covered by the rent: all this and a happy chap at Bank B who has met this month's lending target.

LOUIS ARMSTRONG, RICS CHIEF EXECUTIVE 1998–2010:

There was no nexus between professional judgement and shovelling money at commercial property. Due diligence was for wimps, who missed the deal. It didn't matter what professional advice was proffered about whether a loan against property was sensible or justified: because the prime motivation of lenders was to shovel shed loads of money out the door. Bankers' bonuses very often reflected the amount they lent. Neither they nor their bosses cared that the loans were risky or the borrower uncreditworthy, because the following week some unwitting Japanese bank would own the securitised debt.

Very large amounts of money can be made refinancing when interest rates fall or values rise. If both happen together, the returns are turbocharged. Many a millionaire was made between 2003 and 2007. The really easy money was made remortgaging.

Note to students – this is how it works: imagine you buy a property for £50 million and take out a £40 million mortgage at a seven percent interest rate. The yearly repayments are therefore £2.8 million. Prices rise and interest rates fall, until the worth of your property is £75 million and you can get a £60 million remortgage at five percent interest. The yearly interest payments of £3 million are barely higher than before. You take the £60 million second mortgage and use it to pay off the first £40 million mortgage. You end up with £20 million in the bank. Magic! Wonderful magic...

After having bought the Rolls, the yacht and the mansion, the rest of the cash is reinvested in even more real estate in order then to repeat the trick after the next investment rises in value. And values do indeed start to rise – because everyone is doing the same thing as you. It's how booms start.

That's what began to happen in late 2003. Traditional property companies were still feeling wary, as Sir John Ritblat explains below. But a new generation of "debt buyers" led by Robert and Vincent Tchenguiz were helping change the mood of the market from scepticism towards optimism.

SIR JOHN RITBLAT, THEN CHAIRMAN OF BRITISH LAND:

> *The downturn in 2000 and 2003 was due to the stupidity of South Sea bubbles in all the IT stocks. British Land was absolutely immune; our business model remained intact. We continued to buy and sell property: I think during that period we must have sold about £5 billion. Then we had a sustained burst; we had a real bull market. Money got cheaper – not cheap, but cheaper. Cash poured in and there was huge liquidity. The competition did not affect us much; we were still the first port of call for a lot of lenders, particularly for off-market deals.*

> *The debt buyers were buying buildings that we probably wouldn't have bought. Shell Mex House on the Strand is a perfect example, bought by the Tchenguiz brothers: they paid a high price because they were able to syndicate and securitise the deal using cheap debt. We didn't do that at British Land. We would only buy property on the fundamentals. What was it worth with vacant possession? What was it worth leased to a long-term tenant? If we didn't think it showed the right surplus for our own funding, then we didn't buy it.*

> *What happened was these entrepreneurs found a financing loophole that enabled them to bid on equal terms with the Pru, using cheap money. Shell Mex was exactly the sort of building that would have formerly been bought by Legal & General, or the Prudential. They were granted very high loan-to-value ratios. These loans were often not too long – some of them were, but a great amount of it was quite short money, four or five-year terms. We always said that at the first hint of trouble they would become unzipped. That happened when the music stopped.*

FRANCIS SALWAY, CHIEF EXECUTIVE OF LAND SECURITIES 2004–2012:

> *The upswing that began in 2003 was about too much lending, which led to a bubble in capital values rather than a bubble in rents. Banks were focused on growing the size of their business, and the lending environment became very competitive. Banks began to take lower margins and grant higher loan-to-value ratios. The problem was that at high loan-to-value ratios, the upside sat with the borrower but virtually all the downside with the bank.*

REVVING UP THE RICS

At the time that valuers were coming under fire for overvaluing properties, their professional body was coming under fire for overcharging members with hefty subscription hikes. The Royal Institution of Chartered Surveyors was nearing the closing stages of a three-year restructuring plan kicked off by DTZ's then chairman, Richard Lay, while he was president of the institution in 1999. Lay was followed in 2000 by EC Harris partner Simon Kolesar, then by property investor Jonathan Harris in 2001.

All three stood on a platform in 1999 and pledged to modernise the seventy-five-thousand-member professional body. The man they had hired to carry out the task stood beside them on the dais at the QEII centre in London before twelve hundred members. The Agenda for Change programme was to be implemented by new chief executive Louis Armstrong. This tall and confident former naval officer was a trained barrister who had served on the royal yacht *Britannia* between 1979 and 1981. He rose to the rank of rear admiral before retiring from the senior service in 1998, aged fifty-two, to take command of the Royal Institution of Chartered Surveyors. No one could accuse Armstrong of not having shaken up the institute by the time he retired in 2010. By then, the organisation had globalised and membership had soared to over a hundred thousand.

But back in 2003, the bills for the Agenda for Change programme were falling upon the membership. The tearing-up of divisional branches based upon county boundaries and their replacement by multidisciplinary, city-based centres cost money as well as causing enormous resentment. The active membership, about five percent of the total, saw the Rotary Club-style branch structure as just a good way of making business contacts – or else as offering a way to climb up the tree to the topmost committees in order to give something back to the profession. Subscription fees for fellows had risen from £232 to £320 between 1999 and 2003.

By early that year, Armstrong had nearly completed the tasks set by Lay, Kolesar and Harris. There had been plenty of bumps in the road, but the general feeling was that the Agenda for Change had been a success – at much financial cost. So much so, that the RICS proposed in March 2003 a further forty-two percent rise in the full membership fee from 1st January 2004. This went down very badly, as described in *EG* on 15th March 2003:

For Unity the RICS Needs a Second Vote

The RICS deserves great credit for reforming itself over the past five years. But are the 113,000 members willing to foot the bill? In particular, are the 18,226 practising UK fellows, who currently pay £320 pa, going to accept a 42% increase to £456 in January?... There have been huge improvements in the way the organisation communicates both with its members and the outside world.

Five years ago, when Lay mapped out what needed to change, he did so in an apathetic climate where the only question was, "who cares if the RICS lives or dies?"... Cynics will say that the RICS has become a bloated, over-complex organisation with grandiose views of its place on the planet. There is enough merit in these charges to make them sting.

And sting they did. A campaign led by quantity surveyor Jeremy Hackett failed to attract enough votes to have the rises quashed. He complained that "what used to be a creaky, bottom-up organisation based on a divisional branch structure has now become top-down and unaccountable to the rank and file membership". But the complaints gradually died away. By 2012, members were reduced to moaning about the £320,000 remuneration of chief executive, Sean Tompkins, who took over in September 2010 from Louis Armstrong – whose annual salary had been the considerably larger figure of £400,000. Tompkins' own former post of deputy chief executive was not filled.

RICHARD LAY, FORMER CHAIRMAN OF DTZ AND RICS PRESIDENT 1999–2000:

You have to ask the question: what would have happened if we had not had the Agenda for Change? My view was that the institution would have suffered long-term decline and have become increasingly irrelevant, as the property industry developed in a global marketplace. There were two keys: first to bring in Louis Armstrong as chief executive, who was hired after we hatched the plan, and second to have continuity.

I had always enjoyed listening to presidents at the beginning of their terms giving learned lectures to the great and good, and outlining their plans for the year ahead. However, they found it nigh on impossible to convert the reactionary elements of the membership, who would know that the following year there would be a new president and a new plan. There was no clear continuity – just stop/go. By working closely with the two who were already programmed to succeed me, I was able to say to the membership that we jointly had a three-year plan, which we were determined to push through.

The response reflected the general view that significant changes needed to be made and members were genuinely interested in hearing about the proposed reforms, which generally proved to be a great success. I invited members to write to me with their thoughts and received almost a thousand – mostly helpful and favourable – responses.

The changing of the local branch structure was probably a mistake. It was also done with a lack of sensitivity. A lot of worthy people who had devoted their lives and energies to the promotion of the profession in their own area were very upset. Looking back, I believe that the Agenda for Change achieved most of its objectives but recognise that we could have left a few things as they were, and allowed those changes to evolve.

LOUIS ARMSTRONG, RICS CHIEF EXECUTIVE 1998–2010:

The institution ceased being what I would describe as a cosy gentlemen's club based somewhere in Little England and set in the Sixties or Seventies. The RICS recognised that there was a huge difference between the members' organisation that many people thought we were and a professional standards, qualifications and regulatory professional body working in the public interest that we were actually set up to be.

It was absolutely right to get rid of thirty-two historic county branches that had been the same since the nineteenth century. We had to move away from meetings in the back room of a pub masquerading as continuing professional development. They were simply cosy networking sessions – fine, but not the way professional bodies should operate.

Replacing the branches with twice as many local associations based on towns and cities was not easy. What we had there were dedicated people, often over fifty-five or over sixty, who wanted to help and organise things. They were not happy. We underestimated the emotional attachment of active members to their branches.

We thought they would understand that the future lay in a different direction, even if they themselves felt they should hang up their boots and hand over to a new generation of activists who could organise events of the right type; who could partner with professional staff to deliver the uniformly high-quality co-ordinated programme of CPD that was so needed.

What many critics of the RICS's modernisation programme conveniently forget is that all these changes were approved by a vote of the whole membership: that crucial fact was carefully suppressed by a small, vociferous and hostile minority who wanted to preserve the status quo.

DOWN UNDER

In December 2003, I was off to Sydney. *EG*'s immediate owner, Reed Business Information, had a large publishing business in Australia, where confidence was also clearly rising. Perhaps a real estate weekly, drawing its inspiration from *EG*, could be published Down Under? What I learned was that in terms of both publishing and property, Australia was not just a long way away but in effect on another planet. Developers and landlords controlled the real estate market, while agents were regarded as little more than super-janitors whose job it was to manage property. The owners were a very close-knit group, with the Property Council of Australia their all-powerful lobbying group run by a powerful character called Peter Verwer.

"Your venture will fail," predicted Verwer. I'd met him in London a year or so earlier when he was shipped over by Sir John Ritblat's son, Nick, who thought Verwer would make an excellent head of the British Property

Federation. He would have. But newly installed Liz Peace headed off that idea with some smart media footwork. Why would we fail, I asked Verwer. Lack of good journalists was just one of the reasons he put forward. "There are talented people in Australia, but the gene pool is very shallow," he warned. So it proved: there were only three top-class real estate reporters in Sydney. Back in London, we had three times that number of Antipodeans working at the *EG* office alone. And the home-based variety (all three of them) wanted fifty percent more pay than Reed was prepared to offer.

The publisher also wanted to run the weekly magazine on a shoe-string with just six staff. At the time, *EG* employed more than forty journalists in London, one being Jane Roberts, *EG*'s deputy editor and the most talented and tenacious property writer of her generation.

Roberts ran the entire news section of *EG* and the EGi website from the time I arrived in 1997 through to the summer of 2006, when she became editor of *Real Estate Capital*, a financial spin-off from *EG* which she went on to "take private" in 2009. In early 2004, she headed for Sydney to supplement the gene pool at *Commercial Property Gazette*, which Reed was determined to launch. She came back pretty disgusted after just one week; the magazine closed about a year later. Verwer had been right.

2004–2005: OPTIMISM

In January 2004, I went Down Under again, but this time on holiday. Jane Roberts was running things at *EG* back home in London during the week that influential fund manager Robert Houston of ING became very optimistic at a City gathering in the Mansion House. Here is the start of her leader, dated 24th January:

> The audience at the Mansion House on Tuesday evening must have thought they'd died and gone to heaven. The City gathering of fund managers and investment agents heard ING's property fund management chairman Robert Houston predict that the investment market is in for a sustained bull run. Average yields will fall by up to 1%, he declared, as institutions big and small double their weighting in property, from an average 7% to 15% by 2010; in other words, a return to the golden age of the 1970s before everything turned in 1984 and equities became the only game in town.

Houston was right about the sustained bull run, but wrong about the bull. In 2004 and 2005, institutions sold £9 billion worth more property than they bought, according to DTZ. The biggest net investors – by a factor of twenty – were private property vehicles. These added £28 billion to their holdings in the space of two years. In terms of nationality, the biggest buyers were the Irish (£5 billion) and the Americans (£3.8 billion), while the biggest sellers were the Brits, with net disinvestment of £15.4 billion.

About ten percent of the Irish spending went on one huge deal. In February 2005, the BP Pension Fund decided to sell three-and-a-half freehold acres in Knightsbridge. The fund had already sold its Berkeley Square estate in 2001, for £315 million; now it decided that the time was right to sell an island block of shops and flats sitting between Harvey Nichols and Harrods. This was a better-timed call than Berkeley Square, as it turned out.

The estate, five hundred and twenty thousand square feet in size, went on the market at a guide price of £400 million in February 2005. It sold for £540 million two months later, to Derek Quinlan, the former tax inspector whose empire was later repossessed by the Irish National Assets Management Agency (NAMA) in 2010. Quinlan topped a bid from the Abu Dhabi royal family, which pretty much tells you all you need to know about the Irish property invasion. In the wake of the eventual repossession, Saudi investment group Olayan bought the estate in 2010 (with the help of Chelsfield's Elliott Bernerd) for about the price that Quinlan had paid in 2005.

Interest rates remained fairly static in 2004 and 2005, at between four and 4.75 percent – much the same as they had been since the autumn of 2001. But general economic confidence was rising, if slowly at first. The FTSE 100 gained 350 points during the course of 2004, growing from 4,500 to reach 4,850. In 2005, it rose at nearly double that rate, hitting 5,500 by the end of the year. Capital values rose, again slowly at first. But by the end of 2005, the IPD index measuring offices, retail and industrial values had risen by twenty-four percent, retail leading the way with a thirty percent rise.

Office values, however, lagged behind badly. In 2004, they increased by less than five percent; the following year, the rise improved markedly, to eleven percent. Why the early lag? "Office rents fell from late 2001 to the end of 2004," explains Greg Nicholson. "Hence the sluggish office market. Nationally rents fell fifteen percent – more in the big, central London markets. Yields rose too. A big spike in development completions in London and the South East were quite a factor, as I remember."

Land Securities' Mike Hussey orchestrated the most memorable completion of 2004. An amazing show was put on to celebrate the coming to market of a three-hundred-and-ninety-thousand-square-foot office block at 30 Gresham Street in the City. It was an occasion on a scale unseen since Broadgate opened fifteen years before: an occasion whose budget gave proof to rising confidence. The invitation promised "an evening with Ian Henderson", Land Securities' gentlemanly boss. I walked the short distance from my flat near St Bart's hospital and into a wondrous world, described thus, in *EG*:

Something to Shout About

On Thursday 4 March at 7pm in the City of London an event billed as "an evening with Ian Henderson" opened at 30 Gresham Street, a just completed (but as yet unlet) 390,000 sq ft office block bang opposite the Guildhall. The show closed three hours later with the 60-year-old chief executive of the developer, Land Securities, jigging a little self-consciously to the 55-year-old Lulu belting out her signature tune "Shout" from a makeshift stage.

But first, the show: three laser beams wildly gyrating against a cloudy night sky greeted approaching guests. Once inside the limestone and glass lobby, 125cl bottles of Perrier Jouët champagne, plus straw, were handed out. Sucking happily away, invitees were escorted up gleaming aluminium escalators, and then asked to appreciate a tableau of white-painted females posing gracefully on pedestals.

The guests' gaze was then directed upwards to a group of more muscular female forms twisting slowly within white winding sheets suspended from the atrium roof far above. Then it was on up to a vast empty floor: empty, that is, except for three golf carts gliding around a snaking illuminated pathway. They carried passengers gamely competing in a quiz that necessitated hooking up a yellow rubber duck from a pond and reading the question glued to its belly.

Then off to another vast floor, this time dotted with Islands of Plenty: circular bars laden with food and a good deal more Perrier Jouët. The 150 or so fairly senior property folk gossiped avidly for a while, then listened politely as the Land Securities chief executive delivered a short speech. He then gave away a Smart car to the winner of the quiz. Then on came Lulu....

What was that all about? The official word is that the event is all of a piece with the "capital commitments" advertising campaign, emphasising a commitment to London. Unofficially, it feels much more about expelling the lingering smell of port and cigars and introducing a whiff of fresh self-confidence that will cheer the supporters of property's already rising bellwether stock.

The event succeeded: the entire building was quickly let to Dresdner Kleinwort Wasserstein. Early the next year, 30 Gresham Street was bought by the Government Office of Singapore for £274 million, a 5.6 percent yield. The sap was rising. In October 2005, Land Securities held an even more extravagant event. By then Ian Henderson had retired as chief executive, to be replaced by Francis Salway.

This time, a four-hundred-thousand-square-foot, pointy-nosed block in Victoria by the name of Cardinal Place was the venue for the celebration. The ground floor was turned into a fairground, and later in the evening three rather nervous-looking girls took to the stage and mechanically belted out a few songs. Mutya, Keisha and Heidi were a trio called the Sugababes, and their hit song was called *Push the Button* – an apposite title, given that the entire sector had begun pushing buttons in a big way.

THE AUSTRALIANS COME SHOPPING FOR GOLD

In August 2004, Elliott Bernerd of Chelsfield was finally able to push the button on the £1.4 billion sale of his vast White City shopping centre to German fund CGI. Negotiations had been politely described as "protracted", but a more apt word would have been "tortuous", according to John Rigg of Savills, who acted for the Germans. Transport for London was to thank for this, with its slow and painful extraction of many pounds of flesh in return for agreeing to build an underground station at the mall.

Matters were perhaps not expedited by the fact that Bernerd had been entangled for more than a year in an attempt to execute a management buyout of listed Chelsfield, with endless squabbles over the value of the shares. The deal was finally done in May 2004, with Bernerd holding a fourteen percent stake in the buyout vehicle. Among his backers were the billionaire Reuben brothers, who took a thirty-four percent stake.

Chelsfield and property company Stanhope held development rights on land at Stratford in east London owned by London & Continental Railways, builder of the Channel Tunnel Rail Link from St Pancras to Ashford in Kent. In 2003, the joint venture submitted the largest planning application ever made inside the M25. Sir Stuart Lipton, who switched from Stanhope to Chelsfield in late 2005, had spent years putting together plans for Stratford City, a hundred-and-seventy-acre site bang on the spot of the Olympic Park.

The thirteen million square feet of offices, houses and shops was planned as nothing less than a new heart for east London. On 1st July 2005, four parties each held a twenty-five percent stake: Westfield, the Reuben brothers, Australian builder Multiplex, and Stanhope. On 7th July, London won its Olympic bid, bringing the stakeholders close to each other's throats, as we shall see later.

Resentment was already simmering against the entry of Australian builders and developers into Britain, with much talk about the arrogance that Westfield was exhibiting and the helter-skelter expansionism of Wembley stadium builder Multiplex, which was trying to be come a developer as well as a contractor. *Quelle horreur*. I duly passed on the moans in *EG* on 19th February 2005, after Westfield was caught doing something stupid:

Aussie Arrogance Multiplies the Dangers

"We've seen them come. We've seen them go." A summary of dining club sentiment towards the two Australian companies that have gate-crashed the UK property market. Retail giant Westfield entered the UK in 2000, buying into eight MEPC centres. The £17bn worldwide business last year added a ninth in the hulking shape of Merry Hill – plus a quarter stake in both White City and Stratford.

Multiplex has been in the UK since 1979. But only with the Wembley contract did the Aussie builder register on the radar. The 2,000-strong group led by Andrew Roberts – the 38-year-old son of founder John – now has 400 staff in the UK. There is a stake in a £3bn project in Cricklewood and a £1.5bn bid for the Elephant & Castle.

The two Australian firms have certainly come. Will they go? That depends. To quote Edward de Bono, the key source of stupidity is arrogance. Underlying the breezy can-do culture of both is a touch of "we'll-show-them-poms" arrogance. A small example is Westfield employing the PM's friend, Lord Levy, as a £100,000 a year adviser – a stupid misreading of how UK politics works. A large example is Multiplex's view that it can deal with the UK planning system and successfully build out £10bn worth of development on time and to budget.

Westfield faces far fewer risks than Multiplex: You buy a shopping centre, you sell a shopping centre.... Multiplex has graver problems. Roberts wants his company to be "vertically integrated": a developer, builder and property owner. The cultural reasons why this has never worked in the UK are unconvincing to the more classless Aussies: but it would be perilous to discount English distaste...

This got me a summons to meet Westfield's European boss, Michael Gutman, a tall, dark and lean Aussie of perfectly even temper, fortunately. He explained to me how un-arrogant Westfield was. I later concluded, however, that Westfield had plenty to be arrogant about: the vast malls at White City and Stratford that were built on time and to budget stand testament. I subsequently got to know Westfield's John Burton, the man in charge of Stratford; a less arrogant and friendlier man would be hard to meet.

Multiplex didn't seem bothered about the *EG* article. Its UK chairman was James Tuckey, the genial former boss of MEPC; all I got from that direction was a light ribbing. In June 2007, Canadian giant fund manager Brookfield bought out the Roberts family in a $7.8 billion deal that enabled it to take full control of the Multiplex business later that year. This gave Brookfield a ready-made development platform in the UK, which it later exploited by purchasing Hammerson's City development sites.

IT'S DIFFERENT THIS TIME...
March 2005 brought the most dangerous moment of all in any boom: seemingly sane commentators suggesting that it was all going to be different this time, that the boom would last a generation or more. Phrases like "paradigm shift" or "structural shift" became common currency among deluded proper-

ty analysts. The reason it was all going to be different this time was that property risk was being spread by "securitisation" using financial instruments called commercial mortgage backed securities (CMBSs).

There is no easy way to describe CMBSs. But this, from the US Mortgage Bankers Association, is almost comprehensible, if read very slowly, twice over:

> In a CMBS transaction, many single mortgage loans of varying size, property type and location are pooled and transferred to a trust. The trust issues a series of bonds that may vary in yield, duration and payment priority. Nationally recognized rating agencies then assign credit ratings to the various bond classes ranging from investment grade (AAA/Aaa through BBB-/Baa3) to below investment grade (BB+/Ba1 through B-/B3) and an unrated class which is subordinate to the lowest rated bond class.

> Investors choose which CMBS bonds to purchase based on the level of credit risk/yield/duration that they seek. Each month the interest received from all of the pooled loans is paid to the investors, starting with those investors holding the highest rated bonds, until all accrued interest on those bonds is paid. Then interest is paid to the holders of the next highest rated bonds and so on. The same thing occurs with the principal as payments are received.

> This sequential payment structure is generally referred to as the "waterfall". If there is a shortfall in contractual loan payments from the borrowers or if loan collateral is liquidated and does not generate sufficient proceeds to meet payments on all bond classes, the investors in the most subordinate bond class will incur a loss with further losses impacting more senior classes in reverse order of priority.

What actually happened, of course, was this: because the CMBS market was thought to spread and minimise risk, more and more risk was taken. The very thing designed to create that "paradigm shift" accelerated the crash.

... ACTUALLY, NO, IT'S NOT

On 3rd March 2005, I had lunch with one of the most sagacious agents in London, Alastair Hughes of Jones Lang LaSalle. The reason for mentioning this is to give credit to Hughes for this leader on 5th March. All I did was to précis his views:

Enjoy a Guilt-free Trip While the Ride Lasts

With the investment market red-hot and the occupier market heating up, does the property market face meltdown? Not so far as anyone can see, is the uncomfortable answer. Uncomfortable for two reasons: one, because, after two generations of ups and downs, it must surely come to pass that the current long "up" will be followed by a long "down"; two, because there is now talk of a "structural shift" in favour of property that may last a couple of generations.

Talk of a major realignment of investor sentiment brings derision from those who have seen it all before. But has anyone ever seen this level of global interest in UK property? The fact is, there has been a shift: the number of buyers has widened from a West End coterie to a worldwide community. Like every other market, UK property is globalising. The only difference is that the money needs to be imported to buy goods (property) that cannot be exported.

Actually, there is another difference: this rush of money into property, both from home and abroad, is being strained through some rather fancy financial sieves. This is a bit worrying: hands up those who really understand commercial mortgage backed securitisation? And do the major occupiers splitting their businesses into operating and property companies really appreciate that all they are doing is mortgaging the business?

The last sentence was tagged on because Hughes and I discussed another boom-time fashion. In the Sixties it was called asset stripping. The mid Noughties version was more sophisticated: strip your own assets. Sell the real estate assets of a business into a newly formed property company in which you keep a stake, then lease the space back to the operating company at a profit. There was quite a fashion for what was called the "opco-propco" model – a fashion that died out when property values fell.

CRIMINAL INVESTMENT

Market confidence had reached such a peak in early 2005 that confidence tricksters moved into the market. One group bilked mortgage lenders out of £50 million, in a con that relied upon an RICS qualified valuer overvaluing properties. The valuer was Ian McGarry of Dunlop Haywards Lorenz, while the ringleaders were Saghir Ahmed Afzal and his brother Nisar. In June 2010, Saghir Afzal was sentenced to thirteen years in prison, while his brother Nisar fled to Pakistan. McGarry went down for seven years.

At Southwark crown court, the judge described how Saghir Afzal had led a team in operating a "massive and carefully orchestrated confidence trick" that duped banks and building societies out of almost £50 million. He said the value of the fraud meant that the case was "off the scale" in terms of the sentencing guidelines for fraud cases. Saghir Afzal sent over £26 million of his gains to Pakistan: money that was never recovered.

The husband of *EG* auctions correspondent Estelle Maxwell was chief reporter at the *News of the World*: Neville Thurlbeck. He later became ensnared in the News International bugging scandal. But back then, I asked him to pop in one day to see if the paper could help trace Nisar Afzal and the missing £26 million; he reported back to me three months or so later to say that nothing could be found.

McGarry accepted bribes from the Afzal brothers to the tune of more than £1 million, including lavish overseas holidays in Dubai, an Aston Martin, cash in brown envelopes and three properties in London. In return he prepared inflated valuations for each property, which the lenders relied on when advancing the mortgages. The con worked by using false leases to convince lenders that empty buildings actually had tenants paying rent.

The Cheshire Building Society gave a £11.5 million mortgage in early 2005 to an Afzal front company, Goldgrade Properties, against the surety of an old brassworks in Birmingham. Empty, the place was worth about £1 million. McGarry certified its worth as about £16 million in late 2004, basing his calculation on the fiction that three tenants had signed leases promising to pay rents totalling £1.2 million a year.

If the three tenants were together paying £1.2 million, then twelve to fifteen times that figure would seem to be a reasonable price tag for the property. On the strength of the valuation, the loan was granted. In February 2006, the Cheshire announced a £10.5 million writedown and cried foul; a month later, McGarry was arrested.

The Serious Fraud Office's enquiries revealed that the Bank of Ireland, Société Générale and the Nationwide Building Society had all been defrauded in similar ways. Companies controlled by the Afzals bought the properties from genuine sellers for a total of £5,688,125 – the true market value. Using McGarry's false valuations, the Afzals were able to deceive lenders to loan £49,287,000, which represents a mortgage loan-to-value ratio of eight hundred and sixty-six percent.

The fraud worked like this: a company controlled by the Afzal brothers would buy a property, usually an old industrial building in a dilapidated state, from a genuine seller. The property was then fictitiously "bought and sold" a number of times in a short period, each time for an apparently higher price. The only money that the Afzals paid out was for the initial purchase. All the paperwork was false.

When the final "purchase" of each property was completed, the Afzals obtained a huge profit by virtue of receiving the fraudulent mortgage loans from institutions – which presumably failed to visit the empty real estate. After making one or two mortgage payments, the companies controlled by the Afzals would stop paying the mortgage and the brothers would disappear. In the autumn of 2012, McGarry heard the news in prison that he had been expelled from the Royal Institution of Chartered Surveyors.

MEETING MAXWELL

The summer of 2005 brought a curious meeting with Kevin Maxwell. The son of Robert Maxwell had seen the potential of the nascent property derivatives market – or, more accurately, the potential value of the indices provided by property data specialist IPD to players of a very new game. This game involved betting on movements in the IPD indices, which was far less costly than buying and selling actual buildings. Many hoped that the game would explode into a multibillion-dollar global market. It didn't, but that's not the point. At the time, influential fund managers such as Rupert Clarke at Hermes and Iain Reid of Protego were going so far as to set up "gaming" sessions for those interested in playing the indices without the cost of placing bets.

Kevin Maxwell operated out of sparse walk-up offices north of Portman Square. He bore a startling resemblance to his father at the time, but only in body. He was neither bumptious nor overbearing, unlike the former owner of the *Daily Mirror*, who slipped off his yacht in November 1991 during the collapse of his publishing empire. His plan was simple: buy the fifty-odd percent of IPD owned by half-a-dozen property industry shareholders, then take control from founders Rupert Nabarro and Ian Cullen – who, along with other managers, owned just under half the shares. Fortunes would be made from selling the indices into the booming derivatives market.

Kevin Maxwell had gained the backing of Chelsfield's Elliott Bernerd. However, Nabarro persuaded almost all his external shareholders to stay with him. The constitution of the business founded in 1986 was then altered to make takeover impossible. One shareholder, Cluttons, did sell its ten per-cent stake to Chelsfield for some £1.4 million. That stake would have become worth £7.7 million by December 2012, when IPD was sold for £77 million.

I got a call from Rupert Nabarro in March 2012. He and co-director Ian Cullen were in their late sixties; both they and the external shareholders, including Chelsfield, had concluded it was time to find IPD a new owner. Nabarro asked if I'd provide communications advice; many a happy hour was then spent in Lazard, the merchant bank, trying to coach him and Cullen to be the salesmen they were very clearly not. The sale to US-listed MSCI for $125 million subsequently closed on 30th November 2012. Neither Cullen and Nabarro nor the Americans saw income from derivatives indices as sali-ent to the price.

JANUARY 2006–JUNE 2007: EUPHORIA

MIKE STRONG, CHAIRMAN FOR EMEA AT CBRE:

The boom went on; it went on through 2006, and well into 2007. Finance people who held the belief that there was a new paradigm drove the market. There never is a new paradigm, and it never is different.

ROBERT PETO, THEN CHAIRMAN OF DTZ FOR BRITAIN AND IRELAND:

It was all about the deal, and the commission on the deal. In the end, without any question, it got to the point where people started to lose perspective. They had their eye on their annual bonus. Once you start thinking in those terms, rather than if the deal is good for the buyer or seller, it starts to go wrong.

NICK THOMLINSON, SENIOR PARTNER AT KNIGHT FRANK SINCE 2004:

There was always one more insane person left to buy that investment or that house. What are you going to say? "Yes, we know it's going to stop. No, we don't quite know when. But as long as it keeps going, we'll keep going."

Between January 2006 and June 2007, the FTSE 100 index rose from 5,600 to reach 6,700. That twenty percent leap was more than matched by a rise in the capital values of offices, which jumped a further twenty-two percent over those eighteen months on top of that twenty-four percent rise in 2005. But the first ominous traces of a slowdown could be detected. Retail and industrial capital values rose by half the rate of offices during those eighteen months. During that time, the cost of money – as measured by the fixed cost of borrowing for five years – had started to rise and act as a brake on lending. This is from *EG* on 10th June 2006:

Feel the Relief as the Pace Starts to Slacken

There's still £10 of capital chasing every £1 of property for sale. But is the pace slackening? The Jones Lang LaSalle yield figures for May show the All Property prime yield stands at a record low of 4.64%.... But retail yields, at 4.42%, are almost static now. Industrial property prime yields, at 5.2%, have not moved in the past month either.

What, of course, has moved is the cost of borrowing money to finance deals: what's called the five-year swap rate – effectively, the benchmark borrowing figure – has moved steadily upwards, and now stands at 5.08%. That means it is now possible for those borrowed to the hilt to be paying out more in interest charges than they are receiving in rental income. As JLL suggests darkly: "The pressures on leveraged investors are likely to intensify."

Well, they didn't. Not yet, anyway. DTZ figures for 2006 and 2007 show the volume of purchases at £94 billion, almost the same as in 2004–

2005. There was an upturn in the percentage of foreign buyers, from thirty to thirty-six percent. The hindsight question is: who was lucky enough to be selling, and who unlucky enough to be buying? Well, the lucky included institutions, which were net sellers in 2006 and 2007, to the tune of some £9 billion. The quoted companies divested £2 billion of stock. The biggest buyers by far were the unlucky "private vehicles": typically pools of investors backed by high levels of debt. In 2006–2007, their net investment was £17 billion, half of this falling into 2006 – and the other half into 2007.

PLAYING THE GAMES

The market raced happily along in 2006 like there was no tomorrow. But a deeply unhappy relationship developed between the partners who had won the right to build Stratford City on what was now the site of the London 2012 Olympics. We left the tale on 1st July 2005, at which point four parties each held a twenty-five percent stake in the development rights: Westfield, the Reuben brothers, Australian builder Multiplex, and Stanhope.

On 7th July 2005, London won the Olympic bid. The hundred and seventy acres of land suddenly became worth roughly £120 million more. Twelve months were then wasted as the four parties fought over what was now going to be a much bigger bone. The jostling ended in the summer of 2006, when it was agreed that Westfield would get to build the giant Stratford City shopping centre and Lend Lease was brought aboard to build the Olympic Village. Between times, it got nasty.

In November 2005, London mayor Ken Livingstone had threatened to issue a compulsory purchase order on the whole Stratford City site unless the four parties could agree to work together. By then, it was clear there were divisions between Stanhope's Sir Stuart Lipton, David and Simon Reuben, and Westfield. In February, Multiplex pulled out, selling its twenty-five percent to the Reubens, putting them in the driving seat with half the equity. By then it had emerged that Sir Stuart Lipton personally owned half of Stanhope's twenty-five percent stake – and was heading off to work with his old friend Elliott Bernerd at Chelsfield, the company that had helped Stanhope put together the Stratford City plans in the first place.

The divisions deepened further in March 2006, first at the MIPIM property fair. I questioned Ken Livingstone in front of a packed audience in a marquee holding the London stand at Cannes. It was late afternoon, and the chattering of the crowd had grown loud on champagne, but no one was asking any questions. In desperation, I threw one in myself about the Reuben brothers' commitment.

The mayor said he "wasn't sure" how serious the Reubens were about staying with the scheme. He again threatened a compulsory purchase order. "The developers I'm dealing with want to make a good project. However, I'm not sure everyone in the consortium has that long-term view," he said, referring clearly to David and Simon Reuben. That started a chase.

The following week, Livingstone was questioned on his attitude towards the brothers. "If they're not happy here, they can go back to Iran and try their luck with the ayatollahs; if they don't like the planning regime or my approach." This caused uproar – not least because the brothers were born in India. By May, the talks had reached crisis point. The best way to describe both the situation and the atmosphere is to reprint this from *EG*, published on 6th May 2006:

End This Unedifying Olympic Struggle

"The Reuben brothers have never built a ******* garden shed." The expletive has been deleted from this remark made by one of the other warring parties during the fight for the right to develop the Olympic Village and its surrounds. Well, should the pair of billionaires be allowed to control the most critical development in Britain for a generation? No, not now.

Last Friday, the long leaseholder, London & Continental Railways, rightly called time on the consortium that owns the 20-year development rights to 170 acres of land. For six months, David and Simon Reuben, who now own 50% of these rights, have been in a power and money tussle with UK developer Stanhope and Sir Stuart Lipton, who have a 25% stake, and Australian shopping centre giant Westfield, which owns the last quarter.

A lot of money is at stake: in pre-Olympic days the original partners were effectively given development rights in return for the millions in fees spent over the years in working up the project. Then came the Olympics. At a rough guess, the development rights for the 13.5m sq ft of homes, offices and retail have jumped in value from somewhere south of £30m to somewhere north of £150m. In January, the trio were asked to kiss and make up. Fat chance. Last Friday, L&CR issued a notice terminating the agreement – but gave the warring parties 42 days to think again.

They did not think again. Westfield bought out David and Simon Reuben and went on to finish its 1.7 million square foot Stratford shopping centre a year before the Games opened: an extraordinary achievement. Lend Lease came in to develop a smaller-than-planned Olympic Village that was supposed to be funded privately – but the global crash put paid to that. The Aussie developer ended up as just the builder of the two thousand, eight hundred units, of which half were sold to housing associations and the rest to the Qatari government in a joint venture with Delancey, the property company run by Jamie Ritblat. The plan is to rent them all out.

Just before the 2012 Games, I crammed into a small broadcast studio in Soho alongside Ken Livingstone, Sir Stuart Lipton and the urbane boss of Urban & Civic, Nigel Hugill, who had been instrumental in working up the plans for Stratford City when he was at Chelsfield. The session had been organised by Damian Wild, my wise and calm successor as editor at *EG*. Livingstone showed off the lightweight tan suit he'd worn in Singapore at the bidding ceremony and then gave an account of the first critical meeting, one that was to set the development pattern for the construction of the Games:

At the first meeting of the committee after I came back from Singapore, the senior civil servant came up to me and proposed a committee of civil servants would run the whole project, and we'd all step back. I knew this was a disaster. He said to me: "It's very important this finishes on time and on budget." Loudly and unpleasantly, I just said: "Is there anything in your career that has ever finished on time and on budget?" There was deathly silence. We needed to bring in someone like David Higgins with a record of building things, and keep politicians away.

I'd first come across David Higgins in September 2004, when he was chief executive of English Partnerships, the government's regeneration agency. Developers in London were getting snippy about English Partnerships buying up choice land in London, and I had suggested that the £150 million of public money Higgins had been given by the government was allowing the agency to gazump private developers with ease. I was called in to see Higgins, the former chief executive of Lend Lease – a tall, bespectacled Australian who had given up a very big job in the sun to run a UK quango in the rain. I have never before or ever again been so elegantly chastised, with each of my arguments being carefully demolished before moving on to the next.

It was no surprise that David Higgins was put in charge of the Olympic Delivery Authority, and no surprise subsequently that the physical structures for the Games were built on time and to budget. No surprise either that he was given a knighthood – but a bit of a surprise when he left the Olympic job early to go and run Network Rail.

2006: AN UNSTOPPABLE YEAR...

The headline over the leader on 15th December 2006 was "Stubbornly Refusing to Go Wrong". Here's an extract from this rather frustrated leader, which tried to sum up the year:

- **Quarter one**: "Well, that's it; after eight years, this has all got to stop. Hunker down guys, it's time to take cover."
- **Quarter two**: "Er... those foreign chappies don't seem to have quite got the message and they keep pouring money in. So, let's keep riding the boom."
- **Quarter three**: "This really is ridiculous and will simply have to stop soon."
- **Quarter four**: "Okay, okay, it's not going to stop, slowdown maybe, but, who knows, I give up!"

... 2007: THE YEAR IT STOPPED

By early 2007, I'd given up trying to forecast the end of the boom. But a touch of nervousness could be detected in conversations. Yields had begun moving out. So had interest rates: Libor had reached 5.25 percent, up from 3.5 percent in 2003. Here's the first part of a leader I wrote on 3rd February:

> The All Property IPD index has more than doubled from 100 to 215.5 since 2000. Equities are up only 20.6% and bonds 32%. So, why the undercurrent of nervousness? Property shares fell 7% in January. A short report last week in EG on yields beginning to move out resonated widely. Recently, several large deals have broken down between agreeing the price and signing the transfer deeds.

This skittishness seems to have three root causes: one, the quite unexpected growth in 2006 means that all now firmly expect that 17.9% total return figure to halve in 2007. Second, that last interest rate rise has inflated the cost of money above the lowest yields. Finally, as the feature (pages 62-64) on this "mood swing" shows, funds such as Standard Life saying 2006 was "a turning point" doesn't sound very cheerful.

The "yields moving out" was a reference to a report from Lambert Smith Hampton. The mid-sized agent run by Ezra Nahome had analysed £27.5 billion of transactions reported between July and December 2006, to produce a report that spooked those of a nervous disposition.

Lambert Smith Hampton also said that because the cost of borrowing had risen higher than the initial yield on property transactions, "this could force some debt-backed buyers out of the property market". But the view of Standard Life in *EG* that week was perhaps more important. "The last few months of 2006 heralded a turning point in the UK property market," said Alex Watt, managing director of property investments at Standard Life Investments. "After four years of double-digit returns, on the back of declining yields, property income yields reached the same level as gilts, the 'risk-free' rate. We have been anticipating this trend for some time and have been altering portfolios accordingly." Best call in the cycle. The insurer said it would be reducing its weighting in UK property because it could earn more money by keeping its cash in the bank. Fund manager Prupim also began to retrench, announcing it was to reduce its UK property weighting by £600 million.

This was the beginning of the end of the ten-year boom. Not the end, of course – diminishing numbers of the uninformed and plain reckless continued to buy until the summer of 2008; some right up until Lehman Brothers crashed that September. Back in February 2007, few could see what was coming, including yours truly. In early February, a former deputy governor of the Bank of England, Sir David Clementi, addressed an audience of twelve hundred at the annual Investment Property Forum lunch in the Great Room of the Grosvenor Hotel in Park Lane. I went along. Sir David had taken the chair of a newly formed loose-fit lobbying group called the Property Industry Alliance. He'd sensed the mood shift, but gave a "resounding no" to the idea of a general downturn. He should know, for heaven's sake. So I put his reasons into my 3rd February leader for *EG*:

> First, the financial world – and the property market along with it – has completely changed in 10 years. Property and finance are converging: bricks and mortar, shares, bonds, what's the difference? The business is also globalising. Money flows in from around the world – and out into Europe and Asia. Fund managers now see property as a "third leg" to equities and gilts – even though some may ease their weight to the other two from time to time. And, as Clementi says, "there is now a multiplicity of investment channels" – from Man in the Street's £1,000 ISA to Mr Banker in the Tower's £200m of commercial mortgage-backed securities.
>
> Now, money can flow as fast out of these new channels as it flows in. But there is a second reason for thinking that might not happen – apart from the sheer

inertia and cost of extracting the cash, that is. That is because, even if returns halve in 2007 to 8-10%, it may prove better than leaving the money in the bank or in bonds – provided interest rates rise no further. And that brings to mind the final reason for optimism. Interest rates have been hiked because the economy is doing well, not badly. Retail may struggle and yields may start to edge up. But, to quote Bill Clinton, "it's the economy, stupid" that defines the health of the sector.

Not this time. This time, industrial economies around the world were going fine, only to be crippled by the global banking economy – which in turn had been felled by over-lending into the real estate economy. In other words, this time it wasn't the general economy dragging down property prices; it was the reverse. I'd written a pretty stupid leader, as it turned out.

Meanwhile, plenty of stupid things were still going on. A trio of private equity groups revealed they were considering a £9 billion bid for Sainsbury's. CVC, Blackstone and Kohlberg Kravis joined forces to bring about what would have been Europe's biggest-ever leveraged buyout; the Sainsbury's property portfolio was central to their interest. They had hired DTZ to evaluate the estate, with the aim of carrying out a sale-and-leaseback on the holdings, which analysts believed to be worth over £7.5 billion – billions more than the book value. On 11th April, however, the consortium abandoned the bid, after being told where to get off by the family shareholders.

Two weeks later, it emerged that the Qatari ruling family had been building a stake in the supermarket through its Delta Fund. The advice came from Paul Taylor, a former bricklayer turned banker who had got to know the Qatari royal family while working for Robert and Vincent Tchenguiz. By June 2007, the fund vehicle, Delta Two, owned twenty-five percent of the supermarket chain. In July, Taylor flew David and John Sainsbury to Sardinia to reveal and discuss the potential bid. Oh, to have been a fly on that wall!

The proposed structure involved splitting the business into an operating company and a highly leveraged property company. On 5th November 2007, it was announced that Delta Two had abandoned its takeover bid due to the "deterioration of credit markets". Britain's best-loved supermarket chain was saved by the downturn.

Market stupidity continued well into the late summer of 2007, and in some cases into the spring of 2008. By the time of the annual property beano in Cannes in March 2007, however, it was becoming slowly apparent to those who had seen it all before just how mad everything was getting:

IAN MARCUS, THEN HEAD OF EUROPEAN REAL ESTATE BANKING AT CREDIT SUISSE:

I was at MIPIM in March 2007. We'd done the boat, the villa and the hotel over the last four or five years. I hired a cheap and cheerful apartment directly opposite the Palais as I was fed up of walking three miles when you couldn't get a taxi. We were on the top floor. I opened up the doors and I looked at the Palais directly opposite, and they had these huge banners draped above the entrance. One was for a Russian city I'd never heard of; the other was for Dubai.

I stood there thinking: what has happened to the real estate market that I knew? That was the year when the excesses really came into their own, particularly among the central and eastern European exhibitors. You just thought: this can only end in tears.

Back in the UK, I remember wandering through Waterloo and looking at the New Star billboards offering the public such high returns. I thought: it's going to come to an end soon. Of course, it ran on for another year and more. But I think that was when you began to think: well, the end is coming.

The Russian city Marcus speaks of is Kazan, whose 1.2 million citizens live a thousand miles east of Moscow in Tartarstan. No one had heard of the place when MIPIM opened on the Monday. By Friday, everyone knew the name of Kazan, although not necessarily where it was. We printed a map in the following week's *EG* as an act of enlightenment. The Tartar city wooed delegates on the Croisette with a deep-throated Cossack choir, comely female violinists and long-legged "hot girls" in silky blue dresses barely covering their modesty. One of *EG*'s young male reporters was asked by a senior Tartar official, "You wanna hot girl?" with a suggestion that all he had to do was to write something nice.

Easy to snigger: but questionable practices (of a less physical nature) involving British public authorities and the private sector reached their high point at MIPIM 2007. Cities such as Birmingham, Manchester, Liverpool and Leeds had been exhibiting at the show for years. It provided a chance to woo developers by boasting the delights of investing in their particular bailiwick: nothing wrong with that. The Corporation of London did the same.

But the City paid its own way and told the world how much it was all costing, while less wealthy councils began to have developers "sponsor" what increasingly looked like jaunts to southern France. I attended many an event at which the council's chief planning officer and its chair of the planning committee would be carousing with their "sponsors", often keen to get permission for this or that development. In a fit of moral outrage I suggested in March 2007 that "this crosses the line". But no one could even see the line.

THE FINISHING LINE

The finishing line for the longest boom in modern history was coming closer. Grosvenor chief executive Jeremy Newsum had spotted something. "We are one year nearer the end," he said in the spring of 2007, when announcing the 2006 results for the Duke of Westminster's property business. "We don't like the conditions. It is a hot market and that does not work for us." The group had seen profits jump from £368 million to reach £509 million. Asset values had leaped twenty-three percent to £4.6 billion in the steeply rising market.

Grosvenor had declared an embarrassing £140 million initial loss on the construction of a £1 billion retail-led regeneration scheme in Liverpool, which may have made Newsum grumpy. But, by then, Grosvenor was switching from town centre regeneration to developing residential sites on its own Mayfair patch – and was being constantly outbid in the "hot" climate.

Gordon Brown took office on 27th June 2007. That week, Grosvenor announced it was to sell a fifty percent stake in a £700 million scheme to rebuild thirty-two acres in Preston town centre. A development agreement had been reached between Grosvenor and the council in 2005, since when the duke's property company had struggled to find tenants – until in January 2007, John Lewis agreed to anchor what was called the Tithebarn project.

In came Lend Lease – at precisely the wrong moment, with hindsight. In 2009, Grosvenor pulled out, leaving the Australian company as the lone developer. John Lewis abandoned ship in November 2011, effectively killing the scheme. In July 2012, the council began all over again by trying to attract piecemeal development into the redubbed Market Quarter. You live by the market... a market that began to fade as Blair left office in June 2007.

BOOM, BOOM, BANG

There is no precise point at which euphoria gave way to depression, when boom turned to bang. But the long boom, as marked by the IPD capital values index, did indeed coincide with Tony Blair's time in office between May 1997 and June 2007. The figures below show just that. During the Blair era, the all-property index rose by eighty-one percent, rental values by thirty-five percent (while general inflation pushed up prices by a fifth). The long boom stretched the fundamental link between rental income and capital value to the point where it snapped. Rents fell gently during the 2007–2009 crash, as they are tied to lease agreements. But ten years of capital gains were wiped out in two years. These numbers tell more than any more words:

THE LONG BOOM...

IPD commercial property indices reveal the massive gains in capital values, which grew by four-fifths over the decade – while rents rose by much less

Capital values:	All property	Retail	Office	Industrial
June 1997	125	134	107	147
June 2007	227	255	179	252
Rise (%)	81	90	67	71
Rents:				
June 1997	141	160	118	139
June 2007	191	228	155	172
Rise (%)	35	42	31	23

Source: IPD indices (1986 = 100)

... AND THE SHORT BANG

As the IPD indices show, commercial property subsequently lost almost half its value in just two years; rents slipped only slightly, because of fixed lease terms

Capital values:	All-property	Retail	Office	Industrial
June 2007	227	255	179	252
June 2009	127	139	99	149
Fall (%)	44	45	45	41
Rents:				
June 2007	191	228	155	172
June 2009	180	219	140	168
Fall (%)	6	4	10	2

Source: IPD indices (1986 = 100)

CHAPTER THREE
MONEY, MONEY, MONEY

A billion here, a billion there, and pretty soon
you're talking about real money
Everett Dirksen

Money is what makes Planet Property spin. Leverage makes it spin faster; bankers and fund mangers are the hands that speed up or slow down the rate of rotation. Between 1997 and 2007, the global financial community channelled billions into UK real estate, spinning the market into a giddy delight. The 2007–2009 crash saw this world come to a juddering standstill. Planet Property slowly began to spin again from 2010 – but freighted with more than £250 billion in debt that would take years to shed.

The first part of this chapter looks at how the transaction market slowly grew from 1997, quickly shrivelled in 2007–2008, and then bumbled along until 2012. Who bought, and when; who sold, and when. Part two examines the sometimes shocking role of the banks and their too-close relationships with their customers. Part three considers how the tidal flow of cash washed away the traditional caution and customer focus of fund managers; how fees became more critical than investor returns. How a return to traditional values then began, after the crash. And finally, how globalisation in many industries was matched over those fifteen years by the spread of global real estate funds.

PART ONE: HOW THE MONEY FLOWED

In the fourteen years between 1997 and 2011, a total of £476 billion worth of commercial property transactions were recorded by DTZ in the UK. This works out at an average of £34 billion each year. The agent's *Money into Property* data doesn't record every transfer; some are handled off-market. But the statistics are comprehensive enough to capture a pretty accurate picture of sales and purchases by sector and nationality. The figures also track the rise and fall of the market, plus the ebb and flow of foreign capital.

FOREIGN BUYERS, BRITISH SELLERS

DTZ recorded £4 billion of foreign purchases in the UK in 1997; ten years later, the figure was £18 billion. Foreign capital accounted for twenty-two percent of the market in 1997: ten years on, it was thirty-nine percent. In 1997, the most active overseas buyers were German, spending some £1 billion, with Middle Eastern buyers slightly behind and the US way down the list; Ireland stood near the bottom, spending just £100 million.

Irish investment then leaped like a leprechaun on poteen. Between 1997 and 2003, Irish purchases rose tenfold to reach £1.1 billion, then tripled to £3 billion in 2004, before peaking at £4.5 billion two years later. In 2007, the Irish spent less, but not much less: the figure was £3.6 billion. The following year, the number plunged to £615 million. In 2009, it was a big fat zero. Between 1997 and 2011, Irish investors spent £18.5 billion on buying UK property, £13.8 billion of that between 2004 and 2007. No wonder so many lost their shirts.

DOMESTIC VERSUS FOREIGN INVESTMENT IN UK PROPERTY 1997–2011

Foreign investment rose steadily during the boom, with market share continuing to rise after the crash – mainly because London did not cease to attract overseas capital

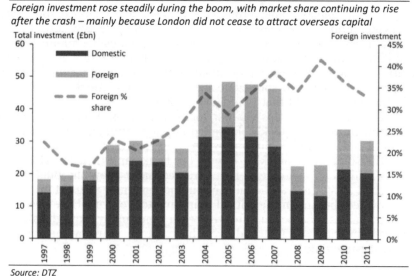

Source: DTZ

The US spent £28 billion between 1997 and 2011, but in two waves. The first £5 billion occurred mainly in 2000 and 2001, before 9/11 and the dot-com crash depressed appetites for a couple of years. Then, whoosh! Investment surged more than tenfold in a year, from £529 million in 2003 to nearly £6 billion in 2004. What US analyst Barton Biggs later called a "jet stream of dollars" began to blow across the Atlantic.

US private equity funds had begun to leave their home shores: Blackstone, Morgan Stanley, Apollo, Carlyle and their ilk started to invest around the world. Enormous sums were raised, both from other funds and from rich individuals, and leveraged with increasingly cheap debt. Research shows that $12 billion was raised in 2003 for global property funds. That number doubled, then trebled, to reach $76 billion by 2005, before soaring to $105 billion in 2008 – then collapsing back to $12 billion by 2010.

In the UK, British sellers appear to have got their timing right. About £100 billion of property moved into foreign hands between 1997 and 2011. Roughly a fifth of these sales occurred between 1997 and 2001, when prices were fairly static, but as prices soared between 2003 and 2007, £53 billion of stock was offloaded by UK sellers. In retrospect, a good move. Who did the selling? Pension and life funds were the biggest net sellers: between 2003 and 2007, they sold down £21 billion of stock. These funds were the first to get back in the market in 2010 and 2011, becoming net buyers.

FLOW MOTION SLOWS

In 2007, foreign and home purchases totalled £46 billion. They shrank by exactly half that figure to £23 billion the following year. But foreign capital did not flee. Overseas buyers continued to account for a third of deals – down from nearly forty percent at the height of the boom, but still well above the twenty-two percent figure of 1999. This can probably be accounted for by the influx into the London market of fresh capital from the Far East, which continued unabated after the crash. Chinese, Korean, Malaysian and Indonesian buyers became increasingly active in London, starting with prime central London purchases before spreading outside zone one of the Tube map. The signature deal of 2012 was the £400 million purchase of the thirty-nine-acre Battersea Power Station site by a Malaysian consortium, from vendor Irish Treasury Holdings.

PART TWO: BLAME IT ON THE BANKERS

The biggest property crash in history was entirely the fault of irresponsible bank lending: discuss. Well, yes, probably it was. But irresponsible bankers do require irresponsible borrowers. One member of the government's own property advisory group was getting worried as early as October 1999, after Bank of England figures showed real estate lending had risen to £45 billion, from £35 billion in 1997.

Paul McNamara, head of research at Prupim, said at that time: "The level of bank lending to property is rising fast – and the propensity to lend on speculative developments is rising with it. There is a history of the banking sector being in denial until the Bank of England sounds the warning bells: remember August 1972 and October 1989."

No one did. Debt more than doubled between 1999 and 2002, from £50 billion to £102 billion, according to the annual De Montfort University study that sends detailed questionnaires to around seventy lending institutions and produces numbers higher than the official debt figures.

In September 2002, the Bank of England did speak out. Deputy governor David Clementi warned of the high level of property debt, suggesting that "the potential for upsets in the property market to cause problems in the banking sector is clear". This was a prescient statement, but unfortunately not one that was acted upon by the Bank of England.

Two years later, one developer spoke out. Mike Slade of Helical Bar warned a roomful of lenders at an *EG*/Association of Property Bankers conference in September 2004 that "debt-driven buyers have inflated prices to unrealistic levels. These new boys have been making merry with your money. We may be missing a trick, but personally I don't think so."

By then, the Bank of Scotland was certainly making merry. A series of adverts for the bank appeared in *EG* showing a face made of money and urging those who weren't "made of money" to apply for loans. "Unlike some other banks our new business team has the authority to make critical decisions quickly," it boasted. As the graph opposite shows, plenty of bankers were beginning to make quick decisions by 2004.

The Bank of England seemed relaxed at the end of 2004, as outstanding commercial property debt reached £150 billion. Its end-of-year stability report mentioned that a third of all loans were going to real estate companies, which did cause a mild flutter. But the Old Lady of Threadneedle Street soothed the market with what was perhaps the most irresponsible statement of the entire cycle: "Commercial property lending provides little immediate cause for concern." *Hooray and away we go*, said the market.

By 2005, De Montfort's debt mountain had reached £172 billion. Not much concern was shown. In 2006, the figure swelled to £194 billion. Still no one was panicking. It was not until a year later that the panic began, in June 2007, when the market started to slide. By then the mountain of debt added up to £231 billion, reaching £255 billion in 2008 as the market collapsed. The property collateral supporting that debt fell in value by forty-five percent by mid 2009.

OUTSTANDING COMMERCIAL REAL ESTATE DEBT

Property debt rose fivefold from £50 billion to £250 billion during the boom, far exceeding what De Montfort regards as its natural level of around £150 billion

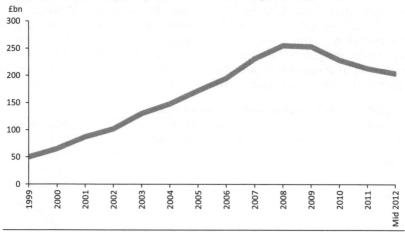

Source: De Montfort University/Bill Maxted

LOAN-TO-VALUE RATIOS FOR PRIME OFFICE INVESTMENTS

Seeking an early indicator? Ratios stayed steady from 1999 until 2005, at around eighty percent, then began to slide towards sixty/sixty-five percent two years before the crash

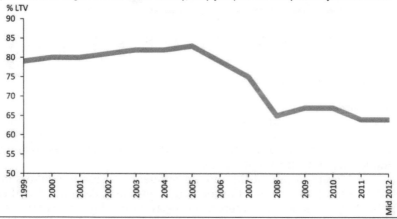

Source: De Montfort University/Bill Maxted

The debt mountain then slowly subsided, falling to £204 billion by mid 2012. I asked Bill Maxted of De Montfort University in December 2012 what bankers thought was the "natural" level of debt. "Around £150 billion," was his reply – which was where it sat in 2004.

Between 1999 and 2006, the margin of interest over the official base rate charged by lenders varied little. It began at ninety-seven basis points – or 0.97 percent, as non-financiers would say. In 2007, the rate jumped sharply to 126 basis points as the financial crisis slowly unfolded, before almost doubling between 2008 and 2010. Tough new banking rules and fearful banks drove the rate higher; by mid 2012, it stood at 335 basis points. Arrangement fees, which floated along at fifty basis points during much of the boom, more than doubled to reach 120 points by the middle of 2012.

Loan-to-value ratios provided warning signs to those watching for a lack of confidence among lenders. These didn't vary much between 1999 and 2005, staying roughly within the eighty to eighty-five percent band. In 2007, they slipped to seventy-five percent, before dropping a further ten percentage points in 2008, remaining at around sixty-five percent until 2012.

FINANCE COST FOR PURCHASING PRIME OFFICE STOCK

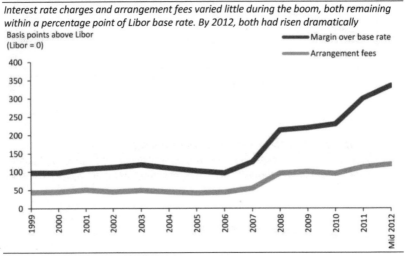

Interest rate charges and arrangement fees varied little during the boom, both remaining within a percentage point of Libor base rate. By 2012, both had risen dramatically

Source: De Montfort University/Bill Maxted

CASTING BLAME

Who was to blame for the unchecked rise in lending? Warnings from the Bank of England were certainly weak and ineffectual. Just as the soufflé was about to collapse in May 2007, the bank said that the sector was "potentially vulnerable" to a downturn. Potentially?

Ian Marcus is one of the most prominent real estate bankers of his generation. One-time president of the British Property Federation and chair of the Bank of England's commercial property forum for four years, he was involved in dozens of big deals as the head of European real estate banking at Credit Suisse until 2012, when he left for a plural existence including roles at Leeds-based Evans Property Group and as a Crown Estate commissioner.

IAN MARCUS, FORMER HEAD OF EUROPEAN REAL ESTATE BANKING AT CREDIT SUISSE:

My own team at Credit Suisse was full of bright young things. In my group of thirty real estate investment bankers, I was the only Englishman; the only one who didn't speak a second language. I was the only one in his fifties, so there was a generational gap. I think the lenders all fell into a trap of what I call MBE: management by Excel. The spreadsheet told you what you could obtain in terms of returns, and no one ever bothered to go and look at the real estate.

There was also no real sense of ownership of loans, since lenders knew that within three months the loan would be out the door because they were going to securitise it. Yes, the analysis was full and complete, but it was done on the basis that most securitised lending of course relied on cash flows. So you looked at the cash flows from the property, and you said, "This company is paying this amount of rent; they're a good covenant," then you'd judge accordingly on what you were willing to lend.

At the time, investment banks could seriously undercut balance sheet lenders. You could lend to your borrower at fifty, sixty, seventy basis points above Libor, knowing you could securitise and sell the loan for more. At the time, balance sheet lenders were struggling to get below a hundred basis points. So you'd undercut them, recognising there was enough in it for you when you syndicated the loans. We did a lot of that.

Then we'd sell the bonds. We'd slice and dice, and believed there were going to be buyers for triple-A rated bonds, double-A and single-A tranches as well as unrated paper. But what we forgot was that these were people who weren't necessarily specialist real estate investors. They were buying it on the rating, they were buying it on the spread, and they were buying it on the fact that the investment banks were sponsoring these deals.

There were hedge funds and other investors who, once the music stopped, weren't able to cope. Look at the White Tower deal: nine London office blocks bought by Simon Halabi and valued on securitisation at £1.8 billion. The securitisation raised £1.4 billion. The portfolio was sold to Carlyle for under £1 billion. Most of those who bought the bonds saw their investment vanish.

THE BANK THAT TOOK THE HIGH ROAD

In August 2008, HBOS reported a seventy-two percent fall in profits for the first half of 2008. The balance sheet showed that £47 billion of the £117 billion corporate loan book was allocated to real estate. Six months earlier, head of corporate banking Peter Cummings had said, "Some people look as though they are losing their nerve – beginning to panic even – in today's testing real estate market. Not us."

I remember a very odd meeting held with HBOS in early 2008. Whether Cummings was there, I don't recall: probably not. Anyway, the pitch was that the bank wanted to give away £30 million with the help of *EG*. Developers who came up with the three best schemes would be granted an interest-free loan from HBOS. The bank would pay *EG* a sponsor's fee in return for getting its logo on the articles promoting the competition.

It felt a bit like talking to folk who had been marooned on a desert island since 2006. (What we did not know then was that HBOS chief executive Andy Hornby was pressuring Cummings to increase his loan book.) HBOS demanded approval of the text to be published in the magazine: we weren't having that, so the bank went elsewhere with its proposal. The £20 million sale of Chantrey House in Eccleston Street, Belgravia, to Native Land in August 2009 was aided by a £10 million interest-free loan from HBOS. This was granted to the developer after winning the first (and last) BoS Corporate Property Entrepreneur of the Year award in December 2008.

As late as August 2008, HBOS remained resolute: "We take the long-term view," a spokesman told *EG* for an article on the bank's troubles. "When we feel asset prices and activity levels are unrealistic, we slow down the rate of lending growth. When common sense returns to asset pricing, we pick up on the opportunities."

The City saw little sense in this thinking. "The strategy under [ex-chief executive] James Crosby and Andy Hornby has absolutely been to bet the bank on property in every way possible," said Alex Potter of brokers Collins Stewart after seeing the HBOS results. Bernstein analyst Bruno Paulson warned: "HBOS is a property bank in a property crunch and thus is in the line of fire."

There was an additional worry: billions in property lending had been advanced to joint-venture companies in which HBOS held equity stakes. "You are going to think a lot harder about pulling a loan from a company in which you have an interest than one you don't," said a banker to me at the time. His comment prompted an *EG* leader on 23rd August 2008, three weeks before the collapse of Lehman Brothers. The doomed US bank even got a mention.

Bubble Blown by Bad Banking Practice

This page, 6 January 2007: A "creeping recklessness" in the market is identified, "a state of mind where greed is outbidding caution – particularly on deals where buyers borrow to the hilt..." This page, 5 May 2007: the Bank of England says property is "potentially vulnerable" to a downturn. The spectacle of a little old lady in Threadneedle Street waving her brolly fruitlessly at hubristic global megabanks and slightly dodgy mini-banks is irresistible.

This week, EG picks on HBOS for examination because it was the boldest and most successful during the boom: and also because it led the way in not just lending but in taking a stake in the deal. Since 1999, HBOS has dished out billions in debt and equity into more than 70 property-related ventures. This has, of course, paid fantastic dividends in a rising market, contributing £2.3bn to the bank's profits last year alone.

But when you own 50% of a business worth £100 that has £90 of borrowings and the value of the business drops to £90, you own 50% of nothing. HBOS's strategy now is to sit tight and hope the market will turn up.... Not that HBOS has much choice but to hold on. Even hinting at a fire sale would be disastrous.

It is not an exact parallel, but take a look at what has happened to Lehman Brothers.

Last week, the US investment bank unwisely let it be known that it would sell its entire $40bn worth of real estate holdings. Panic. On Thursday, an unlikely report had it selling 50% of the entire bank to "South Korean or Chinese parties". Desperate measures indeed, if true: and an indication of how toxic dabbling in real estate can be. For that is what has brought the bank close to the brink.

A subsequent Financial Services Authority investigation revealed that HBOS feared it would have to issue a profit warning in early 2007. Why? Because the introduction of a more prudent policy on home loans had led to falling market share. Hornby convened a meeting of HBOS's divisional heads in January 2007. Cummings was told to "substantially" expand his corporate lending business.

The Financial Services Authority found that Cummings' division had originally proposed targets for 2007 of ten to twelve percent growth in underlying profit before tax. After the meeting, Cummings raised the target to twenty-two percent. It was pushed up again, to thirty percent in April and then to thirty-five percent in June 2007, reported the FSA. You have to read the following conclusion from the FSA twice before the scale of the bank's folly fully sinks in: "HBOS increasingly looked to the corporate division to make up for the underperformance of the retail division."

In other words, an organisation seeing profits drop because of growing caution on residential property bet the bank on commercial real estate – right at the moment when the commercial market was clearly and visibly beginning to turn. All in the name of not having to issue a profits warning. It is scarcely believable.

FSA AND PARLIAMENTARY INVESTIGATIONS
The Financial Services Authority published the preliminary findings of its three-year investigation into the lending activities at HBOS in September 2012. Peter Cummings was fined £500,000 and banned for life from the industry. The FSA said that the head of HBOS corporate division "led a culture of optimism". Optimism "which affected the division's judgment about bad debts, and did not adequately monitor a deterioration in the value of big loans. In 2007 and 2008, when there were growing signs of problems in the economy, he did not mitigate potential risks and instead directed his division to increase its market share as other lenders were pulling out of deals."

Cummings complained bitterly: "For the past three years, I have been singled out and subjected to an extraordinary Orwellian process by an organisation that acts as lawmaker, judge, jury, appeal court and executioner. The fact that I am the only individual from HBOS to face investigation defies comprehension," he said, adding: "Who set the financial targets that the corporate division had to meet?" Chief executive Andy Hornby, according to a preliminary inquiry.

This parliamentary commission on banking, led by Conservative MP Andrew Tyrie, then subjected Cummings and the board of HBOS to a second interrogation. One of the first witnesses was Andy Haldane, the Bank of England director responsible for financial stability. On Monday 3rd December, he concluded: "If we are fortunate, the cost of the crisis will be paid for by our children: more likely it will still be being paid for by our grandchildren. In terms of the loss of incomes and outputs, this is as bad as a world war."

That same Monday in late 2012, the former chairman and both former chief executives of HBOS were hauled in front of the Tyrie Comission. Lord ("Dennis") Stevenson was the three-days-a-week chairman from 2001 to 2008, earning £815,000 a year when HBOS was swallowed up by Lloyds TSB. Sir James Crosby was chief executive between 2001 and 2006. He was also a non-executive director of the Financial Services Authority, becoming deputy chair in November 2007. Andy Hornby was chief operating officer of HBOS from 2001 until 2006, when he took over as chief executive from Sir James Crosby.

The ten-member commission included the Archbishop of Canterbury elect, Justin Welby, as well as former chancellor Nigel Lawson. The grilling began at 3.30pm in the Grimond Room at Portcullis House, just over the road from the Palace of Westminster.

Lord Stevenson was confronted with a letter written to the Financial Services Authority in 2008 in which he had asserted that HBOS was a "highly conservative institution". He had written: "I am not aware of any lurking horrors in our business or our balance sheet. Quite the reverse…" Lord Lawson retorted: "Either you were being dishonest when you wrote that or, if you believed it, you were delusional."

Lord Stevenson said he "deeply regretted" the failure to rein in the corporate lending division. But HBOS's approach to its balance sheet was "much of a muchness" with its UK competitors, he said. "You are living in cloud cuckoo land," suggested Margaret Thatcher's former chancellor.

Justin Welby, incoming Primate of All England, said he was "baffled" by the inability to recognise the "complete failure of culture and strategy" that "led to a bank being wiped out". Referring to Lord Stevenson's insistence on blaming the credit crunch for the collapse of HBOS, the church leader said: "It is like someone who has a fatal heart attack at home and is in a car crash on the way to hospital. And the car crash is then blamed as the cause of death."

Stevenson deflected blame, saying he was "only part-time". Andy Hornby blamed the failure on "too much information". "With hindsight, at times it may have been the case that the sheer volume of information supplied by every division right across operational risk, credit risk and regulatory risk may at times have made it harder for the board to fully understand the potential issues facing the business," he said.

Hornby's mentor and predecessor, Sir James Crosby, told the parliamentary commission he was "horrified" by what happened. Asked what he was apologising for, he responded: "I'm apologising for the fact that I played a major part in building a business that failed." He added: "I wasn't there for the last few years but it would be wrong to disassociate myself from what happened. I was deeply upset by what happened – it was hugely distressing to see what happened to shareholders, colleagues and taxpayers."

Poor health prevented Peter Cummings from giving evidence in Westminster. Instead, the commission visited HBOS's former head of corporate lending at his home in Scotland. The man singled out by the Financial Services Authority for blame said it was "unfair and also a bit sinister" that he was the only director of a failed bank to have been fined and banned from the industry. "We are not the only failed bank," said Cummings in testimony released later. "There are at least four or five of them, and I find it curious that I was singled out. So someone, somewhere decided that that was the appropriate action. I think it is sinister and curious."

He attacked the Financial Services Authority, saying his lawyers believed the FSA penalty was "unlawful" and that, when confronted, the watchdog had reduced its fine from £800,000 to £500,000 on the condition that he did not appeal. "I do think it bewildering and bizarre that in the space of a meeting and two phone calls – because they did not want me to take it to judicial review – they reduced the fine to £500,000," he said. "Frankly, it was like living in an American soap opera. I find it bewildering, bizarre and downright impossible to believe this country has an organisation that is out of control to the extent that it is. I think it is unacceptable behaviour."

The parliamentary commission says his division at HBOS was responsible for £26 billion of the bank's total recorded losses of £40 billion to £50 billion since 2008. Cummings, however, argued that the costly decision to accelerate corporate lending in 2006 and 2007 was the collective judgement of the board, led by Andy Hornby. Although he failed to apologise, Cummings did concede that the losses in his division were "horrendous", saying: "Every day I look in the mirror and ask: what did I do wrong?"

IAN MARCUS, FORMER HEAD OF EUROPEAN REAL ESTATE BANKING AT CREDIT SUISSE:

I very much enjoyed Peter Cummings' company. I think in one sense – it sounds a strange thing to say – he was somewhat of a visionary at HBOS. I think the fundamental mistake was probably the fact that a number of banks – not just HBOS, but it's obviously the highest-profile – went up the curve of being senior, junior, mezzanine debt lenders as well as providing equity.

I don't think the risk was always correctly priced for that capital. And the truth is – this isn't a reflection of intellect – there is a different skill set required to manage and analyse debt/credit exposure versus equity risk. It was the mixing of the two and the fact that there wasn't a lot of joined-up thinking. But I suppose if you're a guy running an organisation that's contributing twenty-five, thirty, forty percent of the bank's profits, you're encouraged to keep going.

You kind of begin to believe your own PR. A lot of it was driven by personal relationships: I'm a fan of relationship banking, but that can't dominate to the detriment of credit analysis. I think the way in

which individuals have been vilified is just not fair or appropriate.
I don't think they were bad people. You can question judgement, but
I don't remember the last time a banker committed murder. We just
forgot (or some never knew) that real estate is a cyclical business.

WHAT'S THE DAMAGE?

By early 2012, it was becoming possible to sensibly quantify the damage. On 31st January, I interviewed Richard Dakin, head of Lloyds' corporate real estate "business support" group: in other words, the workout man, charged with selling the repossessed properties and never-to-be-repaid loans for as many pennies in the pound as possible. By then, both Lloyds and RBS were getting their arms around the problem. RBS had hired the sage former Savills chief executive Aubrey Adams and the wise property fund manager Helen Gordon from Legal & General to help out.

Both banks published their 2011 results in late February 2012. Lloyds then had £65 billion out on loan to commercial property ventures. Within that figure, £21.3 billion of loans were categorised as "distressed". RBS noted £77 billion of outstanding commercial property loans, of which £27.5 billion were distressed. It published a table showing just how distressed: £9 billion lay against assets where the loan-to-value ratio stood at between ninety and a hundred and ten percent, £3.5 billion had ratios of between a hundred and ten and a hundred and thirty percent, and a massive £15 billion had loan-to-value ratios of over a hundred and thirty percent.

The two main UK banks between them thus had £48.8 billion of non-performing loans, three years after the collapse of Lehman Brothers. But should that figure have actually been far higher? The two banks were owed £142 billion from borrowers using commercial property as collateral. The £48.8 billion of loans marked as "distressed" were classified as such only on the banks' own estimate of what the underlying assets were worth.

That valuation was based upon what the banks hoped the land and property would be worth in a slow and orderly sale at a time of their own choosing, not the "mark-to-market" value of an immediate sale. The mark-to-market value is what any RICS trained valuer would have used. But if either Lloyds or RBS had used this as the valuation basis for their commercial property assets, the level of distressed loans could have shot up by billions, doing no favours to the banks' balance sheets.

In June 2012, I got the chance to ask the chief executive of RBS what was the true mark-to-market value of his bank's commercial property assets. The occasion was an event organised by the Investment Property Forum at the newly opened Central St Martin's art college at King's Cross. Chairing the panel was former Bank of England deputy governor Sir David Clementi, who had gone on to become president of the Investment Property Forum. Alongside him was the current deputy governor, Paul Tucker, who would lose out to Canadian Mark Carney for the job of governor later in the year.

But the main attraction was Stephen Hester, former boss of British Land and the man brought in to rescue RBS in late 2008. I thought I'd try my luck with three questions. First: "Will any new regulation prevent banks paying bonuses calibrated to the size of an individual banker's property loan book, rather than the eventual profit earned from the advances?" Second: "Are measures being drawn up to force lenders to demand collateral beyond the properties purchased using the loan?" In other words, was a weapon being fashioned to curb borrower enthusiasm by ensuring they share the pain of default by pledging personal or corporate assets?

Tucker executed an elegant circumlocution around the bonus question with a hint of a yes, saying "institutional shareholders should want a bigger part" of bank profits. The second question went blithely unanswered. Sir David Clementi felt very strongly that three questions was two too many. So that third question went to Hester: "If the UK government copied the Spanish government and ordered independent valuations of RBS's unwanted commercial property loans, how much would the write-down be?"

A deliberately silly question, perhaps. Just that week, the threat of an external valuation on Santander's Spanish real estate loans had triggered financial panic. To be fair, Hester did give a half-answer later. Just before giving me a pat on the back as he departed, he smiled and said: "All things being equal, we should be in good shape in about eighteen months' time." But in the autumn of 2012, there were still real worries in very high-up places about what was called the "extend and pretend" policy: in other words, not calling in loans due on properties where the immediate sale value was way below the book value.

In October 2012, a member of the Bank of England's financial policy committee described the banks' current methods for assessing risks posed by commercial property loans as "bogus". Committee member Andrew Bailey, who was also head of bank supervision at the Financial Services Authority, said "transactions in the sector were so large and so idiosyncratic it was all but impossible to build models to determine whether an individual loan would default and what the losses might be". The Bank of England director warned: "Six months ago, we said it was already the case then that there was some degree of underproviding on commercial property loans. And having looked at some portfolios outside of the UK, we think that the extent of that provisioning might be greater still."

THE IRISH QUESTION IS...

"Where does all the money come from?" That was the title of a plenary session on the Irish property boom which I chaired at the British Council for Offices conference in Dublin on 12th May 2006. A well-lubricated dinner had been taken the night before at Dublin Castle, and those who managed to appear at the Burlington Hotel at 9.30am the following morning exhibited no more than a pale interest in the question.

Not that it mattered. The fountainhead of the money flooding the Irish market was never fully pinpointed. That evening, I sat next to a young agent from the Dublin office of CB Richard Ellis. He told me that he had about €3 million worth of real estate "PA" – an acronym indicating property under his personal ownership. We fell into a discussion about how his other

PA (in the sense of "personal assistant") held €100,000 worth of property herself in the shape of a share in a Dublin office block.

"How?" I asked. "Easy," he replied. "She invested her €10,000 bonus and borrowed the rest." It was apparently easy to take small percentage stakes in commercial property – and even easier to borrow the money. Banks lent like there was no tomorrow; developers developed like there was no tomorrow. Politicians and planners colluded, some illegally.

... WHERE THE HELL'S THE MONEY GONE?

"Where the hell did all the money go?" became the question after Lehman Brothers crashed on 15th September 2008. Two weeks later, the Irish government announced that it would guarantee savers' money held in Irish banks. This effectively prevented a run on the Bank of Ireland, Allied Irish and Anglo Irish. Their property loans were transferred to the hastily formed National Asset Management Agency, or NAMA. It then became possible to quantify what money went where, if not where it came from.

In April 2010, NAMA reported that it held fifteen hundred loans with a total book value of €81 billion. Half of this amount was in loans to a mere one hundred customers. Roughly €7 billion had been lent against UK projects. The Irish banks were given €38 billion in payment for the loans – just forty-seven percent of the assets' former valuation on the banks' books. The great NAMA loan workout had begun.

Large numbers of Irish developers were declared bankrupt, and those that NAMA chose to let live were forced to present plans on how they planned to return the cash. Ballymore convinced NAMA to allow it to continue with schemes to build homes on tracts of land in London. Treasury Holdings, however, failed to put up a convincing plan to build out Battersea Power Station and consequently lost the site. In March 2011, Central Bank of Ireland governor Patrick Honohan described the crisis as "one of the most expensive banking crises in world history".

... WHAT THE HELL WAS GOING ON?

We set up the *EG* property awards in the mid Noughties. These events are great money-spinners: when the sponsorship is flowing, it's possible to make £100,000 on a single evening, even after paying the host £40,000 – as we did Irish comic Graham Norton. He was worth it: privately charming and publicly brilliant, to an audience that included many of his fellow countrymen. The event took place in September 2006, the apogee of the boom.

Anglo Irish Bank sponsored an award and took about a dozen tables (at £2,000 a pop) to entertain its clients. This was the height of relationship banking – a practice of getting so close to the borrowers that it had become unhealthy-relationship banking, according to *Anglo Republic: Inside the Bank that Broke Ireland*.

This 2011 book, by *Irish Times* journalist Simon Carswell, relates how the bank wooed developers with lavish corporate hospitality. As late as 2008, Anglo Irish co-sponsored a golf championship with the *Financial Times*. Companies entered teams of four, who got to play knockout tournaments on top courses like Sunningdale, Royal Birkdale and Gleneagles; the winning teams were invited to the Algarve for the final. English professional golfer Lee Westwood was hired to promote the competition, which cost the bank €304,000 in 2008.

One expensive junket involved flying American customers to Ireland each June to play golf on courses like Ballybunion and Waterville in County Kerry. The annual jaunt, which started in 2001, became so popular that the bank found it more economical to charter a jet than to pay business class fares to convey its clients on commercial airlines. This strategy carried an additional benefit, as journalist Carswell explains: "Putting the clients on a single Anglo charter gave the bank good access to them for the duration of the transatlantic flight."

In 2001, Anglo Irish chief executive Sean Fitzpatrick was asked about his favoured source of information. His reply: "For the real McCoy, you can't beat the nineteenth hole on a golf course." The bank's loan book trebled in size from just under €8 billion in September 2000 to €24 billion in September 2004. Borrowers were attracted to Anglo Irish by the bank's remarkably speedy response to loan requests.

It was commonly charging a €1 million "administration" fee on large loans, plus up to one percent more in interest than rival banks. But you could get loan approval within a week. "You were in thinner air," one developer told Carswell. "It was more high-risk stuff with quicker turnaround. They seemed more like a buccaneer's bank than a Steady Eddy type bank."

Loans over €25 million had to be approved by a credit committee, which met each Friday at 8am. "It was a cross between a Nuremberg rally and the half-time talk to an American football team," one former Anglo Irish manager told Carswell. "There was between fifty and sixty people in the room.... The whole system was set up wrong. No one was going to dissent in that atmosphere." As much as €300 million in loans was being approved every Friday, according to the Anglo Irish manager.

In the year to September 2004, the bank's property profits reached half a billion euros. By September 2005, its outstanding loans had grown to €34.5 billion, including €8.6 billion on London development projects. A survey by financial consultants Oliver Wyman in January 2007 named Anglo Irish "the best bank in the world". By then, the loan book had hit €67 billion.

Then came the crash. What happened next is well-reported history, but here is a short summary. In December 2008, the Irish government effectively nationalised Anglo Irish by taking a seventy-five percent stake in return for a capital infusion of just €1.5 billion. Further amounts followed. The bank took a €30 billion-plus "haircut" on the property loans transferred into the National Asset Management Agency, NAMA. In July 2011, Anglo Irish was merged with the Irish Nationwide Building Society and renamed the Irish Bank Resolution Company – which was later dissolved.

In July 2012, former chief executive Sean Fitzpatrick was arrested, along with Willie McAteer, the bank's former finance director, and Pat Whelan, former managing director of the bank's Irish lending business, after a three-and-a-half-year investigation into the affairs of what was once "the best bank in the world".

PART THREE: INSTITUTIONAL ISSUES

SIR JOHN RITBLAT, FORMER CHAIRMAN OF BRITISH LAND:

I never cease to boggle at the ineptitude of most institutions. The mind boggles at the impoverished nature of the average function-ary; their inability to invest long-term, their shortsightedness, the difficulties they get into, the forced selling then buying back. I have never seen such continued mismanagement over fifty years as from the great pack of the rest of them, apart from the Prudential. I have seen them set budgets for buying properties on an annualised basis, irrespective of the conditions, rushing out at stupid prices to fill their purchasing budgets without regard to the markets.

The Great British Public has a finely tuned nose. In April 2007, unit holders began to withdraw cash from property funds, months before profes-sional investors sniffed trouble. The regulated funds, which allow the man or woman in the street to invest, had done well for their unit holders in the boom – New Star was the best example. Four months later, in August 2007, a survey of sixty-three funds with assets under management of £44 billion brought the bad news. Outflows had doubled between the first and second quarters, rising to £631 million, while inflows had fallen twenty-five percent to £1.1 billion. The squeeze had begun. During 2008, the situation worsened.

It takes minutes for an investor to request their money back, but per-haps months to sell property to provide cash for repayment; this is the Achil-les heel of property unit trusts. Just before Christmas 2007, Friends Provi-dent barred a hundred and eighty thousand policy holders from withdrawing cash from its £1.2 billion fund. The following month, Scottish Equitable was forced to stall a hundred and twenty-nine thousand retail investors. Scottish Widows followed, stopping payouts on its £2.1 billion of property funds for six months: two hundred thousand policy holders were affected. Half a mil-lion investors in all were temporarily deprived of their cash during the crash.

New Star was of course famed for its billboard promises of high re-turns. Its £1.5 billion property fund stayed open, but investors pulled out £500 million and more in the second half of 2007. The company share price crashed. New Star became Death Star. Henderson Global Investors acquired what was left of the business in 2009, eventually dropping the name.

Big life and pension funds tend to hold five to ten percent of their to-tal funds in commercial property. In 2011, Aviva was the largest investor in real estate, with just under £20 billion of UK assets under management. Next came Sir John Ritblat's favourite, Prupim, with £13.2 billion, followed by Standard Life (£10 billion), Legal & General (£10 billion), Scottish Wid-ows (£8 billion), LaSalle Investment Management (£7 billion), and Hender-son Global Investors (£6.7 billion).

Many invest part of their funds into development projects. Hender-son was a one-third partner in the Bullring project in Birmingham, while the Prudential habitually took stakes in out-of-town shopping centres, including one in Bluewater in Kent. In 2012, Henderson was investing in speculative offices close to Holborn Viaduct in London. Funds like Aviva and Legal & General were dipping their toes into investing in the development of residential units for rent. As for any investor in development, if the entry and exit timing is right, large profits can be made. But one prominent developer thinks the funds mostly made a complete hash of their forays into development during the boom, by linking up with inexperienced players.

GERALD RONSON, CHIEF EXECUTIVE OF HERON INTERNATIONAL:

Because the institutions were not able to get the yield, they decided they had to become developers. So they worked with people who thought they were developers. Some of them were. Some of them weren't: some never put a penny of their own money into the deal.

When you don't put any money into something, when you've really got no hurt money, you use this wonderful word "expertise" instead: "I've come along with my expertise to do A, B and C; and you, Mr Fund Manager/Banker, you will give me all the money."

It's not a hundred percent recommendation for disaster. But the only people who are going to make any money out of a high proportion of these deals are those charging fees for their "expertise". For the fund and the bank to take all the risk is crazy.

Instead there were fees for acquiring a property, fees for design, fees for project management, fees for managing the property, fees for selling the property. Fees, fees, fees. In fact, for a lot of these deals, a major proportion of the cost was fees – up to twenty-five percent if you include stamp duty.

Some of these "experts" were amateurs. They were working with young fund managers who had little or no experience. Both sides would talk the product up and convince themselves they were geniuses if they could prove the development would bring in an extra half point on the yield.

PAINFUL RETURNS

Ungeared returns from property funds average five percent. But those borrowing money can make higher annual profits, thanks to the magic of gearing – up to twenty percent in the good times. During the crash, average returns dipped to *minus* ten percent. The funds' investors took that pain, many losing everything. Fund managers had to cope with pain of their own.

In 2007, the top fifty-four funds held £216 billion of assets under management. Over the next two years, that figure shrank by forty percent to roughly £130 billion. To fully feel the pain of £86 million in value evaporating, you need to appreciate that many fund managers' fees were then based on the gross value of the assets, so funds found themselves managing the same physical assets for forty percent less income. The pain eased a little in 2010, when Property Funds Research reported that total assets under management among a group of fifty-one rose £22 billion to £152 billion.

CHANGE OF EMPHASIS

The way real estate funds operate changed greatly between 1997 and 2012. In the Nineties, the focus was on making money for the investors. The charge is that by fifteen years later the emphasis had switched to making money for the fund managers. Here are the views of two eminent investment agents, followed by one from a leading fund manager, who says lessons have since been learned.

ALASTAIR HUGHES, ASIA PACIFIC CHIEF EXECUTIVE AT JONES LANG LASALLE:

I used to speak to fund managers, employed by an institution to make good decisions for the people who invested in that fund. I ended up speaking to investment managers, who were in part focused on their P&L and whose clear objective was to make a profit. That was a distinct change in culture.

I think it took place between 2002 and 2004. Managers began to take assets out of life funds where the fees were low and put them into leveraged funds and joint ventures where the fees were much higher. Pretty much everybody was creating vehicles in order to benefit from debt leverage, to gain access to specialist management but also to earn fees.

So there was a big mind shift in the industry. I remember going to see a really well-respected, highly intelligent, very well-rounded fund manager to get some feedback on our business. He said: "Alastair, I'm not sure you guys get it. All we want is product." I said, "What about the advice that goes along with that?" He said: "What we want is deals." I said, "What you're really advising is that we go out and recruit twenty to twenty-five-year-old 'broker' types to simply introduce stock?" He said: "Yes, exactly."

That was a big shift for us. But, ultimately, we do what our clients want. So the tone in the industry shifted. We were no longer expected to advise to the same extent. The funds would decide whether they wanted to buy or not, based on several criteria. That was the shift. All of a sudden you'd got fund managers who focused on their fees as much as on the performance of their funds. That was a big change in a relatively short period of time.

ANDY MARTIN, SENIOR PARTNER AT STRUTT & PARKER SINCE 2009:

By 1997, inflation was reducing and interest rates were coming down. Investment managers started to say: "I'll tell you what: we can increase funds under management by creating new funds which other people can invest into – and we'll do something different; we'll gear them to extract premium returns." Many joined forces with property companies to gain financing and asset management expertise.

Pension funds and insurance companies had always been equity investors in direct real estate; but they wouldn't take gearing directly on to the balance sheet. But, off-balance-sheet, in new vehicles jointly with other investors, they could. So in the late Nineties you got the growth of the collective investment funds. The majority of these were created offshore to create tax transparency for exempt investors, in places like Luxembourg or Jersey. They were an answer to the growing REIT sector in other parts of the world.

This was the start of the massive growth of a completely new investment sector, investing in UK offices, European industrial, Asian retail and US leisure. In Europe this indirect sector grew to hold assets which totalled more than the listed sector. All of a sudden, the investment manager was taking fees from running the vehicle measured generally as a percentage of the assets under management and a bonus for outperforming the IPD index.

They were also releasing cash from selling property into the vehicle; cash that the fund could reinvest in more property. More cash came from gearing up: using debt to buy more property pushed up the gross asset value of the fund. Fees in the UK were generally paid on gross asset values, and so these funds became powerful in the market and grew very quickly. The unlisted sector began to eclipse the listed sector in advance of REITs becoming established. From the US a new form of collective investment hit the world globally, and funds like the Morgan Stanley Investment Funds became the model.

JAMES DARKINS, MD OF GLOBAL PROPERTY AT HENDERSON GLOBAL INVESTORS SINCE 2001:

The big difference between the boom/bust period in the early Nineties and the Noughties was the growth of fund managers. It all began around 2000, when asset allocators began to see property as attractive. What we saw was property shifting from the dodgy, Porsche-driving, white-shoe-wearing brigade to an asset class managed every bit as professionally as equities.

The growth of IPD and the availability of data made a massive difference to how we were able to measure our performance and professionalism. But we witnessed a number of start-ups, where people made significant investments in opening flash offices in the West End and hiring people at huge salaries.

They were going out to clients and offering returns that we believed were patently ridiculous. But if they said, "I'll give you a five percent income on a ten percent internal rate of return," then they wouldn't have got the equity. So they offered far more; they offered higher returns to drive their capital raising so that they could build up portfolios fast to meet their business costs.

So we'd go and pitch to a client and say: "This is what we think the market delivers," and the client would say to us: "Well, we've just had a fund manager in who is going to do it three percent better than you in terms of total return and one percent better in terms of income." So I'd say: "I'd like to see the buildings they're going to buy. I've got an analytics team who can work out what you need to make those sorts of returns."

It's ridiculous to promise high returns without knowing what you are buying – but that's what they did to attract the equity. There was a whole load of people at it. We saw hedge funds attracted to doing spin-offs in real estate because they had all this money coming in for equities. Then all the investment banks created funds too.

The market became saturated with managers. The majority were paid a percentage of the gross value of the assets they managed. That encouraged managers to increase the amount of debt. If I persuaded you to adopt a fifty percent loan-to-value ratio, I could double my assets under management and double my revenue!

The European association for non-listed funds, INREV, has since addressed this misalignment of interest, which encouraged managers to accumulate assets, rather than maximising performance. As a result, it is now common practice for fees to be based on net asset value, thereby encouraging more prudent attitudes to debt.

Likewise, performance fees were historically paid on an accruals basis. Now, they are calculated on a realised basis, once the asset has been sold and the profits secured. The crisis taught the industry that we could not rely on values only moving in one direction and that you should never count your profits before they are hatched!

PRIVATE EQUITY REAL ESTATE FUNDS

The world of multibillion-dollar global real estate funds is well beyond my experience. They tend to raise hundreds of millions in equity from pension and life funds around the globe as well as from individuals rich enough to run "family offices" to manage their wealth. Hundreds of millions more are borrowed from banks and other lenders. As the figures show, $130 billion was raised in 2008 alone. The typical billion-dollar fund will then go out and buy an office block in Paris, a shopping centre in Poland, some industrial sheds around Moscow and maybe a few thousand rented homes in Germany. Investors are charged hefty management and performance fees by the fund managers, while the actual management of assets is generally outsourced to local agents. The strategy tends to centre on buying cheap in bad times and selling dear when the local economy picks up.

When the global economy proceeded to crash in 2007–2009, these funds were badly hit. Morgan Stanley famously chalked up losses of more than $5 billion on an $8 billion global private equity fund during the crash. Yet these multibillion-dollar funds – run mainly by US groups like Blackstone, Carlyle and Apollo – can make millions for their investors by investing at the right time. In September 2009, Blackstone paid £77 million to British Land for a fifty percent equity stake in the Broadgate office complex in the City of London, then valued at £2.2 billion. The giant US fund also took fifty percent of the £2.1 billion of debt then held by British Land, which badly needed to reduce its gearing. At the end of 2012, Blackstone said it was preparing to sell its half-share in the thirty-acre complex – a stake then valued at £520 million.

Someone a lot more familiar than I am with multibillion-dollar global real estate funds is David Marks of Brockton Capital. As well as becoming president of the British Property Federation in 2013, he is co-managing partner of Brockton, which he founded in 2005. Prior to that, he spent five years with Blackstone, one of the world's biggest fund managers, after working for Jones Lang LaSalle in both London and New York. Here is his expert view on the history and growth of what are now known as private equity real estate (PERE) funds:

DAVID MARKS, CO-MANAGING PARTNER AT BROCKTON CAPITAL:

At the genesis of the sector, in the early Nineties, the funds were initially tagged as "vulture funds". However, by the mid Nineties, they became "opportunity funds", implying that the acquisitions were more about micro-cycle timing and views on an individual sector, rather than simply buying "everything or anything" at fifty cents in the dollar. The term "vulture fund" was fine when you were buying a half-built hotel in Houston in 1993, from Credit Lyonnais. But when you were trying to buy a grade A office block in Washington DC from Equitable Life in 1996, a new terminology was required.

Likewise in Europe, by around 1996 or 1997, the distressed assets owned by the (predominantly) French, UK and Japanese banks had been sold and the "opp fund" moniker became a universal way to describe investors ranging from Apollo to Pelham to Blackstone to Morgan Stanley Real Estate. Virtually all of both the opp fund management teams and the underlying investors were American. The days of the Malaysian sovereign wealth fund investing alongside a Kuwaiti family office alongside a Dutch pension fund, into a pan-European manager, run by French partners out of London, were still some way off.

Around 2006, the phrase "opp fund" was replaced by "PERE", standing for "private equity real estate". The subtle change to "PERE funds" was partially a recognition that as the property market changed, it was the operational aspects of asset management that were becoming a key driver of returns. PERE funds have (post-crunch) targeted either non-performing loan portfolios, entire loan books or in some cases entire banks as key targets. Returns are generated on a combination of buying at steep discounts and then

*"resolving" a non-performing loan with the individual borrowers –
and are far less about adding value at the asset level.*

*This is by far the safest, but also hardest way to add value. An ex-
ample of this asset management approach is when Brockton Capital
purchased a series of pubs in Greater London, post-Lehman, from
late 2008 onwards, in a fifty-fifty joint venture with Realpubs. The
business was heavily asset managed, more than quadrupled in size,
and then sold to Greene King plc for around £55 million in 2011. The
transaction realised over two-times equity profit for the investors in
Brockton and a thirty-seven percent IRR.*

*Many funds were over-levered going into 2007 and 2008. Many
were (incredibly) still purchasing assets into 2008, when it was patently obvious that the world was about to smack into a brick wall.
Many PERE funds had lost their desire or capabilities to asset manage effectively, and had become overly reliant on "levered GDP
growth" as a means of generating their returns. Fine when the UK
was delivering three-percent-plus per annum real GDP growth, but
useless when the economy slipped into recession. Many funds had
grown too large. Business plans, asset by asset, were replaced with
a top-down view on how assets were to be improved and sold.*

*Unlike hedge funds, which literally "blow up" when their investors
decide that they want to withdraw their capital, a pure private equity fund or a PERE fund cannot blow up, as its investors have their
capital "locked in" for multi-year periods. Hence the phrase: "private equity funds don't blow up, they simply bleed to death, slowly".
This entails a painful process whereby both managers and investors
attempt to recover as much of their original equity as they can
(known as "striving for a 1.0x", or trying to recover the investors'
original equity from over-levered assets) but whereby the manager
knows that there will be little or no support for subsequent fund
raisings once the current fund has been sold down and any remaining capital distributed back to the investors.*

*In respect of the top-down view on the wider economy and how crit-
ical it is to get the timing right, it could be summarised by a phrase
uttered by John Schreiber, the legendary non-exec chairman of
Blackstone's real estate team, who used to repeatedly warn the
team, "Hey guys, remember: the macro always beats the micro."*

THE STAGE

CHAPTER FOUR
PLANET PROPERTY

Inside every working anarchy, there's an old boy network
Mitchell Kapor

Imagine a zone in which the sole activity is the trading and development of every type of property, aside from secondhand homes; a place inhabited by those who fund, develop, hold, buy, sell, broker, value, manage, mend and give professional and legal advice on UK offices, shops, industrial property, tenanted homes and new-build apartments. I began to feel my way around the zone after joining *EG* in 1997. It took me five years to see even how the main thoroughfares connect. Over the following six years, I sallied down a few side streets, but rarely through any doors leading to the rooms where bonds are strengthened and confidences exchanged.

Journalists are outsiders. So they should be, even though the zone is a welcoming and fattening place. The more you circle it, the more you appreciate that there is far more there than you will ever see. There are circles of influence within circles of influence within circles of influence. Old boy networks abound. (Old girl networks barely exist.)

This is true for every town and city in the UK. During my tenure as editor at *EG*, the magazine held receptions each year in Birmingham, Manchester, Newcastle, Bristol and Southampton, and it was evident that pretty much everyone there already knew everyone else. By far the biggest part of the zone is, of course, London. I have trampled the grass flat there writing my property column for the *Evening Standard* since 2007.

THE PLANET

But what defines Planet Property? For an answer to that, at least so far as the UK is concerned, we can thank Tony Key of the Cass Business School, who produced these numbers in late 2012.

SIZE AND VALUE OF THE UK COMMERCIAL PROPERTY MARKET

Retail and offices account for most of the value, but industrial has the greatest floor space

	Retail	Office	Industrial	Other	Total
Floor space (million sq ft)	1,432	1,130	4,100	n/a	n/a
Rental value (£bn)	18	13	12	16	60
Capital value (£bn)	259	158	118	145	681

Source: Cass Business School

Only £385 billion of the total £681 billion of stock is what Key calls "investible" – real estate that can be traded. Of that, twenty-seven percent, or £104 billion, is retail property. Offices account for twenty-four percent, or £92 billion. Industrial buildings account for eighteen percent, or £70 billion. The leisure sector, which covers entertainment, food and drink, hotels and sports, accounts for fourteen percent, or £54 billion. The remainder includes education (five percent) and health (two percent); the final ten percent is property that is fairly inaccessible to investors, such as that associated with power generation, sewerage and airports.

Key has calculated who owns the whole £385 million: the biggest group are overseas owners, with a quarter of the entire "investible" stock.

WHO OWNS COMMERCIAL PROPERTY IN THE UK?

Overseas investors own twenty-five percent of all investible property; companies and funds account for almost all the remainder

	Amount invested (£bn)	Share of total (%)
Insurance companies (held direct)	20	5
Pension funds (held direct)	26	7
Unit-linked life funds and pensions	15	4
Open-ended funds	44	11
Closed-ended funds	49	13
Listed property companies	59	15
Unlisted property companies	40	10
Overseas investors	95	25
Charities and estates	13	3
Private individuals	12	3
Local authority and other	12	3
Total 'investible' market	**385**	**100**

Source: Cass Business School

AGENTS, ADVISERS, CONSULTANTS, SOLUTIONS...

By far the largest number of those on Planet Property UK work as agents: the biggest two global agents, CBRE and Jones Lang LaSalle, between them employ some three thousand staff in the UK, and tens of thousands around the globe. The largest two British property firms, Land Securities and British Land, employ around four hundred in total and do not venture abroad.

There is overlap between this zone and the bigger space occupied by estate agents, which sell homes. Firms like Knight Frank, Savills and Strutt & Parker do both. But very few commercial property companies stray into residential – except in London, where soaring residential prices in 2006 began to make it profitable to set up teams to advise on development and sales in the booming residential development sector.

Official statistics show there to be nearly sixteen thousand "real estate agencies" in the UK. But you can forget the fifteen thousand, nine hundred in the residential market: fewer than a hundred "commercial agents" show up in *EG*'s annual survey. But never call a commercial agent an estate agent – that's a bigger blooper than referring to a barrister as a solicitor. Most commercial agents mumble something about being "in property" when asked their occupation by outsiders. They fear being mistaken for an estate agent and subsequently asked whether they think house prices are going up or down. Commercial property agents get to trade office towers, shopping centres or sheds the size of several football pitches.

Each year at the EG Awards I would warn guest presenters such as Graham Norton *not* to use the words "estate" and "agent" consecutively, on pain of losing their fee. The outside world understands what estate agents do and doesn't much like them. Few of the big firms actually call themselves agents. The word is a touch pejorative – and a bit too closely associated with that dreaded word "estate". Jones Lang LaSalle describes itself as a "financial and professional services firm specialising in real estate and investment management" – which is accurate, if rather lengthy. Meanwhile, DTZ does "property services"; Savills is a "property firm"; CBRE tags itself "property consultants"; and Cushman & Wakefield offers "global real estate solutions". Knight Frank meanwhile describes itself as "the world's leading independent real estate consultancy".

From 1997, the trend for agents to align themselves with banking grew. The increasing complexity and globalisation of real estate financing led in the early Noughties to the setting-up of "capital markets" divisions within commercial property firms. This fuzzy phrase is designed to confer higher status on those giving property investment advice and helping raise the cash to buy the real estate. Those working in "capital markets" tend to get the mickey taken out of them by less exalted leasing agents, mainly because no one – including those working in capital markets – quite understands what the phrase means. When you ask, a rambling non-answer usually follows.

The best way to explain what agents actually do is to invent a fictional firm called Commercial Property Services, with a thousand imaginary employees in the UK and five thousand more scattered around the globe. What goes on in CPS's offices around the rest of the world more or less mimics what happens in Britain, but on a smaller scale, so let's concentrate on the home territory.

Half of the home payroll at CPS is made up of those on the "professional" side of the business. This is the more stable part that charges fees for providing expert advice, as opposed to the riskier, brokering side that wins fees only when deals are completed.

The two biggest sub-groups on the professional side are those who value clients' property and those who manage real estate for clients. Valuation is almost a profession in its own right: one that is absolutely critical to the good management of the sector, which is why its practice is governed by a set of rules contained within the Royal Institution of Chartered Surveyors' Red Book. PLCs don't get their accounts signed off without valuations of their property, and bank loans are not given without a valuation from an independent agent. Valuers, in effect, set prices. To facilitate valuation, agents keep databases containing details of deals, which help in forming accurate judgements. The valuation department at CPS employs two hundred staff.

The other main activity on the professional side at CPS is property management. Major property owners like to sublet the management of their assets to agents, just as you might with a rented flat. Collecting rents, dealing with the rates, paying utility bills and coping with maintenance problems can be tiresome, and managing agents will do this for very small fees – in the (usually forlorn) hope that it will bring in higher-paid transaction work. Most FTSE 100 companies employ agents to manage their property assets, as do global banks, manufacturers and IT companies. CPS has two hundred staff in its property management department.

The other hundred or so professional staff at the imaginary firm are split into small expert groups. One team specialises in business rates, another in planning law, yet another in property tax. There are even experts on party-wall disputes at CPS. The boss of this particular group is a member of the (real-life) Pyramus and Thisbe Club, named after mythical Babylonian lovers who whispered their desire for each other through a crack in the wall between their respective homes.

What CPS does not have is a "capital markets" team, as the partners have never been quite sure what this is all about. Nor is CPS in the business of fund management: it reckons that's best left to firms like CBRE and Jones Lang LaSalle. Both manage portfolios worth tens of billions of dollars for clients all around the globe, in divisions that operate behind moderately secure Chinese walls, acting as semi-independent fund managers.

Instead, front-of-store at CPS sit five hundred transaction agents. The bosses are always trying to get them to work more closely together and share information. But transaction agents have a tendency not to want to share clients and crucial information. They tend to see themselves as just as important, if not more so, than the firm itself. And their bonus is based on the deals their team does, so why risk it by giving away critical information the client has asked them to keep secret? This has long been a problem at CPS. Some teams show little loyalty to the firm, frankly – they are even occasionally poached en masse by bigger rivals.

CPS recognises the need to employ the best transaction agents in the business; so, when business conditions allow, it is quite prepared to pinch teams from rivals itself. Then it quietly gets them to bring their clients with them. This is forbidden under an employee's terms of engagement, of course, but there's no point anyone complaining, since everyone does it. Clients have a nasty habit of floating off with the individual agent rather than sticking with the firm the agent used to work for. It's a habitual problem for CPS.

The transactions teams operate within complex hierarchies, with an individual's importance determined by the size and type of deals done, as well as their location (with London superior to everywhere else). Those who trade offices regard themselves as superior to those who trade retail, while retail is superior to industrial – and even more bibulous. "Investment agents drink champagne, industrial agents drink beer, and retail agents drink the cupboard dry," as the saying goes.

Investment and development agents vie for top-dog status at CPS. Those who aid clients on development projects tend to be "mathematical" in outlook, while those who advise clients on which buildings to buy or sell tend to be more financially savvy; each see the other as slightly inferior. But the most presentable agents at CPS, those with the best social skills and the finest connections, work in the lettings department. The job sounds simple: persuade potential occupiers to rent space in clients' buildings. But it's far from easy, especially in a chilly economic climate. The skills of a salesman are needed, on top of up-to-the-minute market knowledge, plus the ability to talk the talk when it comes to the intricacies of lease negotiations.

CPS also employs a few "occupier" agents, who have a strong nose for spotting big companies looking to lease space, combined with the charm and ability to persuade them to move. But the company is not as strong in this area as some of its rivals. The plan at CPS is to pinch a team or two from rival firms when financial conditions allow...

BACK IN THE REAL WORLD
What makes property different from other business sectors is that the traditional "I pay you; you supply me with what I damn well want" relationship does not operate. Transaction agents are not slaves to their clients; they are brokers. They do buy and sell on the customer's instructions. But they have the power to steer favoured buyers in front of favoured sellers, from whom unfavoured buyers are steered away – and of course they can steer unfavoured sellers away from favoured buyers. "Favoured" here means that the broker knows the client, knows they have the money, and trusts them not to renegotiate at the last minute. Price tends to be the bottom line. Many big deals are tendered, but many are not; many assets are sold off-market to prevent invasion of privacy and timewasting.

The best way to understand the power and skill of the broker is to think of a commercial agent as an estate agent (remember not to say that out loud, though). You have a £250,000 flat to sell? It doesn't much matter who you use at this level. Even so, you can come away feeling that the person you're paying to sell your home is actually doing you a favour. It's just what they do, somehow.

Now imagine that you have a £5 million house to sell. The choice of agent narrows down to just three or four firms with experience in this market, and reduces even further after you discover that only two of them employ the right calibre of employee. And if, on the other hand, you want to *buy* a £5 million house, then you'd better prove you have the wherewithal before an agent will waste the time even sending you the brochure.

If you want to buy or sell a £100 million office block in London, there are barely a handful of commercial firms to enlist – even fewer if you're talking about a £500 million mall in the Midlands instead. In either case, the choice of individual broker within a firm can be as important as the choice of firm. Personal reputation trumps company brand in many cases. "We're using Bloggs & Co because they employ John Smith" is a common refrain; one that leads to John Smith getting very well paid to prevent him being pinched by other agents (then paid even more when he does get pinched).

The "broker as kingpin" scenario is more extreme in the US. In October 2006, I spent a week in New York – much of it in the offices of CB Richard Ellis, the world's largest agent. Here I met several of the firm's top brokers, including the very topmost, Stephen Siegel. Another, Mary Ann Tighe, unfortunately didn't have time for a chat. She was busy closing the world's biggest real estate deal, the $5.4 billion sale to Tishman Speyer and BlackRock of eleven thousand, two hundred apartments on the eighty-acre Stuyvesant Town/Peter Cooper Village in New York. Four years later, Tishman Speyer defaulted on a $3 billion loan taken out to finance this deal.

But that's another story. The story I took back from New York was that individual brokers really are more powerful than the firms for which they work. Transaction fees in America can be six percent of the agreed price, three times the UK rate. Up to half of that goes to "the house", but the rest goes to the individual agent and whichever minions he or she agrees to "put on the ticket". This can make successful agents not only very rich but also as powerful as movie or sports agents.

At CB Richard Ellis the top brokers inhabited large corner offices filled with their own furniture, while the lower ranks toiled in cubicles outside. Tighe's office was furnished like a five-star hotel suite with a feminine touch; Siegel's was gentlemen's club meets boardroom. What was very clear was how the broker dominated the client. Siegel – who was later burned by Bernie Madoff – sat high in his chair; on a low settee sat a major client who had come to discuss the imminent development of a million-square-foot skyscraper. I was there to interview both. Siegel was clearly the alpha male in the room. It's not quite like that in the UK, but the picture is a telling one. There are certainly plenty of alpha male brokers in London (although few alpha females).

PROPERTY OWNERS

Those who own real estate are more disparate than agents. Most visible are the listed property companies, active developers, investors and traders of every type of real estate. They are the physical face of property: most people have heard of FTSE companies like Land Securities, British Land, Hammerson, Segro, Great Portland Estates or Derwent London. But a far larger range of enterprises hold property assets; most obvious among these are "the corporates". Retailers such as Marks & Spencer and Tesco directly own and manage millions of square feet of real estate. So do banks like RBS and

Lloyds, as well as Unilever, Shell and Vodafone. Most FTSE companies contain small divisions to manage their corporate real estate.

Property shown on PLC balance sheets is just the tip of an iceberg. Government statistics list over forty-six thousand firms engaged in "the renting and operating of own or leased real estate". The Office for National Statistics calculated the total value of UK commercial property to be somewhere around £560 billion in 2010. Billions more are invested in property by trusts benefiting aristocratic and non-aristocratic families alike, with further billions of property investment by charities such as the Wellcome Trust. Hence the higher, £681 billion figure estimated by the Cass Business School.

Unlisted property companies come in a multitude of shapes, sizes and degrees of transparency. Some operate in just one town, city or region; a few operate countrywide. Some specialise in one sector, such as retail, leisure or industrial; others are diverse in their activities. Some are limited companies, others limited liability partnerships. Some are open and welcoming, others closed and very private. But all are in the same game of making money from commercial real estate.

FUNDS

There are as many fund varieties as there are bricks in the walls of the Tate Modern. But all of them do much the same thing, for a fee: pool other people's money and (often) borrow more to buy and sell bricks and mortar. In "geared" funds, half the cash tends to come from investors as equity, the other half in the form of debt from the banks. You can take a stake in funds that specialise in anything from luxury flats to clapped-out industrial sheds. You can invest in Russia, Japan, America – in fact almost anywhere, if you have the cash and the nerve.

Some funds let the public invest directly, and these "retail" funds are strictly regulated. In times of boom they suck in money from the man in the street: the best-known example in the Noughties boom was New Star, whose billboards seemed to be everywhere. But these funds are few. They are just the visible tip of a £150 billion market built to serve the professional investment community and high-net-worth individuals.

The biggest group of property-investing funds belong to the pension and life insurance companies, such as Prudential and Aviva. It's only a smallish portion of their total assets – typically between five and ten percent – that goes into real estate, but the Pru and Aviva still hold billions of pounds' worth of commercial property assets. Most of their stock tends to be "dry": in other words, well-maintained property let to blue-chip tenants on long leases, needing little more than the rent collecting and an occasional lick of paint. These estates are managed carefully, and so only in times of plenty do insurers and pension funds dabble in development.

In the Seventies and Eighties, around eighty pension and life funds were investing in commercial property, with some putting as much as twenty percent of their total assets into bricks and mortar. Since that time, consolidation has reduced the number of funds that are around, and three boom and bust cycles have shrunk the appetite of actuaries to allocate much more than ten percent of funds' total assets to bricks and mortar.

Perching further up the risk curve are the thousands of unregulated funds, both large and small. They take rich people's money, add more borrowed from the banks, and then try to make returns of up to twenty percent for their investors – as well as big, fat fees for themselves. There are worldwide and continent-wide funds operated by big banks such as Goldman Sachs or Morgan Stanley or by giant American private equity houses such as Blackstone, Carlyle and Apollo. It's common for a single fund to hold billions of dollars' worth of real estate. These funds are not for widows and orphans, note: Morgan Stanley lost more than $5 billion in one highly leveraged fund during the crash.

Smaller funds tend to specialise either in a sector or in a geographical area. Typical would be a £150 million London residential fund, or one looking to invest £80 million in secondary shopping centres. Towards the top of the risk curve are funds that include the word "opportunity" in their name – at least, that used to be the case until the word became synonymous with "risky". By 2008, the more acceptable acronym of "PERE" was in common use instead, to cover the entire sector labelled "private equity real estate".

The perinatal death rate of funds is very high. Trial balloons appear all the time saying that "so-and-so is to set up a £500 million fund to invest in such-and-such". Conceiving funds this way costs little more than a press release. If the investors bite, then the real and expensive legal legwork of giving birth to a live fund can begin. But even then, many die soon after birth. They die of starvation, because there turns out to be no real estate to be had. If I had a tenner for every fund that promised a fortune by investing in luxury residential property, I could buy a flat in Mayfair.

FINANCIERS

Property finance is almost a separate subculture. A dinner is held each year by the Association of Property Bankers (or the Association of Property Lenders, as it is now known, following a rather wise name change in the wake of the banking crash). At these dinners, which I have attended many times, an elongated top table would always be placed on a platform after the fashion of an Oxbridge college's high table. From this exalted and rather embarrassing position I would look down upon eight hundred or so black-tied bankers – and not recognise a single face among these quietly powerful financiers who fund the property industry. It is bankers who provide the cash used to fund between fifty and ninety percent of each real estate transaction. At least, that was the case up until 2007. After the crash, insurance companies and private equity funds began to lend. Most cash is provided as debt in return for interest, but banks also hand out cash in return for equity in the venture with the hope of making a profit.

The first thing a property financier will tell you, on being introduced, is "Oh, I'm on the debt side" or "Actually, I'm in the equity team". Apart from a vague feeling that it is more prestigious to dole out equity rather than debt, that's about as much as I know of this semi-separate world – except that it's not just banks that lend. Rich individuals also back property deals, while not-quite-so-rich individuals form syndicates to lend money and take equity. Money floods into UK real estate from around the globe in this way. But the high-street banks such as RBS, Lloyds and Barclays remain the mainstream source of funds, despite their near-death experiences in 2008 as a result of their activities in this sector.

LAWYERS

The last – and least appreciated – group to have offices on Planet Property UK are the lawyers. Some solicitors attend upon the immense complexities that seem to surround every deal; others make a living from the litigation that follows. Yet others specialise in planning and development. All profit from a sector that provides enough fodder to fill a dozen or more pages at the back of *EG* every week – much of it written by members of the Property Bar Association, which has three hundred barrister members.

In 2012, *The Lawyer* magazine listed fifteen major law firms possessing separate property departments. At the head was DLA Piper, with two hundred and twenty-seven real estate partners dotted all around the globe, bringing in fees of £164 million – about £720,000 each.

Topping the table in terms of fee income per head, however, was Linklaters, where the twenty-seven property partners clocked up £2 million each. Second came Ashurst, whose thirty partners – earning an average of £1.93 million each – include the head of the City Property Association for 2012, Ann Minogue, who is the long-time lawyer to Sir Stuart Lipton. Just below Ashurst stood Herbert Smith, with £1.91 million being pulled in by each of its twenty-one property partners.

Eversheds, Clifford Chance, CMS Cameron McKenna, Berwin Leighton Paisner and Freshfields each employed between thirty and eighty property partners in 2012. But special mention must be made of Hogan Lovells, whose thirty-one partners earned an average of £1.68 million in fees in 2012.

Most lawyers hate being dragged out by their new, bushy-tailed press officer to meet the press, but Lovells was different – and so was the head of its property department: Bob Kidby wore a large moustache and played guitar in a band. The company held themed party nights for the press every year and gave generous use of its conference theatre to *EG* for events. The firm merged with US practice Hogan & Hartson in May 2010 and rebranded itself as Hogan Lovells. When Kidby went off to help run Welbeck Land in 2012 with his band partner Alistair Watson, he was replaced at Lovells by his deputy Michael Stancombe, who was just as genial, only without the guitar. The law is not all claret and choral singing.

Stancombe, who became a partner in the early Eighties, explains how the role of the real estate lawyer changed over fifteen years: "In 1997, the market was still dominated by domestic institutions and property companies. Property lawyers (as we were then known) always took the lead on deals with support from other disciplines.

"Now the deals have become so much more complex, reflecting the development of the offshore funds industry and the flood of overseas money.

In consequence, the real estate lawyer has become much more of a ringmaster, co-ordinating a significantly wider range of separate streams of advice. For the successful real estate lawyer, project management skills are now almost as important as lawyering skills."

CONNECTIONS, CONNECTIONS, CONNECTIONS

That's a short guide to the majority of the players in the zone. But it does not tell the whole story, because the unwritten rules of how the game is played are what perhaps matter most. This is not a transparent market. The business is fluid: opportunities come and go, as do personalities; reputations wax and wane. Many of the ideas that generate business are sparked over conversations meant to be about something else – chats in bars, restaurants or dining clubs, on the golf course or at the shooting range; banter between people with a common heritage or education who have slowly learned to trust one another over the years.

Time and again, deals emerge from such encounters. But not just deals; it is here too that critical market and financial intelligence is swapped. EM Forster's injunction from *Howard's End* to "only connect" is what the best operators in property understand instinctively. Connections must be made and maintained, because the most valuable market knowledge is only ever transmitted face to face. Those in the sector are convivial because it is profitable for them to be so. If you want to see the modus operandi in motion, then fly down to the MIPIM international property show, held in March every year at Cannes.

If more than a dozen people share a common interest and the desire to do business with one another, almost inevitably a club of some sort will be formed, even if it's just a standing arrangement to "meet at Fino's" (in Mayfair) on the second Friday of every month. Or it could be an old boys club – both Eton and Harrow have alumni associations for those working in property. There are formal and ancient dining clubs too, some called after the date they were founded. I was once taken to dinner at Boodle's as a guest of the 1872 club, but only after promising not to report a word.

The citizens of Planet Property have loyalties each to their own clan as well as to their employer. Clans are formed by those of the same background, or by those who went to the same school, or were educated at the same university, or had their first jobs at the same firm. It sounds not much different from the business world in general, but it is more necessary and more significant, because of the fluid, deal-driven nature of property.

In London there is a strong and powerfully connected Jewish network, for instance. Those property companies, agents, bankers and solicitors with Jewish roots or ties have a propensity to deal with one another. But there appears to be little anti-Semitism in the industry– or little anti-Gentile feeling, for that matter. Those from different backgrounds are about as interested in your religion, race or culture as they are in which football team you support: they can be initially wary, but certainly not enough to let their feelings get in the way of business.

Other clans in the zone include those based on educational ties. Reading University is the Oxford of real estate. The College of Estate Management in Reading is to Reading University what Oxford Brookes is to Oxford University – not as posh, but still a pretty good pedigree. Many of today's bosses went to the College of Estate Management, which sits on the same campus as Reading University. Cambridge is, well, the Cambridge of property. Superior. Oxford Brookes is Durham. Those who went to Cambridge are more at ease in dealing with other Cambridge alumni than with graduates of Reading, and vice versa.

Planet Property remains a man's world, at the top at least. The *EG* 2012 agents survey found ninety-three percent of senior staff were male. Still, thirty-seven percent of the four thousand, eight hundred fee earners were female. "There are now plenty of very bright females coming out of college," I was told once by an eminent agent whose son found himself in stiff competition with women for a job in 2010. He said, stiffly, "It will be good for the profession."

What is delicately called "diversification" is advancing less rapidly. Periodic attempts are made by the colleges, but with little success so far. In late 2012, for instance, British Land put up £200,000 to fund an education programme to give youngsters from diverse backgrounds a taste of the industry. But such initiatives are making slow progress, and the population of Planet Property is still mostly white and still slightly upper-middle class.

When editing a magazine, it is an important exercise to bear in mind one's imaginary typical reader. Through a mixture of research and intuition, the typical reader of *EG* was pinned down in 2006 by magazine staff as being a white male aged forty-three, living in Hazlemere, Surrey, going by the name of Charlie. Charlie was a gregarious, rugby-playing fellow, then earning £80,000 a year as a mid-level investment surveyor with a top-ten firm. He was educated at a minor public school before going on to Oxford Brookes. Charlie lived in a five-bedroom, modern, detached house with his wife, named Hazel, and their two children: Chloe, aged eleven, and seven-year-old Tom. His BMW sat on the drive next to Hazel's 4x4. The *Telegraph* and the *Mail* landed on the doormat each morning. Meet the typical inhabitant of Planet Property: a man happy in his skin and in his job.

CHAPTER FIVE
MAINLY FOR STUDENTS

The only thing that interferes with my learning is my education
Albert Einstein

That's the way the money goes...
    If you appreciate how gearing can magnify profits and losses, then you don't need to read this chapter. If you know perfectly well that a property sold at a five percent yield costs twice as much as one sold at a ten percent yield, skip to the next chapter. If you can decipher the acronym "IRR" and readily comprehend its significance, move on. If you understand that every extra square foot squeezed into a development is worth between ten and twenty times the extra rent, then too move on. If you know perfectly well that fees tied to the value of the property for an army of brokers and money managers can be either a blessing or a curse, then this chapter is not for you. But if, on the other hand, you feel you could benefit from a simple introduction to how so much money can be made and lost, read on. For all else in Planet Property is easy to follow, once the following is grasped.

GEARING: THE BLACK AND WHITE MAGIC SHOW
The black and white magic of gearing has been the prime driver of property cycles for as long as there have been those with money willing to lend it at a profit to those wanting to buy property to sell later at a profit. In other words, pretty much forever. History was merely repeating itself during the ten-year boom between 1997 and 2007 and the bust that followed.

WHITE MAGIC FOR MR LUCKY

Take the example of imaginary Mr Lucky. Let's pretend he bought an office block in Anytown for £10 million in May 1997, just as Tony Blair moved into Downing Street. Then imagine that Mr Lucky sold in June 2007, the month Blair gave way (somewhat reluctantly) to Gordon Brown. To keep it real, we'll base the example on prevailing interest rates and the actual index of capital values, as tracked by IPD since 1986. IPD monitors capital values and rental incomes for around £150 billon worth of property in the UK.

The reason Mr Lucky was happy to pay £10 million is because Solid & Solid, Solicitors, occupied the block. They had signed a fifteen-year lease in 1995 which committed them to paying £800,000 a year in rent until 2010, with upward-only reviews every five years. In 1995, the going rate for an office block like this was about 12.5 times the annual rent; hence the £10 million price tag. So Mr Lucky was initially receiving £800,000 each year in income as a result of his £10 million outlay. That, in property speak, is an eight percent yield: but more of yields later.

HERE'S WHAT HAPPENED NEXT...

Between May 1997 and June 2007, the price of office blocks rose by two-thirds and rents by a third, according to IPD. So it is safe to pretend that by the time Mr Blair left office, rent reviews in 2000 and 2005 had raised S&S Solicitors' rent – let's say to £1 million a year, to keep it simple. By 2007, the market was hot. Buyers were willing to pay up to sixteen times the rent, rather than 12.5 times. S&S was paying £1 million in annual rent. The block was therefore worth £16 million. That's sixty-six percent more than Mr Very Lucky had paid for it.

Time to sell: enter Mr Unlucky, waving a cheque for £16 million. So, a handsome £6 million profit for Mr Lucky? Not quite. Up to £1 million will have disappeared in costs and in buying and selling fees to agents and solicitors, all taking their cut as a percentage of the property's increased value. But the £15 million left is still £5 million more than Mr Lucky paid in 1997. Not bad? Even better: Mr Lucky is luckier than you might imagine. For he laid out only £2 million of his own money in 1997. He is walking away with his original £2 million, plus that additional £5 million.

Thanks to the magic of gearing, Mr Lucky has made a two hundred and fifty percent profit on his original stake. That's because in 1997 he borrowed £8 million from Mr Banker. Which was okay by Mr Lucky: the rent paid by Messrs Solid & Solid matched the eight percent interest rate he was being charged by Mr Banker. Which was fine for Mr Banker: his cost of money was tied to the London interbank offered rate, or Libor. Mr Banker was making a healthy margin of 1.75 percent – or 175 basis points (bps), which are otherwise known as "bips" – on a Libor rate of 6.25 percent in 1997. Mr Banker's cost of money dropped as Libor fell to 3.5 percent by 2003 – which was very good news indeed for Mr Banker.

Cheap money rocket-propelled the boom over the following four years. As the economy grew, so did confidence in property; new lenders entered the market, and competition drove down margins. Margins fell to less than 100 bps, as banks vied to lend. Mr Lucky paid eight percent for his money in 1997. By 2007, borrowing rates had fallen to around four or five percent. Rents had either stood still, or risen, thanks to leases tying tenants to rents that could go up but never down. So every commercial property investor in the land was being tempted to buy by the so-called "yield gap" between the low cost of borrowing, say five percent, and rents, still yielding seven to eight percent.

BLACK MAGIC FOR MR UNLUCKY

Back to Mr Unlucky, and his bankers. He agreed to pay Mr Lucky £16 million, but only if both sides' deal costs were included. It is a matter of honour to chip the asking price, even at the top of the market. Fine, said Mr Lucky, who was selling because things were feeling very "toppy". Mr Unlucky borrowed £14 million from a very eager-to-please Mr Banker – eager, because Mr Banker's bonus was linked to the amount he was able to lend. Mr Unlucky had previously been lucky (as had everyone), so he had £2 million to hand from his last deal. He was eager to do another before prices rose any higher. Receiving his £14 million loan in June 2007, he added his own couple of million and paid £16 million for Mr Lucky's office block. Mr Unlucky agreed to pay Mr Banker five percent interest on his £14 million mortgage: interest that cost just £700,000 a year, against the rental income of £1 million. What could go wrong? Try a global banking collapse.

Pop! Mr Unlucky's office block halved in value to £8 million by June 2009 – a fall even harder than the forty-five percent drop in the IPD index over those two years. Mr Unlucky's block was in Anytown, not London town, where values did not fall quite so far. There was a little-noticed "margin call" clause in the 2007 loan agreement, obliging Mr Unlucky to ensure that the £14 million interest-only loan never exceeded ninety percent of the market value. This had been no problem when the offices were worth £16 million, but became a terrible problem when the value fell to £8 million. Mr Banker turned very nasty, calling on Mr Unlucky to hand over £6.8 million in order to reduce his mortgage to £7.2 million, ninety percent of the much reduced value of his property.

Not a chance. Mr Unlucky was obliged to hand over the property to the bank, under another little-noticed sequestration clause. But Mr Unlucky wasn't stupid, just unlucky. So the loan agreement with Mr Banker had contained no "PGs": no personal guarantees that would allow Mr Banker to seize his personal assets, such as his £5 million home in St John's Wood. Bonus-hungry bankers had long stopped asking for PGs for fear that borrowers defect to a rival. And Mr Unlucky had taken another precaution: the office block was registered as a separate company from the Unlucky Group. Eager Mr Banker had failed to ask for a guarantee that the PLC would repay the loan if the separate company could not. Mr Unlucky wrote back to Mr Banker to say: "Sod, off, I haven't got £6.8 million. Here are the keys to the property – good luck." Why not? He had neither personal nor corporate obligations.

NOT JUST MR LUCKY AND MR UNLUCKY

Imagine the white magic trick being played with infinite variations over the Blair years. Imagine the trick being played by those who could persuade the banks to lend them not just eighty percent but ninety-five percent or even a hundred percent of the purchase price. Imagine the multiplication of riches delivered by the increase in bank lending to investors in commercial property from £34 billion at the end of 1997 to £250 billion by the end of 2008. That fuelled an eighty percent increase in capital values over ten years.

Imagine the trick being played by anyone with an interest in buying not just offices but sheds, shops and anywhere the population takes its leisure. The group includes pension and life funds, the far larger private equity funds, property companies, rich individuals and family trusts. DTZ figures show £388 billion was spent between 1997 and 2008, including £109 billion by foreign buyers. Who knows how many billions were made?

But then imagine the gearing wheel going into reverse, and all those billions gained turning into billions lost. Gordon Brown became prime minister in June 2007. During the first two years of his tenure, values almost halved. Office values plunged by forty-five percent, to the level they were at in both 1997 and 1986. By mid 2012, the level of outstanding property debt was £204 billion, according to De Montfort University. Over seven thousand, seven hundred loans with a total value of £23 billion were in default. Now try and imagine how many Mr Unluckys there were – and not just individuals. How many property companies, private funds and pension funds were all dazzled by the white magic then ruined by the black magic of gearing?

YIELDS: WHERE LESS MEANS MORE AND MORE MEANS LESS

The "yield" on a property is the annual rent expressed as a percentage of the building's value. Sounds easy enough – except that the numbers are counter-intuitive. The higher the capital value in relation to the rent, the lower the percentage yield – and vice versa. It took months before it sank in with me. Here are a couple of examples.

The £800,000 annual rent paid by Solid & Solid, Solicitors, on the block bought by Mr Lucky for £10 million in 1997 represents a yield of eight percent. The £1 million annual rent being paid by S&S when Mr Unlucky bought the block in 2007 for £16 million is a yield of 6.25 percent. So: the lower the yield, the higher the price; the higher the yield, the lower the price.

Take a simple example: If the rent is £5 and the value £100, the yield is five percent. If the rent remains at £5 and the value falls to £50, the yield doubles to ten percent. This is worth getting fixed in the brain before proceeding: for the numerical yield is the basis on which all commercial property is priced. That is because the rent tends to be the one fixed constant, thanks to the leasing system that normally commits tenants to pay a fixed amount over a fixed number of years.

When property values rise, yields are said to be "coming in" or "compressing". When prices fall, they are said to be "rising" or "going out". Yields tend to fluctuate broadly between four and fifteen percent. Within that range lie three bands: prime property, secondary property, and only-touch-with-a-barge-pole property. In good times, prime yields for top-class property in top spots let to safe-as-houses tenants on long leases range in the four to five percent price band. In bad times, they go out to seven or eight percent. In good times, secondary properties start in the six to seven percent band; in bad times they shift out to between nine and ten percent, meaning a buyer will only have to pay ten times the annual rent. Don't-touch-with-a-barge-pole properties stand at ten percent in good times and up to fifteen percent or even more in the bad times.

You might think it clearer if the value of a property were expressed as a multiple of one year's rent. This is what used to be called the "YP" – or year's purchase – price. But there are two good reasons for sticking to percentages, expressed down to two decimal points. Firstly, it is very handy to compare the yield against the annual interest rate charged by lenders. The gap between the two provides a quick and easy way to see whether the deal is worth doing. Secondly, yields are used for more than a simple calculation of one year's rent. There is the yield you are getting at that moment in time (the running yield), the yield you might get after the lease expires (the reversionary yield), and the yield you might get if you fill the place up or redevelop (the potential yield). Whole books are written on the topic. Let's move on.

INTERNAL, OR INFERNAL, RATES OF RETURN

Whole books are also devoted to the subject of "internal rates of return". The official definition is "the annualised effective compounded return rate that makes the net present value (NPV) of all cash flows (both positive and negative) from an investment equal to zero". To fully understand just what that means, read those books. Old-fashioned property companies generally tend to stick to trying to turn £100 into £120 and calling it a profit margin. The newfangled IRR method came to the UK from America around the turn of the millennium. The key element in IRR is the word "internal". That simply means it's about your own money: the equity invested in the project that comes from the pockets of those investing. Rate of return means profit made over time on that equity.

Why fund managers like to quote IRR numbers is that they can seem quite high. "We're looking for an IRR of twenty percent on this £2 squillion opportunity fund." The reason a twenty percent IRR is normal is that it's the profit on the equity, not the profit on the total sum invested. Imagine again Mr Lucky and that office block he bought for £10 million, using £2 million of his own money and £8 million from Mr Banker. If he sold it twelve months later for £11 million, he would have made £1 million profit on his £2 million investment. That's an IRR of fifty percent.

It is, of course, not quite as simple as that. The IRR measures cash flow over time. You pay for the building – money out. The rent starts coming in – money in. You pay interest on the loan – money out. You lease a vacant floor – money in. This can go on for years. Then the building is sold – big chunk of money in. The idea is to forecast these cash flows over time and work out how much profit that brings you in today's money. So, again, let's move on.

SWELLING DEVELOPMENT PROFITS

Money can be made trading existing properties in a rising market by employing the magic of gearing. Even more can be made by redeveloping a site. But development is a lot harder, takes far longer and costs far more than inexperienced developers ever anticipate. You expect planning permission to be achieved in twelve months: it takes two years. You think the project will cost £30 million to build: it costs £40 million. You're confident you can sell for £50 million: no, it turns out to be £40 million. That's why experienced developers build in hefty provisions for cost overruns and add up to twenty percent profit margins. They then allow between twelve months and three years for the property to lie vacant once the builder has finished. But the rewards can be huge for those who are able to squeeze more space into the site than anyone else had thought possible.

It works (very) roughly like this: two developers are vying for a site. Developer A's architect draws up sketch plans showing that a hundred thousand square feet of rentable space can, under existing planning rules, be squeezed into the site on which a building of forty thousand square feet now stands. Developer A then works out the rent he might charge: let's say £50 per square foot, which is £500,000 a year. Then let's say that he counts on selling at a five percent yield – twenty times the rent, remember? That's a £10 million price tag. Take off twenty percent profit and the cost of construction, and you're left with what can be paid for the land: in this case, £2 million. This is what is called the "residual value". In goes the bid. But Developer B is far more aggressive and reckons that a hundred and twenty thousand square feet can be squeezed into the land, if a risk with the planners is taken.

Let's not go through the whole cost exercise again. Instead, examine the financial impact of Developer B getting away with an extra twenty thousand square feet. The building will cost a bit more to build, granted; but what rises far higher is the value of the completed building. Why? Because the possible annual rental income has risen from £500,000 to £600,000. That extra £100,000 a year in rent translates into a £2 million increase in value, because buyers will be willing to pay twenty times the annual rent – that five percent yield. Developer B does his sums based on a sale price of £12 million rather than £10 million. That leaves a residual value of £4 million to pay for the site. But Developer B knows his plans are a bit more expensive as well as riskier. He holds back £1 million, offering £3 million. A grateful seller takes the fifty percent higher offer. Developer B makes £1 million more profit than Developer A might have done.

Perhaps the most extraordinary example of a developer increasing the floor area on a site came with the construction of the Walkie Talkie tower in the City of London. This "upside-down" tower was designed by architect Rafael Viñoly, to the instructions of Land Securities' then development director, Mike Hussey. The old offices on the site had a gross area of 369,000 square feet. The gross area of what is officially called 20 Fenchurch Street is now 1,015,000 square feet. This 2.75 multiple could not have been achieved by building a straight tower. The floor plans show the effect on the amount of lettable space by the way the tower slowly swells as it climbs into the sky.

If all the floors had been the same size as floor three, that would have clipped 193,000 square feet of net lettable space from the 681,000 square foot total. The gradually increasing floorplates in the Fenchurch Street building begin at 14,900 square feet on floor three and rise in increments of five hundred square feet to reach 29,489 square feet by the thirty-third floor. At £60 per square foot, that 193,000 square feet of space would bring in more than £11 million in extra rent, making the tower worth up to £200 million more to an investor willing to pay eighteen times the annual rent. Hussey's genius was to persuade the City Corporation that increasing rather than decreasing the floor size in a tower, floor by floor, was architecturally acceptable (a strategy that was greatly helped by hiring an acceptable architect, in the form of Viñoly).

FEES: THE BLESSED AND THE CURSED

While lawyers and accountants tend to charge by the hour, property brokers, valuers and fund managers prefer to charge a percentage of the value of the property for transactions. This is an ostensibly crazy system, since the cost of buying, selling, valuing or managing real estate is largely unconnected with the value of the asset. And it gets crazier. Property prices rise far more slowly than inflation. IPD set up an index of property values, using as a starting point their value in December 1986, which was indexed at 100. In December 2012, the IPD all-property index stood at 142. Over roughly the same period, the Office for National Statistics' retail prices index rose from 100 to 242. Income up forty-two percent, expenditure up a hundred and forty-two percent. Result – unhappiness?

Not really. That's the way it's always been, and there are good reasons why it works. The percentages may be small, but commercial property is priced in millions. A fee of half a percent for selling a £50 million office block might not sound much. But in a bull market, £250,000 could be made in a couple of weeks by a small team of experienced investment agents. In a bear market, the client pays nothing if the block fails to sell. Clients like the arrangement: they don't mind the broker making plenty in times of plenty, because then they're making plenty themselves. In times of famine, the client pays nothing unless the property is sold. The system is both a blessing and a curse if you happen to be broker: oodles of cash in the good times, with the risk of getting fired in the bad times.

How it works is described well by Greg Nicholson, who retired from CBRE at just shy of sixty in 2012, after more than thirty years as an investment agent. The former Hillier Parker partner was involved in seventy major shopping centre deals worth many billions of pounds. Says Nicholson: "The problem is there is a very low cost of entry to broking. All you really need is a desk, a phone, a bit of nous, and away you go.

"The holy grail in terms of a fee in the Eighties was always one percent of the selling price. This gradually got eroded with increased competition among agents, and particularly so during the 1989–1991 crash. The market came back in the early to mid Nineties: then you could sell a £50 million plain vanilla product for fees between 0.6 and 0.7 percent.

"By 2012, fees had been further eroded. Some businesses were struggling to survive on 0.25 to 0.35 percent," Nicholson adds, and gives an example: "Every big agent competed for the sale of a £1 billion portfolio owned by St Martins Property Corporation and put up for sale by the Kuwaitis in 2010. No one bid more than 0.35 percent. Savills won it with a bid of circa 0.25 percent. Their rationale in a difficult market would probably have been 'If we can get £1 billion of stock to sell, we can probably get not only fees on this sale but more too down the line'."

But it's not always like that. You have to work hard and build up personal relationships with clients. It can take a long time. Says Nicholson: "But then, suddenly a deal comes along and they only want to use you. We sold a shopping centre for £98 million and got a fee of just under £1 million from a client. If they had had a beauty parade, the job could have been done for £250,000. Frankly, the business of fees is a bit all over the place. A lot of fees don't get properly agreed and documented until after the deal is done, believe it or not. Some agents are hopeless at negotiating fees."

CHAPTER SIX
POLITICS, PLANNING AND TAXES

If you want to make enemies, try to change something
Woodrow Wilson

POLITICS

Tony Blair's New Labour was welcomed into power by developers. "There was a mood of optimism," says Sir John Ritblat, then at the helm of British Land. "The Tories were discredited. They had been in office eighteen years and hadn't spent any money on the infrastructure. Thatcher boasted she'd never spent sixpence on the Tube. It had begun to show."

Blair appointed John Prescott as deputy prime minister, giving the rambunctious MP for Hull East a new "super-ministry". This took the cumbrous shape of the Department for the Environment, Transport and the Regions. Prescott promised "to adopt a more coherent and integrated approach to the planning of development", saying: "Experience has taught me these things must be looked at as a whole rather than individually." Thus began the top-down era of planning control, given flesh by the creation of regional development agencies.

"I was never a great fan until after the event, but John Prescott actually did a huge amount for the property industry," remembers Liz Peace, who as well as having been chief executive of the British Property Federation since 2002 is also a former civil servant. "He may never have quite understood what he was doing. Prescott persisted in thinking that most of my members were house builders. But he actually believed in regeneration.

"We all laughed hugely when he coined the phrase 'sustainable community'. I remember one of my directors saying: 'I thought a sustainable community was a town. Why do we have to have a fancy new title for it?' But Prescott sort of put property on the map as being capable of delivering something more than profit, pinstriped suits and Rolexes: suddenly commercial property actually delivered some of the things that – wait for it – a Labour government wanted."

Louis Armstrong, chief executive of the Royal Institution of Chartered Surveyors for most of the Labour administration, reckoned the new regime initially misunderstood the property sector. "We had to embark on a campaign to get them to understand the industry wasn't just a milch cow for spivs covering the country with concrete, an industry that didn't deserve sympathy, or a group that were just a necessary evil who had to be tolerated." The former naval officer, who retired from running the surveyors' body in 2010 after a decade, felt that "a lot of work had to be done to try and encourage the young, bright, overconfident twenty-year-olds in the Treasury to understand the contribution we made."

A long-time friend and colleague of Gordon Brown when he was prime minister argues that the Treasury had a far wider agenda than simply appeasing developers. "At one level, you could say that what Labour wanted to deliver was an end to boom and bust," says Lord Stevenson, who ran the Smith Institute think tank as plain Wilf Stevenson for over a decade before joining the prime minister at 10 Downing Street as a senior policy adviser between 2008 and 2010. In May 2009, we met in a cramped, top-floor room at No 10, filled with hospital waiting-room style furniture.

LORD STEVENSON, FORMER GOVERNMENT POLICY ADVISER:

The determination of the Treasury was that there would no longer be incredibly cyclical changes in the economy. They had given away responsibility for interest rates to the Bank of England. They recognised that too little was being done on the supply side.

So when you look at the main constraints and bottlenecks, you are looking at matters that improve the flexibility of labour, increase competition, and reduce cartels. All those things had largely been the policy preserve of right-wing governments. But the centre-left felt that they were at the heart of a new paradigm for centre-left governments.

You have to look hard at where productivity gains were coming from. They were largely coming from smaller companies breaking established monopolies. The majority of productivity gains were largely coming from new companies. Research from Harvard showed that productivity gains were not going to come from supporting middle and lower ranking companies that were inefficient and ineffective.

You had to let those go and be much tougher in what you do. That is a long way of asking: what do you do to help the newer companies to increase their productivity? The answer that came back was that they couldn't – without government support.

And one of the biggest calls was to reform the planning process. This was, after all, just around the end of the Heathrow Terminal Five saga, which was in some senses the end point of the dirigiste era that began with the 1947 Planning Act. These two events invited the conclusion that they ought to do some work to change things.

If you look at the regional development agency plans at the time, nearly all of them came up with a hit list that suggested they needed major changes in infrastructure in terms of roads and airports. They also wanted housing to go with these changes. And nationally the case was being made for a step change in the amount of housing that was needed. Planning and housing became hot topics.

They have of course been hot topics from time to time. But the fact that this time the Treasury was driving them made a huge difference. The model up to 1997 was very much that the Treasury was the guardian of the money and its job was to stop things happening. But from 1997 things changed. The chief economic adviser to the Treasury, Ed Balls, was instrumental in this drive.

The Treasury became a department that became involved in managing the economy. It became a finance ministry. It became a department that was involved in the growth of the whole economy. It is a little-known fact that it changed its objective in 1997 to full employment. That in itself changed the nature of the organisation.

The chancellor may have been behind the wheel on this one, but in the back seat was Stevenson's Smith Institute. What was at the time half-jokingly referred to as "Gordon Brown's think tank" is in fact an independent mechanism for exploring policy options – although the Conservatives didn't agree, judging it not independent enough to warrant charitable status. A Charity Commission investigation, however, eventually found otherwise.

The institute commissions and publishes a diversity of monographs – a word that I had to look up when Stevenson asked me to edit one in 2003. It turned out to denote a series of essays on a single topic, written by experts in the field. Called *Solving the London Housing Crisis*, this one included a contribution that nicely balanced the Brownite tendency, from the former Conservative environment minister John Gummer.

JOHN GUMMER

I'd met John Gummer in September 1995 when he was secretary of state for the environment. I was editor of *Building* magazine at the time, and a construction industry trade mission led by Gummer was going to South America for fourteen days, visiting Brazil, Argentina, Chile and Peru. I'd been on one of these jaunts to China two years earlier, with junior environment minister

Tim Yeo. The rules of engagement for me were "everything off the record until the end", at which point I'd get to interview the delegates.

China was spellbinding in 1993. We attended the official opening of the Yangpu Bridge to Pudong, which bore a close resemblance to the desolate Isle of Dogs circa 1983. There was plenty of whizzing around in big cars in Beijing, Shanghai and Guangzhou, an abundance of meetings in horseshoe formation with high-ranking Chinese officials, the odd twelve-course banquet – oh, and one tipsy karaoke session with high-up British officials. Unbeatable for bonding.

So too was the trip to South America with Gummer. Except that since he was a cabinet minister, we got to mingle with a higher pay-grade of politician than junior minister Yeo had met in China. I will resist reminiscing further – except to say that watching John Gummer in action was a revelation. A man mainly remembered for feeding his daughter a beefburger in 1990 during the BSE scare, he had the constitution to match Winston Churchill's and political skills not far from those of former US president Bill Clinton.

Soon after I arrived at *EG* in 1997, I asked Gummer – a former journalist himself – if he would write a weekly column. He did so, fifty weeks a year, without a single break, for ten years. For quite a while, *EG* would hold regular breakfast meetings at his house behind the Home Office. Gummer would persuade other minsters, shadow ministers or high officials to turn up, while I'd invite along a dozen relevant people from the property sector.

We would meet in a reception room where Gummer's satirical doppelganger from the *Spitting Image* puppet show was on view, before heading downstairs for the "full English", followed by an off-the-record discussion. A good deal of the political, planning and housing coverage in *EG* was informed by those discussions, so adroitly chaired by Gummer. The MP for Suffolk Coastal would later switch chambers, in 2010, to become Baron Deben. He was "the best environment secretary we've ever had," according to Friends of the Earth.

THINKING ALOUD AT No 11

My main task for the Smith Institute was to write an introduction to the monograph in question and then, a little later, to stand up in 11 Downing Street to introduce the experts who had contributed their thoughts to that particular volume, which tended to be around fifty to a hundred pages in length. Although designated as the editor, my actual editing input was minimal: the copy editor, Kate Ahira, did a good deal of the work, and very well too (as she has done on this book). The seminars were fascinating occasions. The relevant minister would come; housing and property experts were in attendance – but the core of the audience of seventy to a hundred comprised senior civil servants, who rarely left the shelter of Whitehall.

In the autumn of 2004, the Smith Institute decided to air ideas on "sustainable development", which was a newish buzz phrase at the time. Fringe meetings were organised at all three party conferences; all were sponsored by Tesco – something that the retailer may have come later to regret. I got to hold the ring at two of these meetings. The Labour seminar, held in the Grand Hotel in Brighton, passed peaceably enough; the Conservative event at Bourne Hall in Bournemouth, however, did not.

Tesco director Lucy Neville-Rolfe was in the room. She is a formidable woman, but was matched on this occasion by two equally formidable women sitting expectantly in the front row, arms folded. The pair were Tory councillors from a Home Counties town opposing a Tesco development. There was a short, restrained debate on the need for more homes, followed by a longer, rather more bitter debate about how Tesco was allegedly destroying this fair land.

I got to "edit" seven more monographs, mostly housing related. The last of these was in 2008, on the future of the private rented sector, interest in which flared again in 2012. My only non-housing topic was *The Green Shift*, published in 2006 and considered to merit not one but three seminars at No 11. The Tories had started taking the environment seriously and were gaining support on the topic. Climate change had suddenly begun to matter a lot to Labour.

Therefore the essayists included Gordon Brown, David Miliband – who was then environment secretary – and the government's chief scientific adviser, Sir David King. As well as being editor, I was asked by Stevenson to contribute an essay on how parliament needed to adapt to provide proper oversight of "green" policies and how Whitehall structures should change to implement meaningful actions.

After I had stopped laughing, he provided a list of names of those with whom he wanted me to conduct off-the-record interviews. My job, I realised, was simply to be the amanuensis for those who could not speak on the record. One such was London's then mayor, Ken Livingstone, whom Labour were busy wooing back into the fold at the time. He came to one of the seminars on the topic.

Others interviewed included a recently retired permanent secretary, and a senior Treasury adviser – a man so bright it was scary asking him questions. Most memorable, though, was a left-wing Labour politician on whose tattered living-room couch I sat for forty-five minutes, inhaling the strong aroma of dog while I waited for him to come home. Eventually he arrived, having forgotten the appointment. He picked up the hall phone and began plotting loudly against Tony Blair, oblivious of my presence.

Needless to say, no meaningful actions followed from my long and naive essay entitled *Taking Meaningful Action*. The only action I recall was the disdain poured on me by David Miliband at one of the No 11 seminars, for sounding alarmist in my introductory remarks. The experience turned into a fascinating lesson on how Whitehall absorbs, squeezes, then gently suffocates new ideas: even those to do with saving the human race.

TREASURY, NIL – KEN, ONE

In late 2012, the coalition government launched a Treasury-driven initiative to spark economic growth by introducing measures to boost housing and spending on infrastructure. There is nothing new in politics: fifteen years earlier, New Labour had had the same idea.

Well, that was the plan. One of New Labour's first actions was to ask the architect Lord Rogers to head an "urban task force" to figure out ways to revive the inner cities. That yellow-jacketed document fed into an urban white paper published in November 2000, full of good intentions but carefully filleted of ideas that might cost money.

One big idea that was being floated around that time was the elimination of both VAT and stamp duty on brownfield sites in needy areas. Not a chance. "A white paper that has been reduced to another forgettable piece of top-down fiddling" was *EG*'s verdict at the time. Just before the general election in May 2001, Labour brought out *Ambitions for Britain*, a forty-five-page, best-forgotten manifesto pushing the virtues of regional development agencies in promoting growth.

Far more influential on events was Ken Livingstone's London Plan. In July 2001, the mayor produced a highly detailed draft plan for development in the capital, four hundred and fifty-eight pages long. The core idea was that residential as well as office development should be densely concentrated around transport nodes. The notion may seem obvious now, but at the time it was the One Big New Idea. Building fifty-storey private blocks of flats adjacent to Tube and rail stations was a revolutionary suggestion.

The idea gave political impetus to the building of the Shard in Southwark for instance, giving permission, as it were, for developer Irvine Sellar to dream a very tall dream. In July 2008, I went to Genoa to interview the architect of the thousand-foot tower, Renzo Piano. He made it very clear that without Livingstone's 2001 plan there would have been no Shard.

In June 2002, the final document of the London Plan was published, helping to ignite a building boom in the capital on a scale unseen since the Victorian era. The London Plan influenced other English cities to relax planning restrictions and permit far more dense urban development.

PLANNING

IAN COULL, FORMER CHIEF EXECUTIVE OF SEGRO AND LABOUR PARTY SUPPORTER:

Planning is a vote loser. No politician has ever won favour by allowing developers to do more. So Labour was quite brave in 1997 by openly recognising that planning was a major obstacle to international inward investment and economic growth. They then set about trying to do something about it. Not easy.

The best planning minister was Charlie Falconer. He was very outgoing, a terrific guy and somebody who understood the industry pretty well. Labour did try to address the sector's concerns. What we wanted was more certainty, a quicker and more transparent process, with a greater level of consistency across the country.

But Charlie Falconer didn't last very long, as he was whisked off by Tony Blair to do other things. We then went through a series of planning ministers over the following two or three years. Every time a new one came in, the proposals were watered down a bit. The bill was a bit of an improvement, but not much.

A green paper suggesting ways to alter the planning system for the better was published in December 2001, and a bill was subsequently promised by planning minister Lord Falconer, who heralded it as "the greatest change to the system since 1947". Falconer left for the Home Office in 2002. The watered-down bill finally became law in the spring of 2004.

"Charlie's big idea, which was a good one," says the British Property Federation's Liz Peace, "was that if you put all the effort into making proper plans first for an area, then the decisions become easy. All you do is look at the plan. If the plan allows for it, you can have it; if the plan does not, the answer's no. That was the whole basis of the 2004 act of parliament.

"The idea was not new – a 'plan-led' system existed; it just wasn't terribly effective. But Labour made the revised system too complicated. No local authority found it very easy to write a plan." Indeed not. As late as 2012, only half had done so. Here's why, according to former Royal Institution of Chartered Surveyors chief executive Louis Armstrong.

LOUIS ARMSTRONG, RICS CHIEF EXECUTIVE 1998–2010:

The desire to control everything from eco-towns to the numbers of houses built was well beyond the capabilities of any government. Nor could you control local councils who did it their way whatever anyone else said. So there was a big debate on what to do.

Falconer got frustrated because there wasn't a magic wand that even a sharp, carefully focused minister could wave and get results. It was a quagmire into which he sank further and further; the more stones you turned, the more the alligators materialised.

Liz Peace, chief executive of the British Property Federation since 2002, was heavily involved in industry-government discussions.

LIZ PEACE, CHIEF EXECUTIVE OF THE BRITISH PROPERTY FEDERATION:

During Labour's time the planning system, for lots of reasons, became far more complex: partly because of Europe and partly because people are more litigious. Objectors merely see not getting what they want as the first stage in fighting it all the way to the European Court of Human Rights.

The local politician is elected in order to say, "In the interests of the community, we are going to do this." But what they tended to say on any big development was, "Sorry; no, we can't make a decision." It gets shoved up to the Planning Inspectorate and ultimately to the secretary of state. Local authorities abrogated their responsibility.

One of the principal problems of the new system was the difficulty of getting developers to take part. Fine if you are the Duke of Westminster and you own half of Cheshire. But most of the development industry doesn't know where it is going to be in five years' time. They were not going to pay consultants to help them to read and comment on local plans in every one of the 367 local authorities – or even in half of those where they think they might be active.

So private developers did not get involved in the plan-making process, but then they came along later and said, "We want to do something and are told it's against the plan. Well, in that case we'll fight." So the whole thing just didn't work. Like communism, the idea was great idea in principle: if you could get this plan, this blueprint drawn up, all would be fine.

But it became far too bureaucratic. Have you ever seen any of these plans? They tend to be huge, badly written, and don't actually say anything. On top of that, Prescott stuck in the concept of regional planning. That, fortunately, did not take off. The English are not interested in regions – a point the coalition seized upon.

One of the first acts of the incoming government was to scrap regional agencies and top-down housing targets. Then Communities and Local Government, led by secretary of state Eric Pickles and planning minister Greg Clark, rushed headlong into planning reform underpinned by the concept of "localism".

This certainly put the wind up the property industry, with the suggestion that planning would become a neighbourhood issue where local communities decided whether or not they would accept development. But this localist approach has been substantially moderated by the need not to impinge on the Treasury's growth agenda.

The result is a government statement of planning policy (the National Planning Policy Framework) firmly focused on ensuring that planning supports rather than impedes growth. The policy actually goes further than the development industry had ever imagined.

The Clark proposals were well received in the spring of 2012. The MP for Tunbridge Wells radically simplified the planning rulebook, slimming down the number of pages from over a thousand to around fifty. His review raised fears among conservationists that the green belt would be unbuckled. The National Trust got rather upset, and the passions of nimbys in general were inflamed by a melodramatic "save our countryside" campaign orchestrated by the *Daily Telegraph*.

Clark somehow managed to assuage their fears as well as keep developers happy. Planning peace and love reigned over the Olympic summer of 2012. In September, though, war broke out again. The emollient Greg Clark was promoted in a government reshuffle, to be replaced by a new, more aggressive planning minister: Nick Boles, who was explicitly tasked by prime minister David Cameron with turning words into actions, as the government was coming under growing pressure to increase house building numbers.

A grand plan was announced to stimulate the economy, partly by freeing up the planning system with measures like allowing change of use from offices to residential. War naturally recommenced. The last word goes to Liz Peace: "Every ten years, there is a great review of the planning system, and *it's all going to change everything and make it better* – and then it sort of fizzles out and then we start all over again. That's just what happens. You could fill a room with reports on improving planning."

TAX POLICY

Taxing transactions, taxing land deals, but not taxing capital gains – those were the three fiscal policies that marked the relationship between government and real estate between 1997 and 2012.

- The quadrupling of top-rate stamp duty between July 1997 and March 2000 invoked outrage that gradually muted into acceptance as prices adjusted to account for higher rates.
- The "land tax" proposal to claw back a proportion of the uplift in value conferred on a piece of land by the granting of planning permission eventually became the community infrastructure levy.
- Real estate investment trusts (REITs) were introduced, after what began as a no-hope campaign ended in a surprise victory for the sector – but a victory that came at the wrong moment.

STAMP DUTY LAND TAX

Chancellor Gordon Brown doubled top-rate stamp duty from one to two percent in July 1997, just two months after Labour took office. In March 1998, the top rate was hiked up in the budget by a further one percent, hitting three percent. One year later, it rose to 3.5 percent. Then in March 2000, Brown took the rate to four percent.

The industry was furious, the Treasury highly pleased with itself. Stamp duty revenues from residential and commercial property jumped from not much more than £1 billion in 1998/99 to £4.1 billion in 2001/02. By 2007/08, the take had soared to almost £10 billion. Income then collapsed, slumping to £6.1 billion in 2011/12. The hikes maddened the commercial sector, where almost no deals are done below the top rate. Into this arena stepped Liz Peace.

LIZ PEACE, CHIEF EXECUTIVE OF THE BRITISH PROPERTY FEDERATION:

When I joined the BPF in January 2002, two things struck me. First of all, the industry was still reeling, furious over the stamp duty rise. The leaders saw the rises as a sort of personal attack on each and every one of them. The feeling was that this was a government that clearly thought property didn't matter; that it was an industry easily crucified with unjust tax rises. They were deeply bitter and afraid that it would go up even further.

Tied to this was a feeling that government did not understand and didn't want to find out about the sector. They actually believed that the government had a conspiracy to extract large amounts of cash out of commercial property.

I remember having a conversation with a senior official in the Inland Revenue, as it was then called. When I told her of the conspiracy theories, she fell about laughing. She said, "Oh, my God, how incredibly arrogant your industry is, thinking civil servants and ministers sit around working out a plot against the sector."

Her reaction was both amusing and quite scary – because what it did show you was that government doesn't plan whom it is going to tax. It just taxes where it thinks it can make money, and if you happen to be in the wrong place: tough. Senior figures were mortified by this reaction. I remember one chief executive going on and on about how the rises were affecting the industry. Mind you, it didn't stop him taking a huge salary and bonus that year or the next.

So, why did Gordon Brown quadruple the tax? "You have to go back to Adam Smith for the definition of a good tax," says Lord Stevenson. "The one thing we do not tax well here is land. So stamp duty is a surrogate for a land tax. Fair enough, it is a blunt instrument. But it is nonsensical to say the government can operate without raising revenues, and it has to 'tax well' when it does so."

Not well enough, according to Liz Peace. "One BPF member from the North said: 'Look, we consider ourselves to be a good, law-abiding company. Yes, we make money, but we are doing our bit for society. We don't want to not pay tax, but stamp duty at four percent is the difference between doing a deal and not doing a deal.' He said they'd gone to some fancy and very expensive lawyer who came up with some incredibly tax-efficient offshore structure, which meant they paid nothing. He actually felt bad about it: because if the duty had stayed at two percent, they would not have bothered."

The British Property Federation opened negotiations with the government, telling it the rises were stifling the sector, says Peace.

LIZ PEACE:

They turned round and said: "You don't look as if you're suffering. You have told us it will be the end of development or transactional life as you know it, but look what is happening." That was because the market had picked up after the 9/11 blip. So it was hugely difficult to say to government: "This tax is crucifying the industry."

They would say: "Excuse me; we don't actually quite see that happening." Then the government launched their stamp duty modernisation project in 2002/03. This they dressed up as how to respond to the digitisation of the Land Registry. In practice it was how to turn stamp duty into something that is more difficult to avoid.

The property press didn't help. Stories would appear in Estates Gazette *or* Property Week *saying "so-and-so is going offshore". Officials would get a rude note from the financial secretary to the Treasury saying: "What the hell is going on? Why aren't we stopping this?" The line I got from ministers was: "If you want us to look at stamp duty then your industry had better start paying it first."*

Stamp duty land tax ceased to be an optional tax. Avoidance was a lot more difficult, because you could not register your deal with the Land Registry unless you had actually paid the tax. So more stamp duty was paid. But lawyers continued to find ways round the tax; there was a clever loophole that involved inserting property into limited partnerships.

The Treasury closed this loophole, so a lot of limited partnerships simply took themselves offshore. I remember the great rush of that happening. We warned the government at the time that this would happen, and how it would damage the sector. But they wouldn't relent. So the baby went out with the bathwater – and most LPs of course went offshore.

By mid 2012, the government was coming under pressure to curb tax avoidance by the likes of Apple, Google and Starbucks. In December of that year, the chancellor, George Osborne, announced a series of measures to close tax loopholes. I went to see property lawyer Melville Rodrigues of CMS Cameron McKenna, an expert on the subject. His words shaped the following article published on 7th December in my *Evening Standard* column:

Osborne's Easiest Revenue Stream Is in the Channel

Capital gains tax on commercial real estate is routinely avoided by setting up offshore vehicles. Common locations for the vehicles are the Channel Isles and Luxembourg, given their tax-treaty networks.

Hundreds of office blocks and shopping centres in the UK are officially "owned" offshore – via structures that create an illusion of "management and control" from outside the UK, a legal necessity to avoid paying UK capital gains tax. Yet the property managers of the offshore vehicles operate from respectable property companies and pension funds based in the UK.

To maintain the fiction of local control the managers fly to the Channel Islands, Luxembourg and sometimes more exotic locations for occasional directors' board meetings that last just a few minutes, then off for a beer. Does Osborne see this as abuse? No idea. But lawyers say it's by far the biggest and easiest loophole to close.

THE COMMUNITY INFRASTRUCTURE LEVY

"One thing that causes public upset is the windfall gains that come from conferring planning permission," says Wilf Stevenson. "When the good times rolled, that exacerbated the issue." It was in the early Noughties that the idea of a land tax was born – or rather, born again. At least four serious attempts had previously been made to extract tax from increases in the "value" of land, the first made in 1909.

Each of these attempts foundered, and in every case it was for the same reason: they failed to address the conundrum of how on earth to tax an *opinion* of what the price of a piece of land *might* be *if* it were to be sold. One expert will say that the value is X; another expert will say that it is Y. This fundamental flaw led to a century of delay.

David Lloyd George's famous "people's budget" in 1909 introduced "increment value duty". This was a twenty percent tax chargeable on the difference between the value of the land at 30th April 1909 and its value at the date of any subsequent sale, or grant of a lease, or transfer of an interest: it applied to all land, including that beneath individual homes. Uproar ensued, and the Lords refused to pass the bill. Lloyd George even threatened to create five hundred new peers to ensure its passing, but instead a bill removing the Lords' veto on the legislation was passed.

The land tax proposals became law. *EG* produced a *Land Union Journal* – a "monthly periodical to assist persons called upon to deal with valuations and assessments under the new act". In fact, the journal exposed and ridiculed the fundamental assumption that you could retrospectively – or even contemporaneously – fix accurate values to land. The law became unworkable and was repealed.

The next serious attempt came in a "development charge" inserted into the 1947 Planning Act by Labour. Twenty years after that, Labour set up a Land Commission and introduced the "betterment levy". A full-blooded Development Land Tax Act was made law by Labour in 1976 – that one brought the sight of builders hastily digging trenches on empty sites so that developers could avoid the levy by saying work had already started before the tax became law. Each of these measures failed in the end – although the 1976 act lingered and was only fully repealed by Margaret Thatcher in the late Eighties. The next attempt surfaced not much more than a decade later.

Liz Peace explains what happened next.

LIZ PEACE:

> *Labour ministers said they didn't mind people making a profit by using enterprise. What they did mind was when they made a profit out of doing nothing, like simply sitting on a piece of land and scooping a profit once the state gave them planning permission.*

> *The planning green paper put out by Lord Falconer in the autumn of 2001 suggested a tariff: an idea that was backed by John Prescott. Suddenly the Treasury popped up and said, "If it's a tariff, it's a tax. Therefore this is our job." Officials then spent the next twelve months looking around for a different way to tackle it. They came up with something called an optional planning charge.*

> *Then they announced Kate Barker was going to do a housing review, so the charge idea got subsumed into that. That review came out in March 2004. Out of the document came the idea that we might have what they called a planning gain supplement or PGS.*

> *Barker had particularly focused on landowners who made a huge amount of money out of the grant of planning permission for new homes. The trouble was the government took it one step further and*

said: "We'll apply it across the board, not just to housing." Calculating the tax based upon the increase in value on complex commercial projects would have turned the PGS into a developer's nightmare and a lawyer's dream.

But that did not stop Labour trying. In 2004, I edited a monograph on the topic for the Smith Institute. The publication was entitled *Building Sustainable Communities: Capturing Land Development Value for the Public Realm*. The subtitle was of course the real title. In the booklet, Treasury housing expert and economist Kate Barker argued for the introduction of a planning gain supplement that would encourage development by providing funds for public amenities like new roads and schools.

John Gummer argued forcefully against a PGS in the monograph, on philosophical grounds: "A betterment tax is wrong in principle and like most things that are fundamentally wrong, it will always fail in practice. We should insist on the right to property as one of the fundamental supports of freedom and accept the planning system as an unfortunate necessity. Property must not be stolen from its rightful owners, even by men of goodwill with the best of intentions."

The intention to impose a planning gain supplement was attacked over the next year or so by the property industry. Louis Armstrong of the Royal Institution of Chartered Surveyors recalls: "There were always issues around valuation. I think our professionals were concerned that what was a logical and superficially attractive idea was flawed. The moment you tried to find out at what point you value the land, it opened up a quagmire into which professionals would sink and lawyers would make a lot of money."

The property industry decided to come up with its own alternative proposals to minimise the damaging effects of the planned legislation. Says Peace: "The [government's] proposal did not deal with complex developments in city centres. The key issue was to get the industry bodies to coalesce around one way of doing it. Sir Stuart Lipton helped bring together house builders and developers to agree a tariff system that applies a fixed sum per square metre of development."

The Treasury eventually agreed to a tariff-based tax, which came to be called the community infrastructure levy or CIL. The idea was given the power of law in the 2008 Planning Act. But it took until April 2011 for all the complex regulations to be published. The Conservatives were originally opposed to the tax, but their objections quietly dissolved after the coalition government was formed in the summer of 2010.

"We all thought we had hit upon probably the best outcome," says Peace. "But experience so far suggests that it may turn out to have been a horrible mistake, with local authorities seeming to be in the process of setting the CIL charge at levels that will choke off development. We may find ourselves having to go back to the drawing board!" In late 2012, the rules were still being tweaked.

REAL ESTATE INVESTMENT TRUSTS

Unlike traditional property companies, real estate investment trusts (or REITs) don't pay capital gains tax when selling assets. In return for this relief-, the REIT has to obey all sorts of complex rules and financial dictates – rules that could fill another book.

The big property companies began lobbying the Treasury on the topic almost as soon as Gordon Brown became chancellor in 1997. Why? The argument for REIT status turned on the point that it is unfair for property to be burdened with "double taxation". Not only did property companies have to pay capital gains tax and corporation tax, but their shareholders also then had to pay further capital gains tax as well as dividend tax on the income from those shares.

REIT conversion would be tax-neutral, it was argued. The capital gains tax lost would supposedly be compensated for by the increase in tax income from higher profits. These would come because REITs would develop and trade their assets far more frequently.

These arguments were drawn together in a paper with the abstruse title of *Property Securitisation in the UK*, early in the Labour administration. Now-defunct accountants Arthur Andersen did the brainwork, while additional input and sponsorship came from the British Property Federation, the Royal Institution of Chartered Surveyors, the Investment Property Forum and the Corporation of London.

In other words, the entire property establishment put its intellectual weight behind this document. Sadly, it was gibberish, to all but a student of higher mathematics. Liz Peace is not much kinder. "It was a hugely erudite mathematical study, containing all sorts of incomprehensible equations to show how REITs would be tax-neutral. The Treasury had lots of people with mathematics degrees who turned round and said, 'The sums are fine – but we just don't believe the assumptions in your model.'"

In May 2000, the Treasury chose a brutal method of delivering the message to the property industry. The big "No" came unheralded at a conference organised by the Investment Property Forum, where the delights of REITs were on the agenda. Treasury official Dilwyn Griffiths, who had been negotiating with the sector since 1998, stunned the audience by saying: "We see no point in stringing along the industry forever.... The ball is now back in your court." As the British Property Federation's Peace puts it, "At a stroke, years of expensive work was totally dismissed."

She explains: "The mood when I came into the BPF in early 2002 was 'Don't bother with REITs: you will never get them back on the agenda'. Then (I don't know why) suddenly there seemed to be a glimmer of interest. I was sitting next to a Treasury official at a conference in late 2002 – it was after the French announced their version of REITs. He said, 'If you want to push the case for REITs, you really need to look at how it will benefit the end user.' I said, 'What do you mean by *end user*?' He said: 'The occupier.'

"So I said, 'What about investors? And what about pension funds, the savings of the man in the street?' 'Oh, I hadn't thought of that,' he said. Anyway, there and then he sketched out what he thought were the sort of arguments we should make. Others were starting to get similar encouragement."

A central figure in the successful, second REIT campaign was Francis Salway, who joined Land Securities in 2001 and served as chief executive between 2004 and 2012. Salway explains the renewed push for REITs:

FRANCIS SALWAY, CHIEF EXECUTIVE OF LAND SECURITIES 2004–2012:

You have to remember 1997 was the start of the dot-com boom, and property was seen as being "old industry", and hence out of fashion. The stock market ratings applied to most property companies were pretty low. Property companies were trading at big discounts to net asset value. A number of people exploited that by taking their companies private. Not all names disappeared, but quite a few did.

Then as the dot-com boom collapsed, property began to come a bit more back in vogue. That led to a reappearance of the old question of listed companies being taxed on capital gains and profits, and shareholders then being taxed again – double taxation. So there was a renewed push to introduce real estate investment trusts, particularly as REIT status was increasingly being used as a filter test by global investors when considering whether to invest in listed real estate in that country.

"We began to talk to the Treasury," says Liz Peace. "In due course, they came back with a series of questions. They were just ten simple points on what were the benefits: 'Can you prove they will work?', that sort of thing. A group led by banker John Gellatly began to work up the answers. The back-and-forth process began; John's papers got longer and longer. He is a seriously clever chap. From time to time, I had to ask him to put them into something the man in the street could understand. In the end, a government green paper went out for consultation."

That consultation paper was published alongside Brown's March 2004 budget. But problems remained. "The draft legislation had a number of serious drawbacks," says Salway. "So Stephen Hester of British Land and I engaged in pushing for a number of key changes. Originally, there was proposed to be a gearing test stipulating that the REIT's level of debt had to be no more than a fixed percentage of asset values. If we'd had the original proposals, a lot of companies would have faced a real risk of failing that REIT qualification test when values dropped in any subsequent downturn."

A prescient thought, as it turned out, when REITs were established in 2007. Two years later, values had nearly halved. In June 2004, a joint industry response was sent to the Treasury; the proposals were then largely accepted. In March 2005, Gordon Brown promised legislation in his budget speech. Says Peace: "It was classic Gordon: 'I intend to introduce British REITs to help solve the housing crisis.' The whole industry went into panic. They thought: 'My God, he's going to specify that we have to have a certain percentage of residential stock in order to convert?'

"Then one of his officials rang me up: 'Don't worry, Liz, what he really meant to say was...' I subsequently discovered how Gordon Brown did his budget speeches. He would take material from different sources, and then write the speech. Points would be circulated to the relevant departments. They would write back with a correction; if they were lucky he took it into the speech and if he didn't that was it. That is how you got these idiocies creeping in. But at least he gave the official green light."

In March 2006, the chancellor set a date of January 2007 for REITs to begin trading. "That was an example of effective lobbying on practical issues," says Salway. "Within an amazingly short period of time after REITs were introduced, the new structure was severely tested by the fall in values. It came through: the REIT legislation held up well, and no company was at risk of losing its REIT status. The REIT entry charge for Land Securities was just over £300 million. But that was recouped over just three years through corporation and capital gains tax savings."

Peace says: "The REIT structure we got clearly suits quoted companies. When you look at who was paying my salary and who was on the group, and how influential people like Francis Salway, Stephen Hester and Ian Coull were, it's not surprising. Subsequently, officials said, 'We only introduced REITs to preserve the quoted sector.' They certainly did not. It was all about helping housing, helping regeneration, democratising property, making it possible for the ordinary man in the street to invest in REITs. Ironically, it did keep the quoted company sector going. I'm sure there would have been more buyouts, going private, if we had not had REITs."

Thanks to the initiative being seized by the big property companies, the legislation ended up promoting their financial interests. But the timing was very costly. Ian Coull was chief executive of Segro at the time: "If I could wind the clock back, we probably wouldn't have converted to a real estate investment trust on 1st January 2007. The conversion charge was two percent of your gross asset value. So we were converting at the peak of the market. But we were also keen to get on with it and bring in all the benefits that REITs undoubtedly did bring. So we all did it.

"If we had done it a couple of years later, it would have cost about fifty percent less. But there we are. However, having tried for about ten years to persuade the government to introduce the legislation, the industry was hardly in a position to say: 'This is a great idea, but can we have it in three years' time, please?'"

A LESSON IN THE LONG ART OF POLITICAL PERSUASION
Lobbyists seeking lessons on why it took one false start and a decade to persuade the government to legislate on REITs should heed Lord Stevenson, who came up with this final piece of political advice:

LORD STEVENSON, FORMER GOVERNMENT POLICY ADVISER:

Saying you have a very strong case for doing something that will help development means the government will listen. But it is also right and proper that the government should take its time to make up its mind on the facts. So it is up to you as the proponent of the scheme – and there are eighty industry sectors, all with their pet schemes – to put forward the case. But the task is to argue your case on economic grounds: to say that at worst it is revenue-neutral and at best revenue-positive.

The problem is it can take five years. The first year, the Treasury tells you to go and get lost. The second year, they will look at it and give you some comments on why it doesn't work. In year three, they will invite you in to discuss the proposals and listen very carefully to see if they think what you are proposing is a goer. In the fourth year, they will give you proposals – which you will hate. In the fifth year, it goes into the budget. That is what happens all the time. Anyone who thinks differently is just bonkers.

REITs were a classic. You have to get the arguments right. Where the property industry went wrong was simply sending in their arguments and then going around saying, "Why don't these buggers do something about this?" When the truth is that you have to sit down and do some really hard work. It happens through hard work and graft – and the five-year rule.

The industry was not recognised as being very effective. They did get their act together, but this was only levelling up to where many other industries have been for a long time. You may feel some distaste for the lobbying profession, but Whitehall is a complicated place and it needs people who understand what is happening to give guidance.

Simply sending in a letter saying "Please do this because I would like it to happen" does not work. And the days are long gone when you could use your friends in power to get what you want done.

THE PLAYERS

THE PLAYERS

CHAPTER SEVEN
DEVELOPERS' WORLD

People who enjoy meetings should not be in charge of anything
Thomas Sowell

FORTY YEARS AGO...
My first visit to the home of Harry Hyams was in the early Seventies. Ramsbury Manor is quite a sight: the Grade I listed Queen Anne mansion, built in 1680, sits in four hundred and sixty acres of Wiltshire parkland through which the River Kennet flows. I sputtered up the looping driveway in a tiny, red Hillman Imp and parked beside the garage. The tin can of a car was supplied by Wimpey to allow me to tour building sites: in this case to tot up the costs of tending the house and gardens of Britain's most famous developer. Hyams had paid £650,000 for the manor in 1964, a record sum at the time.

Stainless steel drip trays lay under a powerful sports car and a gleaming limousine; alongside sat a Ski-Doo. The white-tiled garage was as spotless as an operating theatre. Formica-lined birdhouses sat in the grounds, providing shelter to a flock of pink flamingos. Beside the river, a revolving oak hut gave protection from variable winds to anglers fishing in the Kennet. That was my first introduction to the great riches that property can bring. I never saw Hyams in person: I only got as far as the servants' quarters. The sole evidence of the man himself was his looping signature on cheques paying for the work.

Oliver Marriott describes the reclusive figure in his 1969 book, *The Property Boom*, as "the daddy of all developers", adding: "He was a rather tall, extremely elegant figure with a black Spaniard's beard, neatly trimmed.

In a quiet way, Hyams was the living legend of the property world." He was still a living legend at the end of 2012, when the eighty-four-year-old remained lord of Ramsbury Manor.

But the visibility of the man who would (allegedly) sue you for suggesting he left the Centre Point building on Oxford Street deliberately empty had almost faded by the time I reached *EG* in 1997. All I remembered was that George Wimpey had built the thirty-five-storey tower in the late Sixties, and that Hyams was on the board of what was then one of the world's largest contractors. Wimpey held a forty percent stake in Oldham Estates, a shell company Hyams bought in 1959 entirely because it was listed on the Oldham stock exchange (which did not shut down until 1965, believe it or not). By 1966, the value of Oldham's assets had risen from £22,328 to £38,978,403. Marriott estimates that during those seven years Hyams made a £27 million fortune, which is equivalent to £411 million at 2012 prices.

Hyams flared briefly into public consciousness in 2000 during the contentious taking-private of publicly listed MEPC, in which he held a small stake. Then he hit the headlines again in 2006, when Ramsbury Manor was burgled and millions of pounds' worth of antiques were stolen. Back in 1999, I received a letter on handcrafted paper from the great man himself. The millennium was approaching, and *EG* was preparing a special supplement. Might this most legendary of developers break his silence, I had enquired. Perhaps specially for an ex-Wimpey surveyor who remembered sending him bills for flamingo houses and a circular oak fishing hut? A wry "No" from the Howard Hughes of property was the response.

Hyams is the last of a trio of post-war developers well known to the general public; Jack Cotton and Charles Clore being the other two. I recall as a child seeing newspaper headlines in the Fifties containing the names of Cotton and/or Clore as if no explanation were needed. Developers luxuriated in public approval from the early Fifties until the late Sixties, as Britain rebuilt itself after the war. This was the era of new towns, new city centres – a mood well captured in the *The Power Game*, a TV series starring Patrick Wymark and Peter Barkworth that ran between 1965 and 1969.

Jack Cotton died in the Bahamas in March 1964, aged sixty-one. In the last five years of his life he had become ever more famous, says Marriott. "His photograph, with spotted bow-tie and carnation, and phrases peppered with vivid imagination were continually in the newspapers."

Sir Charles Clore died in July 1979 aged seventy-four in Monaco, after building a huge fortune in property and retailing – he owned Selfridges at one stage. This fortune is now administered by his daughter, Dame Vivien Duffield. He was a more private person than Cotton, but still just as famous. Contemporary songwriters Michael Flanders and Donald Swann included a reference to the developer in a verse of their song *Sounding Brass*, a skit satirising social climbing and status symbols:

> *Hell has just been taken over*
> *By a friend of Charlie Clore's.*
> *We've acquired a private furnace,*
> *Bigger, hotter, far than yours.*

On 25th October 1960, an ill-fated corporate marriage took place between Cotton's City Centre Properties and City & Central, owned by Clore. The partnership split in a blaze of publicity four years later, shortly before Cotton's death. But while Cotton and Clore were stealing the headlines, a quieter man than Clore was building a legacy, and one that has lasted. His name was Harold Samuel; the company he founded was Land Securities.

LORD SAMUEL

Baron Samuel of Wych Cross died on 28th August 1987, aged seventy-five. Forty-three years earlier, on 15th February 1944, the companies section of *The Times* announced that Harold Samuel had acquired the Land Securities Investment Trust. The thirty-two-year-old chartered surveyor paid £20,000 for a business founded in 1863. The assets consisted of three houses in Kensington, together with £19,321 of government gilts. By the time of Samuel's death, Land Securities held assets worth £3 billion and was Britain's number one property company.

Land Securities' success was founded on doing the reverse of what was to happen sixty years later in the West End, when offices would begin to be converted into flats. Samuel bought apartment blocks that had been requisitioned for war-time use as government offices. The 1947 Town and Country Planning Act contained an obscure clause allowing these requisitioned homes to continue in use as office space, which was then worth far more than housing. This clause was something of which few owners were aware, and many thus sold too cheaply to Land Securities under the assumption that the properties were to be converted back to apartments.

"A thorough understanding of the laws and the loopholes affecting property could be crucial to success," says Oliver Marriott. "Harold Samuel realised this absolutely. This was the cornerstone of his great fortune." In August 1950, the *Evening Standard* reported that Land Securities shares, which stood at £6/15s, were worth sixty times their 1944 price. If they were to reach £8, the paper said, "Harold Samuel will become the first post-war millionaire." In August 1953, Land Securities moved into palatial offices in Devonshire House on Piccadilly, where the home of the Dukes of Devonshire once stood, and which the company had bought for £1 million in 1949.

The Finchley-born former estate agent made a bid for the Savoy Group in 1953 – but was defeated by the concerted efforts of the Establishment, who were horrified at the possibility that Land Securities might turn the Savoy into an office block. Samuel, then forty-one, merely turned his attention elsewhere. Giant town-centre developer Ravenseft was fully absorbed into Land Securities in 1955. But perhaps the sweetest deal done by the man who coined the phrase "location, location, location" was his takeover of what was left of the Clore/Cotton empire in 1968.

A year later came the £144 million acquisition of The City of London Real Property Company, which owned four million square feet of space in the City as well as the five-acre Stag Place site in Victoria. Samuel was knighted for his charitable work in 1963 and made a life peer in 1972 at the age of sixty. Six years later, he handed over the reins to Peter Hunt, a cigar-smoking extrovert who had been with the business since 1964. Hunt ran the company for nine years under Samuel's watchful eye, from 1978 until Lord Samuel died in 1987. The man who acted as go-between in this sometimes-strained relationship was Ian Henderson. "I was Harold Samuel's office boy," he says.

IAN HENDERSON

In late 2012, the man who ran Land Securities from 1997 to 2004 sits as the grand old man of property, aged sixty-nine, in an office in Grosvenor Street, headquarters of Capital & Counties. Here this sage and humorous character – who describes himself as a "farmer" in *Who's Who* – holds the role of deputy chairman. The listed property company, which is run by Ian Hawksworth and Gary Yardley, owns Covent Garden and is embarking on the development of some seventy acres of Earls Court – a project on the same scale as that undertaken by the extraordinarily energetic Roger Madelin of Argent at King's Cross, which took twenty years to gain traction.

Henderson started his working life with Chesterton, in 1962. "I remember visiting the home of Lady Diana Cooper as a young surveyor to inspect the plumbing, during a stint at Chesterton," he recalls. "Her chihuahua began chewing my ankle. I shook the dog roughly from my trouser leg. She complained. I had to leave Chesterton."

He joined Hillier Parker on £500 a year and made a name "bringing in business from tripe dealers in Manchester". In 1971, Henderson moved over to Ravenseft, the provincial arm of Land Securities. Two years later, it was back to Devonshire House to work on the Elephant and Castle shopping centre, among other projects. By 1978, he'd become the "office boy" detailed to smooth relationships between Lord Samuel and Peter Hunt: "I used to have dinner every Monday night at the Caprice with Peter to brief him before his Wednesday meetings with Lord Samuel." So, just the man to provide a bridge between the Sixties world described so well in *The Property Boom* and the world of the late Nineties, in which *Planet Property* really begins.

IAN HENDERSON, CHIEF EXECUTIVE OF LAND SECURITIES 1997–2004:

> *Harold Samuel was a man of remarkable integrity. He paid himself £65 a year when he started the company in 1944. He never paid himself any more, relying entirely on the appreciation of his shareholdings. He was very enigmatic. I'd give him his quarterly cheque for a trifling sum. He'd always say, "Do you think I'm doing a good job?" I'd back out saying, "Yes, of course, sir."*

> *I had my worst negotiations with Lord Samuel – far worse than with the other side. If there was ever a query as to whether we had misled somebody, he used to say to me: "Henderson, have you said anything that could possibly have led the other side to believe that that was our position?" If I havered, he would say: "Give way." But when he thought we were right, he was stubborn.*

> *We once reached an impasse on a lease renegotiation with Kleinwort Benson in Fenchurch Street, on the site that is now the Walkie*

Talkie. Harold was getting grumpy; he would not give way. I suggested we might persuade them to agree – by flipping a coin. He looked at me hard and said: "What do you mean – toss for it?" I said: "Sir, it's a fifty-fifty chance, isn't it?" I was dismissed.

About ten minutes later, the red buzzer went. This was the way he communicated – you had to drop whatever you were doing. I went back in. He agreed we should toss for it. Kleinwort's agreed. One of our directors, John Moore, was instructed to ring Kleinwort Benson. Moore called and said to the Kleinwort director, "Are you going to call, or am I?" The Kleinwort man said, "I'll toss; you call." So over the phone, and with no other witnesses, he did. John Moore shouted: "Heads!" And a voice came back down the phone, "Oh, bugger; it is." That was some measure of trust.

The Seventies

We had seen this tremendous boom in 1973. Our assets were valued at £1 billion at the start of the year. Then, that autumn, Harold decided he wanted to buy in company shares. Before doing that, he felt he had an obligation to have a revaluation of the assets: that showed fifty percent uplift in six months to £1.5 billion.

We then had the miners' strike and the three-day week in early 1974. I used to travel up to London with huge jerries of paraffin for the oil lamps in Devonshire House. Values collapsed. We went from £1.5 billion in late 1973 down to £700 million or £800 million, less than a year later.

It was a very tense period, because the Palestinian movement was out to bump off leading British Jews. Edward – Teddy – Sieff of M&S was shot, just after Christmas 1973, supposedly by Carlos the Jackal. Teddy lived next door to Harold Samuel in St John's Wood. The police tried to persuade Harold to take a different route to work, but he refused. But we did have the most amazing security at Devonshire House, as he was considered to be a prime target. There were lengthy discussions with the anti-terrorist squad.

Harold was very concerned about our banking covenants at the time. I said to him: "Sir, as far as I'm concerned, if we have problems, everyone else has much worse problems." He said it was a question of principle and honour that we maintained our covenants. We sold building after building. I had the experience of taking major investors round the City, walking them around Victoria and saying: "Is there anything here you would like to buy?" And the answer was nearly always: "No, not at any price."

The secondary banking crisis meant the market shut down completely for about three months, I think, towards the end of 1974. Eventually we did two deals with the BBC, one a new building in

Hanover Square (now demolished to make way for Crossrail), the other in Burlington Gardens. Godfrey Richardson of Knight Frank was acting for the BBC. We called him Cassandra, because he could find anything wrong with everything!

We gave those two buildings away, effectively. But at least it started the market. The BBC bought them for their pension funds. Godfrey Richardson had the courage to say to the BBC: "You should buy them, because they're a steal." They were – at about half their previous valuation.

The Whitgift Centre in Croydon had to go, along with a number of provincial shopping centres. We had to sell a tall office tower on Cavendish Square, just behind Oxford Street, for £27 million. I think it sold recently for £450 million. I remember arguing with Lord Samuel about it. I said: "I don't think this needs to go, sir." And he said: "My banking covenants are still under pressure."

It was all very slow. Peter Hunt and I used to work night after night trying to put heads of terms together to get people to buy, because we had to realise an awful lot of cash to get the right side of the banking covenants. It was pretty depressing. There were probably technical breaches, but interest payments were always covered. So the breaches were never called into question, as there were so many other dire problems in the market.

The Eighties

In the early Eighties, we added an extra storey and a half to Devonshire House and refurbished the building. That was the first big refurbishment after the recession of the Seventies. Then things started happening in central London. My role was to deal with the government; at the time, they were renting eight million square feet from us. That's because Lord Samuel had focused on developing the right sort of offices in the right places to suit the various ministries.

Nobody was prepared to offer them more competitive terms. I just did deal after deal with them. There were all these buildings in Victoria: they served Land Secs extremely well as raw material for the next round of development thirty years later, some of them having been residential mansion blocks before the war.

Just before I went on the board in 1987, Harold gave me an exercise to do. He said, "Tell us what would happen to our banking covenants if rental values halved?" It was a mammoth exercise. I thought, "What other company can possibly be doing this?" – and the answer was they weren't. Things were still going up. He saw the result of this exercise, but Harold died on August bank holiday 1987, a full two years before the crash.

Peter Hunt and I actually implemented the strategy in the early Nineties, which enabled Land Secs to come through, although we had been very careful. We viewed developments as an element of gearing. In other words, the schemes were treated as debt until we signed a tenant. I think other people used to assume the schemes would be all let up and everything would be hunky-dory.

The early to mid Nineties

We could have been more active in the early Nineties. We did build up a fantastic retail warehouse portfolio, but for one reason or another weren't as active as we might have been. We should have acquired the Metro Centre and Meadowhall. There were things like London Bridge City, which we nearly purchased. But on the other hand, the restraint enabled us to do a lot of mixed developments in the first few years of the next decade.

One of the reasons for this inactivity during the early Nineties was that Peter Hunt had a stroke in 1993 which left him unable to speak for three or four months; it took him a full year to recover. The City was unaware of the seriousness of his illness. He was knighted for his services to property in 1995. Ian Henderson was appointed deputy managing director in 1996, and was groomed to take over upon Sir Peter's retirement, scheduled for July 1998. But the appointment came eight months early as a consequence of Sir Peter's death at the age of sixty-four, on 8th December 1997, following a heart bypass operation.

SIR JOHN RITBLAT

There is of course a second and steelier character who can also provide a bridge between the Sixties and the time in which the story of *Planet Property* begins, around 1997: a man who built Britain's second-largest property company from small beginnings in 1970, before retiring in 2006. And who was still working away in December 2012, at the age of seventy-seven, alongside his chip-off-the-old-block son Jamie in the marbled offices of Delancey on Berkeley Square.

Henderson's opposite number at British Land was of course John Ritblat, who was knighted in 2006. The UK's second-largest property company was the creation of the son of a north London dental surgeon, born in 1935. Ritblat's uncle, Dudley Samuel, was a successful agent. He persuaded his Dulwich College educated nephew to try estate agency instead of stockbroking. A job with Edward Erdman was secured for young John in 1952, at the age of seventeen. In 1959, he set up on his own with Neville Conrad, a friend from his uncle's firm.

A detailed account of the rise of Sir John Ritblat can be found in Alastair Ross Goobey's *Bricks and Mortals*, published in 1992. But to cut a long story short: during the Sixties, John Ritblat turned from agent to principal, partly with the help of financier Max Joseph. In 1969, Joseph asked him to rescue the failing Union Properties, whereupon Ritblat bought into

Union and revived the business; the following year, he purchased control of the British Land Company from financier Jim Slater for a round £1 million.

"I said to Slater that £1 million was an awful lot of money for a shell company," recalls Sir John. "He said, 'It will be the best buy you ever make.'" British Land was a corporate oddity with a great name. The company was founded in 1856 as an offshoot of the National Freehold Land Society, which later became Abbey National. The society had been formed in 1849 by supporters of a movement to extend enfranchisement, because at that time it was necessary to be a landowner in order to qualify for the vote.

Slater's prediction was proved right. In 1972, John Ritblat was trying to raise £15 million by tempting Swiss investors to buy British Land bonds paying eight percent interest. Little interest was shown by investors at road-shows in Zurich, Basel or Bern – but in Lugano on the Italian border, the issue completely sold out. "The Italians had suffered a banking crisis. Investors came over the border, clearly attracted by the idea of investing in a company called British Land," says Sir John. Why? "Because they thought we were part of the British government."

John Ritblat took over from Max Joseph as chairman and managing director of the company in 1971. Over the next twenty years the portfolio bloomed, growing in size from £37 million to £1.6 billion. There were a few downs as well as lots of ups, as Ross Goobey relates in his book. The first down was in 1973, when British Land was pipped to the post in a deal to buy the Uris Corporation, one of New York's biggest office owners. "We were gazumped at the last minute by the two sons-in-law of the owner," says Sir John, who had arranged twenty-year fixed-interest loans through NatWest. The bank was going to take twenty-five percent of the equity in both Uris and British Land as part of the deal. Imagine if it had...

The successful bidders had only short-term loans and were hit by rising interest rates and the mid Seventies crash. The rump of the liquidated company was sold in 1977 to Olympia & York, which was then a little-known Canadian firm – a "critical element" in the prehistory of Canary Wharf, according to Ross Goobey.

The same crash hit British Land as hard as it did Land Securities, as Ross Goobey relates. Just one vignette: on 30th September 1974, the company was due to complete on the purchase of a £4.4 million office block in Aldersgate. There were worries that the money would not be available; a month before, Ritblat had threatened to sue Mercantile Credit for failing to honour a £10 million credit facility.

The secondary bank didn't have the money. Happily, its banker, Barclays, agreed to give British Land the credit. "The fact that Barclays lent us the money is an indication of the strength of our balance sheet at the time," says Sir John. "The whole industry was effectively bust. But we never sold anything. Our loans were non-recourse; none tied to individual properties. What we did was batten down the hatches and sit tight."

From the mid Seventies to 1991, it was pretty much onwards and upwards, with a dazzling series of deals that took the asset value of the company up to that £1.6 billion number. Ritblat then sidestepped what British Land still calls on its website "the city development debacle of the early Nineties" – a tilt perhaps at Sir Stuart Lipton and Godfrey Bradman, who had developed the huge Broadgate office complex near Liverpool Street Station. Here is Sir John's recollection of the time:

SIR JOHN RITBLAT, CHAIRMAN OF BRITISH LAND 1971–2006:

Coming into 1989, the market was overbought, overpriced and over-rented. People had lost sight of the underlying fundamentals and were getting carried away. This was an accident waiting to happen. I was on record in 1989 on this – much, I think, to the annoyance of my shareholders.

I was a real Jeremiah and suggested it was a very good moment to liquidate British Land and to leave the majority of the old assets behind, but keep some of the income-producing assets in New British Land. Virtually everything that could potentially go wrong with a sound market was in sync for disaster.

The economy turned down and the property market collapsed. I felt by 1991–1992 the gloom had probably been overdone. Because we had anticipated it at British Land, I had built up a large treasury of cash and long credit facilities. So, from about 1992, I started to buy in a major way. Between 1992 and the end of the decade, I think I spent £7 billion, which was a colossal amount of money.

In 1994, I bought most of Broadgate that we didn't already own. I was able to finance it very comfortably. We paid, all up, at Broadgate something just over £1.5 billion, refinanced it for £2 billion – and it was worth £4.5 billion. So it was a good day's work, you might say.

Sir John Ritblat's successor, Chris Grigg, sold a fifty percent interest in Broadgate for £1.064 billion to US fund Blackstone in September 2009. To make the purchase, the giant US fund paid £77 million in cash and took on £987 million of borrowings, paying five percent interest to those holding the securitised debt.

By 2012, Blackstone's equity stake was valued at over £500 million, as the value of Broadgate had risen from £2.1 billion to £3 billion. I had lunch with Sir John on 10th November 2009. He was not best pleased that half his legacy and inexpensive debt had been sold for a song. "When Chris joined, my advice was: don't do anything, just sit there – the storm will pass." Grigg says he simply had to reduce the company's debt to match a savage reduction in asset values.

When Sir John retired from British Land in December 2006, the company held properties worth £14.4 billion, had debt of £6.6 billion, and therefore enjoyed net assets of £7.8 billion. Up from roughly zero, thirty-five years earlier. In 1969, the company's shares were listed at sixpence in old money (2.5p); they peaked at 1,630p in December 2006, and at the end of 2012 stood at 562p.

Veteran property analyst Alan Carter has followed British Land for much of that time. He says: "John Ritblat is a brilliant financier. The way he got control of Broadgate was extremely well executed. But he was always obsessed by size. John's only weakness was that he just wanted to be bigger than Land Securities. The other drive, which he never quite got to, was merging British Land and Land Secs. He even registered a company called British Land Securities.

"John came up through the bulk of his career through a period where inflation did the trick and raised capital values. British Land tended to be more highly geared than others – a great play if values move up. He did tend to ignore the fact that values can fall."

That's not how to look at it, according to Sir John, who reveals the secret of British Land's enduring success during his reign: "Parts of the City never understood our model. We always secured long-term funds at fixed rates, never tied to individual assets. The key question is this: will the rental income from the property cover the interest payments on the loan? If it does, you can ride out ups and downs in value. The reason we wanted to get bigger and more powerful is because you can command lower financing costs. We never failed to repay our loans. We never had loan-to-value issues because we always borrowed corporately. Nearly all the debt was unsecured. When we sold assets, the cash went into the BL community chest. We never changed this business model over thirty-five years. Our strategy was always to take the long-term view; we were never persuaded by the siren calls of short-termist analysts and traders."

But it's true British Land did indeed acquire the "British Land Securities" name in the early Seventies. "Land Securities was a hundred times bigger than us at the time," explains Sir John. "We were expanding and had bought retailer Dorothy Perkins and companies in America. We needed a name that would tell those abroad what we were about. Later on, it did upset Harold Samuel at Land Securities that we were using our subsidiary's name to do deals; he felt we were confusing the market. We used to have lunch twice a year. On one occasion, he demanded I sell him the name. I said no, but ribbed him by suggesting 'British Land Securities has a nice ring to it, doesn't it?' It was two years before we had lunch together again."

British Land was difficult to get to know in 1997, when I began to work at *EG*. John Ritblat did not encourage journalists: but on a couple of occasions he rang to discuss something I'd said in a leader. I'd listen, but not really understand the financial points he was making. Not his fault, mine: I'd only been in the job five minutes and barely understood property finance. Who was I to disagree, anyway? The man was a living legend. Not one regarded warmly by analysts at the time, however. The City is supposed to judge companies by their results, not by the personality of their chief executives, and British Land's results were terrific, right up to Sir John's retirement in 2006. But Sir John did not have much time for what he calls "the scribblings of analysts".

THE WARS OF SUCCESSION

In 2000, British Land made a 500p per share bid for 29.9 percent of Liberty International, the seventy-five percent owner of Capital Shopping Centres (now Intu). Liberty boss Donny Gordon checked the move with an offer of another 75p. "The shares were grossly undervalued," says Sir John. "We had bought seventeen percent of the company before announcing the bid. So we did make a lot of money."

I suggested in *EG* that the rebuff had "made the grandmaster of property chess look vulnerable" – a view influenced by alienated City analysts, who had been restless since the late Nineties about the dictatorial way Ritblat was running British Land. A year later, the attack became more personal. I wrote this in *EG* on 26th May 2001, after Robert Fowlds of Merrill Lynch attacked the man himself:

Listen to Your Analyst, He's Talking Sense

The John Ritblat factor at British Land is costing shareholders 66p per share – or £700m. At least it is if you believe that Ritblat's departure or Damascene conversion from autocrat to democrat would push up the price to levels now enjoyed by a reformed Land Securities; its shares trade at a 21% discount to NAV, in contrast to BL's 34%.

This conclusion can be drawn from a note produced by Merrill Lynch late last week. The slightly schizoid analysis makes two charges – while still insisting that BL is a quality buy. First, the company is too big with its £8bn of assets. This seems an odd charge given the expressed liking for Land Securities, which produced a set of OK-ish results this week.

The 65-year-old chairman and chief executive, they say, is "very autocratic" and "the only likely candidate for CEO would appear to be one of the sons of the current chairman and CEO". This is not news. That said, analyst Robert Fowlds should be congratulated for putting into print what the property world has whispered for three years.

So, let's stop whispering. John Ritblat is autocratic. His greatest fault is that he tends not to admit to fault in himself, only in others. He tries to run an £8bn plc like a £100m private fiefdom. It is embarrassing that his very capable son Nick is seen as a shoo-in for dad's job. There is a worrying lack of other talent: and nobody, until now, has dared tell him all this.

But, as Merrill Lynch admits, BL has the highest-quality assets of any large property plc, the longest leases and the most efficient capital structure. What do they want, blood? The answer appears to be yes. The question is driven by that discount to net asset value figure. If BL's discount matched Land Securities' the shares would be worth over £5.63, not £4.97. That £700m is what the shareholders grumble over.

There are only two unanswered questions: what are the institutional shareholders going to do about it? And what is John Ritblat going to do about it? On past form the answer to both is: not much. The institutions are famously weak-kneed and Ritblat is famously combative. The former will (probably) continue to hand-wring and the latter will (most likely) produce a decent set of results next week, announce some changes but march on, saying he is the only soldier in step.

I got a long, stern letter from British Land's bankers the next week, giving a detailed rebuttal of the charges. Looking back, you do have to wonder what the fuss was about. Ritblat weathered the attack, but another came in the summer of 2002, from activist shareholder group Laxey. British Land shares had recovered ground, narrowing the "Ritblat discount" to £155 million. But Laxey thought it worth creating a stir and attacked the running of the business. This *EG* leader from 20th July 2002 gives some idea of sentiment at the time.

Succession, Not Abdication, Is the Issue for BL

John Ritblat vows that he will never split his chairman/chief executive job — and that he will leave the £9.3bn company when he chooses. Great sport has been had in the City since Isle of Man-based "active value investor" Laxey bought a few BL shares (and borrowed a lot more). They did this to create a stir that would see the shares rise — and then sell at a profit. The stir was all too easily created. Ostensibly because many in the City feel that BL has underperformed in the past five years.

But the real reason is City distrust of a 67-year-old autocrat running Britain's second-largest property company with no obvious check on his power, and no obvious successor but his son Nick. At the AGM on Tuesday, Ritblat countered with the promise of two new non-executive directors and an independent deputy chairman. He also pledged that the role of chief executive and chairman would be split: but only after he leaves. A date left unclear....

This short struggle has left the property industry — as opposed to the City — feeling uncomfortable. Most stand in awe of John Ritblat. Most feel he is doing a good job and should carry on. Most feel his son would make a fine successor — if only his surname were not Ritblat. Last week, one of the most respected fund managers of his generation wrote in EG that until governance and "the question of succession" were settled, the quality of BL as a company was "not going to be properly reflected in the share price". That was the judgment of Alastair Ross Goobey...

That week, analyst John Gellatly of Credit Suisse, who went on to help the British Property Federation shape legislation on real estate investment trusts, said of John Ritblat's length of tenure: "I think it's twelve to eighteen months. Beyond that, it's going to start pissing institutions off. Three years would be far too long. I don't think Laxey has much of a mandate for anything, but it has got [the vote of] quite a lot of people who abstained from reappointing John, and that's pretty significant."

Sir John says the "Ritblat discount" argument was irrelevant. "The value of the assets is always rising and falling. What matters is: are your finances sound?" He says his son Nick didn't want to become chief executive and Laxey "was a sideshow. They lost a fortune." During the 2002 spat, he hit back, hard: "How Laxey could think we live and work in a vacuum is inconceivably amateur really. We know that we've got strong support from our shareholders. We've got ninety-five percent of the shareholders to consider, and we've got to run the business and continue to perform well, and that's what we're doing. I think everybody accepts that British Land is an absolute Rolls-Royce." He told *EG*: "I've no plans to go. But we have always had in hand proper procedures for planning the succession."

It was two years before Ritblat brought in a successor, in late 2004, in the formidable shape of Stephen Hester, former chief operating officer of Abbey National. "I pushed Stephen to come and do it," says Sir John, who stayed on as chairman for two years.

I had never visited the cream-coloured offices overlooking Regent's Park until almost two years after Stephen Hester took over as chief executive. On 24th October 2006, I was invited to come and have a chat with Hester, an Oxford-educated banker who was slowly opening up British Land to the press and, more importantly, to the City.

The discussion centred on Hester's plan to bulk up Broadgate, announced a couple of weeks before. An extra 1.2 million square feet of space would be added to the four million square foot estate by rebuilding fifteen of the twenty-five-year-old blocks. This was the genesis of an idea that led to the tearing-down of two blocks and their replacement by the huge, silver headquarters for UBS that was rearing out of the ground in late 2012.

On my October 2006 visit to British Land, Sir John – who was due to give up the chairmanship that December – walked into Hester's enormous, dark office to say hello. He was completely charming; we talked about this and that. He promised to send me some information, which promptly arrived by courier along with a handwritten note later that day. Hester sat politely silent, returning to life only after Sir John left the room. When Hester departed from the company two years later to rescue RBS, I wrote this in the *Evening Standard* on 24th October 2008:

How Hester Avoided the Pitfalls at British Land

Stephen Hester's four-year tenure as chief executive of British Land ends on Friday 14 November. On Monday 17 November the imperturbable 47-year-old becomes chief executive of the Royal Bank of Scotland and gets to sit in the chair vacated by Sir Fred Goodwin. So what will Hester do at RBS? Those seeking clues will naturally take an interest in how the former head of Abbey house-cleaned this rather dusty property company during three years of boom and one year of bust.

Actually, what Hester didn't do is more interesting. But before coming to that, it is worth allowing the man to speak of the things that he did do after joining Britain's second-largest, and by far oldest, property company in late 2004. "It is fair to say British Land has been comprehensively modernised. A whole new generation of people have been brought in. We have turned from a business that buys things and sits on them into one of the most active property companies in the market."

The ageing board has gone, replaced with some very bright young contenders for Hester's job. The HQ has been shifted from a Regent's Park terrace to a bustling modern office block near Marble Arch. The second thing Hester did was throw open the doors and windows. "I think our whole presentation to the outside world has changed. Our level of disclosure has got us considerable support and we now have the most international share register of any property company."

The amount of financial information disclosed on the British Land website will make directors of RBS blanch. Happily for them, most of what's posted is impenetrable to all but bankers. Hester also did what the man he is replacing at RBS never did: foster good relations with the media. This wasn't something that Hester's predecessor at British Land was much interested in either. But what Sir John Ritblat left was a house in very good order indeed.

Hester had the good fortune to enter a well-built house in a still-rising market. The value of the properties rose to £13.5bn by 2006, before falling back to £12.2bn at the end of July this year. But what has also fallen is the debt — by nearly £600m to £5.8bn in July. That trick was helped by some sales. The critical thing Hester didn't ever do was overborrow in a market that was mad to throw money at real estate.

"He had a very positive effect," says analyst Alan Carter. "Hester was quite dispassionate. REITs were introduced on 1st January 2007. In late November 2006, he had sold two crap shopping centres in Slough for £175 million rather than wait until January 1st, when relief from capital gains tax would come in. I think he was good, because he sold more property ahead of the crash than anybody else of the major companies. That's probably not a bad yardstick."

Hester's successor was dealt the worst of hands. Former Goldman Sachs banker Chris Grigg joined in January 2009, the pit of the worst recession since the Thirties. Grigg had joined from Barclays, where he was chief executive of the commercial banking division – a good training for what was to come. His first job was to persuade the City to subscribe to a £740 million rights issue to prop up the balance sheet. New shares were offered at 225p – way below their depressed price at the time, of 468p. British Land's share price was 550p by the end of 2012.

In November 2009, Grigg had to cope with the defection of retail director Andrew Jones and his two senior lieutenants, Valentine Beresford and Mark Stirling. On leaving British Land, Jones and his colleagues quickly formed Metric Property. The trio had joined British Land in the summer of 2005 from Pillar Property, a company purchased for £811 million from proprietors Raymond Mould and Patrick Vaughan, two of the savviest investors of their generation. The pair set up listed London & Stamford after pocketing a fortune from the sale of Pillar. At the end of 2012, Mould and Vaughan linked up with their younger former colleagues from Pillar to form London-Metric Property. Planet Property is a small world.

Back in late 2009, it must have felt a very dark world for Chris Grigg, who went on to change the spots of British Land. That year the company's net asset value had shrunk to £3.4 billion, from £8.8 billion in 2007. But thanks to Sir John's legacy, net rental income was close to £600 million, earning underlying profits of £288 million. Hester had opened things up, but he had essentially carried on with his own version of Sir John's stern "accumulate and prosper" strategy.

Grigg changed the atmosphere as well as the strategy. Personnel changes like the hiring of cheerful Charlie Maudsley from LaSalle Investment Management and down-to-earth Steve Smith from Axa lightened things up. Smith announced his intention to resign in 2013 to strained assurances that the parting of the ways was friendly, but by then British Land had adopted a more relaxed persona, with press dinners hosted by an open, affable man happy to enter property politics as British Property Federation president.

In July 2010, I had lunch with Grigg in the boardroom of the company's offices behind Marble Arch. On my arrival, I noticed a large portrait of Sir John Ritblat hanging in reception. A year later, when I was invited back to act as quizmaster at a board dinner where business minister Mark Prisk would be guest of honour, the picture of Sir John had gone.

By then, British Land's new opportunistic strategy was emerging – to some criticism. The £130 million purchase of an island site in Clarges Street, Mayfair, raised eyebrows. "What on earth are British Land doing getting into the luxury flats market?" was the view. There was also a fifty-fifty joint venture in Whitechapel with house builder Barratt: "Very off-pitch – and with a common house builder! Sir John wouldn't do that" was a common criticism. Whether such reactions were justified, only time will tell; so let us move on to a more traditional British Land project. The Cheesegrater skyscraper in Leadenhall was moving steadily towards its full height of seven hundred and thirty-seven feet by December 2012, but this was a development disapproved of by another esteemed industry grandee, the man who developed Broadgate.

WIGGLY WOBBLY TOWERS

SIR STUART LIPTON:

After the Big Bang in 1987, the trading houses became very expansive and demanding in their use of floor space. Floor space typically had a life of eighteen months before it was "restacked", often at a cost of £10 million or more, as the traders became ever more profitable. Buildings became one-size-fits-all, as all potential occupiers were considered to need trading floors.

After this period of success, developers in the City began to think of larger, taller buildings. A new building type where computer design allowed unusual shapes and engineering feats emerged. The first of these buildings was for Swiss Re, the Gherkin: a very clever solution by Ken Shuttleworth for a small site.

Other towers built on the limitless forms and shapes allowed by computer design, to create what might be called wiggly wobbly architecture: 122 Leadenhall Street (the Cheesegrater), 20 Fenchurch

Street (the Walkie Talkie), the stalled Pinnacle, the Shard at London Bridge, and yet-to-be-built 100 Bishopsgate are examples.

All have unusual shaped floorplates: these are driven by a desire to provide interesting architecture to make the City an architecturally distinguished place. These new, twenty-first-century buildings have floorplates that vary at almost every level. The Eighties buildings were very cost-efficient; these new buildings are not.

With poor net-to-gross efficiency, high construction costs and long build periods, rents to substantiate overall costs had to rise. At the same time, occupational densities increased from a hundred and fifty square foot per person to half that area per person. These densities were understandable for trading floors, where the need is for the whole floor to understand market activity by close proximity.

What isn't understandable is the high densities now assumed by almost every city occupier. The drive to lower costs seems to have forgotten that the real cost of every building is its personnel and their efficiency. Towers take twice as long to build, cost fifty percent more at least than a groundscraper, and are at least five percent less efficient than a conventional building.

A tower needs a prelet. The problem with the wiggly wobbly shapes is that, for the tenant, they are more complex to occupy. These City buildings were built in sharp contrast to Canary Wharf, where American-style buildings of great quality were built with highly efficient floor plans, but much less interest in presenting themselves as architectural statements or additions to the civic fabric.

The one tower not criticised by Sir Stuart is the slender and uniform-floored Heron Tower on Bishopsgate. The genesis of the Gherkin and the Pinnacle are discussed in chapter two of this volume, while the Shard appears in chapter eight. The Heron Tower merits mention here, as it became the battleground between City developers and the forces of conservation at the start of the boom.

FIGHT THEN FLIGHT OF THE HERON TOWER
In June 1999, reports appeared that Gerald Ronson had "secret plans" to build a tower on Bishopsgate. His company, Heron International, announced in May 2000 that an application would be made to build a thirty-seven-storey tower containing four hundred thousand square feet of space on the corner of Bishopsgate and Houndsditch. "No, no," said London mayor Ken Livingstone, "make it higher." Designer Lee Polisano, then working for US architects Kohn Pederson Fox, added five more floors.

The City Corporation granted permission for the forty-two-storey tower in January 2001. English Heritage and Westminster council complained that the six-hundred-foot skyscraper would block views of St Paul's. Former environment secretary John Gummer, then an influential MP, later Lord Deben, inflamed opinion in his weekly *EG* column. On 20th January

2001, he wrote: "The horrible tower will break every planning rule and yet is supported by the planning officers. It is likely to be the first in a group of oversized skyscrapers conceived by greed out of vulgarity."

The following month, deputy prime minister John Prescott called in the planning application on the advice of English Heritage, despite the fact that the conservationist group's London arm took a positive view of the proposed tower. Prescott ruled in favour of a public inquiry, which began on 23rd October 2001. The six-week hearing proved to be the bitterest fight in planning history. Before it began, the Commission for Architecture and the Built Environment announced it was to back Heron against its bigger and better-funded fellow quango, English Heritage.

The *Daily Telegraph* claimed the tower would "vandalise a sublime moment in Western architecture" by sullying the views of St Paul's. Writer Giles Worsley feared the "erosion and eventual extinction" of "the visual pre-eminence" of Sir Christopher Wren's cathedral. Ken Livingstone savaged English Heritage, accusing it of being a "Taliban of architecture" and "the greatest threat to the economy of London since Adolf Hitler".

Rallying opinion for the tower was CABE commissioner and former *Architects' Journal* and *Building Design* editor Paul Finch: a man whose wisdom is equalled by his wit. Commander of the City battalion was chief planner Peter Wynne Rees, a highly articulate character who has almost literally shaped the City since joining the corporation in 1985 from Lambeth Council. Just after he started, when I was features editor at *Building*, we had lunch at Scribes, a *Daily Mail* haunt off Fleet Street. The then bearded thirty-seven-year-old made a great impression, eloquently articulating his views of how the City was going to develop in future.

"We always go and see Peter to discuss our ideas before doing anything" was a refrain I was to hear time and again over the years, in reference to Rees. Another was: "There is no point in trying that on Peter; he won't wear it." The gay character was great copy: who else would dare commend tall buildings because they give one more time to make love in the lift? I'll never forget him at an *Evening Standard* party for London's most influential people, where he turned up in an exquisite silk suit with the trousers tucked into knee-high burgundy leather boots.

In early December 2010, a lunch was organised by Sir Stuart Lipton in a chilly City Livery Hall to celebrate Rees's quarter-century as chief planner. It was an event attended by the leading developers and architects of the age, with luminaries such as Lord Rogers sitting alongside Rees at the top table. A hard act to follow.

Back in 2001, there was real fear that rejection of Ronson's plans would cause permanent damage to the reputation of the City. But victory became Heron's in July 2002, when the tower gained planning approval. The battle left English Heritage licking its wounds – and without the heart to do more than whimper opposition to any subsequent towers.

Five years passed before work began, however. There were two reasons for this delay, explains Peter Ferrari of Heron. Economic confidence had dipped after the 9/11 tragedy, just nine months earlier. A more immediate issue was that Norton Rose occupied the site: the solicitors were looking to move, but it took a long time. They finally left for the South Bank in 2007.

Heron had not been idle in the meantime. In 2006, permission was granted to add a further three floors, taking the tower with a spike on top to seven hundred and fifty-four feet – and making it the tallest building in the City. Detailed plans for the skyscraper and an adjacent twenty-three-storey hotel and residential tower were also finalised.

This allowed the £495 million of funding to be put in place. Two European banks, Eurohypo and Landesbank Hessen-Thüringen, agreed to advance £370 million of development debt; an Omani sovereign wealth fund, alongside other Middle East investors, provided the remaining £125 million. Work began in April 2008, and topping out took place in April 2010, with Gerald Ronson herding wobbly-kneed journalists (myself included) around the half-finished tower.

The Heron Tower – including a giant fish tank in the lobby – was completed in March 2011. By late 2012, half the four hundred and forty thousand square feet of space was let. The plan to build an adjacent hotel and residential complex was put on hold when Heron decided to seek a partner or, failing that, to sell the site. Meanwhile, Gerald Ronson got on and built the Heron, a sleek and successful residential tower in the Barbican. Peter Wynne Rees was so impressed he bought one of the flats.

PAY AND RATIONS

In 1998, *EG* produced a league table listing property company bosses by their total remuneration, adding together basic pay, bonus and share grants, based on information taken from annual company reports. Many of these individuals were still active in 2012.

John Burns sits at the base of the 1998 table, on £304,000. In 2011, at the age of sixty-seven, his basic pay alone was £550,000. That was doubled by a £550,000 bonus, then nearly doubled again by his share rewards, taking Burns' total remuneration to just over £2 million at the greatly enlarged Derwent London.

Few of his contemporaries in the property world would argue that that is too much for the man who founded Derwent Valley in 1984. His peer group would probably vote for the urbane Burns as the most respected developer of his age. (I'd vote for him as the best-dressed developer and the one with the best taste in restaurants and wine.) The former Hillier Parker surveyor built up his £2.5 billion company by sticking to the inner London fringes, then – with the help of fellow director and stepbrother Simon Silver – employing fine architects to design inventive schemes that squeeze valuable new space into old buildings.

THE PROPERTY COMPANY PAY LEAGUE

Many of the same names are still active and still earning, fifteen years on from this 1998 directors' pay survey showing who earned the most in basic pay, bonus and share grants

	Company	1997/98 pay (£)
Million-pound men		
Michael Slade	Helical Bar	1,285,000
Gerald Kaye	Helical Bar	1,044,000
Over £500,000		
John Ritblat	British Land	580,004
Paul White	Frogmore	571,000
Patrick Vaughan	Pillar	548,000
Raymond Mould	Pillar	531,000
£400,000–£500,000		
John Whittaker	Peel	496,000
Richard Peskin	Great Portland Estates	489,000
Elliott Bernerd	Chelsfield	473,000
Nigel Kempner	Benchmark	451,000
Peter Thornton	Greycoat	447,000
Martin Landau	Development Securities	441,500
£300,000–£400,000		
Martin Barber	Capital & Regional	392,622
James Tuckey	MEPC	389,904
Ron Spinney	Hammerson	389,000
Adrian Wyatt	Quintain	388,000
Andrew Rosenfeld	Minerva	375,000
Benzion Freshwater	Daejan	370,105
Ian Henderson	Land Securities	366,000
David Garrard	Minerva	359,000
Nick Leslau	Burford	358,000
David Tye	Rugby Estates	346,000
Sir Nigel Mobbs	Slough Estates	340,000
Larry Lipman	Safeland	331,000
Philip Lewis	Milner	305,300
John Anderson	Burford	304,000
John Burns	Derwent Valley	304,000

Source: Estates Gazette

There was private restiveness about high bonuses back in 1999. Rewards were being boosted by the misuse of property data company IPD's indices. I never discovered the names of the guilty parties; IPD founder Rupert Nabarro was too discreet. But he called me in to tell me that "certain board directors in certain companies" were using IPD data as cover to justify dodgy bonus schemes. He was worried that this practice would bring the reputation of his company into disrepute. I wrote this perhaps too well-coded leader for *EG* in December 1999, after our meeting.

Applying Stock Market Values to Bonus Pay

There is an undercurrent of disquiet at the way the Investment Property Databank indices are manipulated to justify high pay. This is not a carp at high bonuses. Measure Helical Bar either way – NAV or shareholder returns – and the

£1m-plus bonuses look earned. But the less talented have a natural tendency to want high rewards as well. Against them the complaint is directed.

There is a tendency for working directors to regard the firm as "theirs" – whatever the size of their equity stake. After all, staff numbers are small. So performance is particularly personal. A more than human desire to take a larger slice of the pie than perhaps is equitable to the non-active shareholders grows.

So complex bonus arrangements are drawn up. Opacity rather than transparency is their hallmark. As is a sky's-the-limit upside, and a severely limited downside. It has long been thus. But can anything be done? Mmm. It could be argued that at the financial fountainhead the institutions could wag their fingers a lot harder at funds managing property shares. Don't count on it.

External pressure could help. The IPD is in a delicate position, relying as it does on the goodwill of all. It has suggested a way of making NAV-based schemes fairer. Perhaps members who operate perfectly fair schemes could encourage the formulation of "IPD-approved" guidelines. The influential Investment Property Forum might like to initiate some debate. Should below average performance be punished? Should performance be rewarded if it's only average?

Improvements were made, and the remuneration section of annual reports began to take up several pages of small print. Bonus payments mostly disappeared in 2009. But directors' pay continued to climb, and this put me in the mood to carp in my *EG* column on 5th November 2011. Why? Because three people had separately grumbled to me about swelling boardroom pay. At the time, the subject was in the news; bankers were getting bashed. It struck me that however big the balance sheet, a property company's management challenges were minor, compared with trading companies of ostensibly similar size.

LandSec vs Wolseley

Here is a seditious thought to entertain on Guy Fawkes Night. A notion prompted by the news that FTSE 100 company bosses enjoyed a 55% pay rise last year: do the otherwise admirable chief executives of Land Securities and British Land really deserve to be paid on a par with fellow FTSE 100 chieftains?

Francis Salway of LandSecs and Chris Grigg enjoyed far smaller rises in their total remuneration last year than that inflammatory 55% figure given by Income Data Services last week for all FTSE directors. Salway took a 16% rise to £1.4m, Grigg an 11% rise to £2m. About average for FTSE companies of similar size.

But. Both firms are minnows compared to the FTSE 100 whales in terms of staff numbers, turnover and geographical spread. LandSecs and BL are positioned at numbers 54 and 62 respectively in the index because their balance sheets contain property worth £10.5bn and £9.6bn respectively.

A privatised Forestry Commission would make the FTSE if the value of each tree lay on the balance sheet. A wounding comparison perhaps. But property company directors are essentially asset farmers. Not an easy task; but surely easier than running most other FTSE 100 business.

LandSecs employs 182 full time staff and receives semi-automatic revenues of £275m in the form of rent. One below in the table sits Wolseley. The world's biggest builders merchant has 45 000 employees in 23 countries earning revenues of £13.6bn. Hands up, which company *you* would rather manage?

BL employs 179 full time staff and receives about the same in rents as LandSecs. Just below BL sits Capita, with £1.4bn of revenues, earned by 35 000 staff working in a multitude of public and private sector service industries. Again, hands up, which company would *you* rather manage?

The aggregate remuneration of the chief executives of Land Securities, British Land and Hammerson shows a nearly one hundred percent increase in total income between 2003 and 2012. There are hiccups; bonuses fell away in the crash. Compare this to the income of "Mr Average Property". Average pay among fifteen hundred or so respondents to the 2003 annual salary in *EG* was £47,520; in 2012 the comparable figure was just £46,738.

TOTAL REMUNERATION OF CHIEF EXECUTIVES AT THE TOP THREE UK DEVELOPERS

Land Securities, British Land and Hammerson chiefs, taken as a group, doubled their total personal remuneration between 2003 and 2012. Staff did not enjoy a similar rise

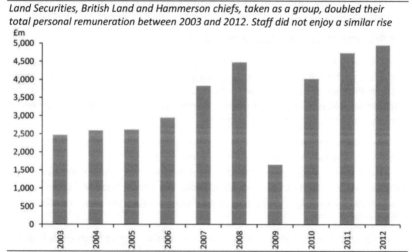

Source: Land Securities/British Land/Hammerson

MILLENNIAL ANGST

As real estate analyst Alan Carter explains, "The sector was deeply unloved at the turn of the century, on the basis that real estate and 'hard' assets were going to be of no use once the internet had all-pervaded. So the sector had been sold off aggressively. Shares were trading at a thirty to forty percent discount to their net asset value."

Against this background, the British Property Federation met at the Grand Hotel in Brighton in February 2000. British Land and Land Securities were seen as stuffy, secretive and complacent: Old Property holding out against New Property. The latter was represented by Nick Leslau, an agreeable and charismatic figure with flowing locks, given to wearing white, open-necked shirts. "The Viagra this industry needs is disclosure, and what we need is more management fear," he told delegates.

Credit Suisse analyst Mike Prew supported Leslau. He attacked the listed companies for "destroying shareholder value". The stage was set. On the platform in Brighton that day was Norma Cohen of the *Financial Times*, the feisty property correspondent who later maddened Sir John Ritblat with what he saw as negative reporting of British Land.

Mike Slade of Helical Bar was sitting beside Cohen. When she bent down to pick up a fallen pencil, her head drew close to Slade's lap. "Oh, Norma! I didn't know you cared," he cried in mock surprise, to guffaws from the almost entirely male audience. Cohen smiled. She stuck to her script, savaging listed company bosses for opacity and "treating their shareholders with contempt".

Land Securities boss Ian Henderson could only reply limply from the floor, in a debate that was giving Old Property a drubbing: "We disclose as much as other industries. We do not treat our customers with contempt. We've moved away from the feudal concept." The dawning of a new millennium and the rising dot-com frenzy influenced the mood of the conference, which I attempted to capture in an *EG* leader on 5th February 2000:

Old Property Must Adopt New Property Ways

NewProperty gave OldProperty a bloody nose in Brighton on Wednesday. At the BPF's gathering of the great and the good at the Grand, those once automatic members of the G&G were trashed. Secretive, unimaginative and destroyers of value were the brickbats hurled at the two unnamed targets – namely, British Land and Land Securities.

In a recession, these two pillars of property would surely be regarded as safe havens for capital. But, today greed is ascendant over fear. Capital is flowing into hope stocks. Freeserve, with the income stream of one second-tier shopping centre, is valued at £6.25bn. Land Securities can be had for £3.8bn, a 38% discount to NAV. British Land, distrusted and disliked by the City, is trading at a 44% discount.

NewProperty makes telling points. One: if you raise capital from shareholders they have a right to view transparent accounts. Want to run a private fiefdom? Fine, go private. Point two: low inflation now precludes just sitting on assets – money costs more than the returns made. Add value – or give way and let someone else try.

Freeserve, incidentally, was an internet service provider whose value evaporated as fast as dry ice when the dot-com boom went bang.

In June 2000, the directors of MEPC decided it was better to run a private fiefdom than be pilloried on a stock market that undervalued its assets. The decision was a controversial one. Real estate banker Richard Cotton was involved in the deal. The influential mergers and acquisitions expert, who spent twenty-two years at JP Morgan Cazenove before leaving in 2009 to join investor and asset manager Forum Partners, explains the rationale.

RICHARD COTTON, FORUM PARTNERS:

> *Jamie Dundas and Robert Ware of MEPC felt they could produce a one-off uplift in value if they privatised the business. We talked to a small number of potential buyers. In the end, Alastair Ross Goobey of Hermes said he would do the deal. I'd said to Argent boss Michael Freeman, who had a number of joint ventures with Hermes, to go and tell him they were thinking of selling. Alastair took the bait.*

> *I remember Alastair turning up at Rothschild's in his dinner jacket after the opera to sign the deal. Hermes paid effectively the NAV, which was ten to fifteen percent below the current share price. There were some very angry institutions – we had to go up to Scotland to see Standard Life, which was a big shareholder. They were very unhappy; it was a difficult meeting.*

IAN MARCUS, FORMER HEAD OF EUROPEAN REAL ESTATE AT CREDIT SUISSE:

> *There were a whole series of property companies, great names and brands, which between 2000 and 2003 were taken private, either because the management got so fed up with the increasingly vigorous regulation imposed on them, or because they were trading at such a wide discount to their asset value. The property assets were worth, for example, £100 million; the stock market value of the firm was £70 million – who can blame the management for buying out at £90 million, knowing the assets might rise to £120 million? That is of course what happened.*

> *Hazlemere went private during that period; Nick Leslau took Burford private. The big one of course was MEPC going private – quite extraordinary. But the City was undervaluing these businesses, as history showed. If you traded out, then you did very well. If you refinanced, you did very well. The boom time for delisting businesses was between about 2003 and 2005, before share prices rose again and the market began to look toppy.*

FROM SLOUGH TO SEGRO

Public property companies that were simply too big to go private, however, had to opt for change in response to City angst against Old Property. One such firm was Slough Estates, as it was called before its 2007 rebranding as Segro. The industrial property giant began the process of change at the beginning of 2003.

Until then, the company – founded in 1920 by Sir Percival Perry and Noel Mobbs (who was later also knighted) – was run as something of a family fiefdom by Sir Nigel Mobbs, grandson of Sir Noel. It had originally been formed with a single asset – five hundred and eighty acres of flat government surplus land along the Bath Road in Slough – but by 2003 had accumulated an eclectic set of additional assets, including a golf complex in Florida as well as a US energy company.

Sir Nigel (who would die suddenly at the age of sixty-eight in October 2005) was a tall, genial character, whom I once heard compared to "a slightly lumbering but affectionate and appealing Great Dane" – rather a harsh judgement on a man who was a Barclays bank director and a lot sharper than he let on. As editor of *Building* magazine in the early Nineties, I briefly sat on a College of Estate Management advisory board chaired by Sir Nigel, and found him to be more bloodhound than Great Dane. But in 2003 the City wanted fresh blood, not a man who dressed up in uniform to meet the Queen as Lord Lieutenant of Buckinghamshire. On 1st January 2003, former Sainsbury's property director Ian Coull joined Slough at the age of fifty-two to become the new chief executive.

The Labour-supporting Scot, who had given up a main board seat at Sainsbury's to take on his new role, began slowly to modernise the business. It proved a long and delicate undertaking, but Coull was a careful man. During our occasional lunches he would be very frank about the scale of the task and how long it would take to change the culture and pare down the assets into a cohesive business. Too frank, probably: I'd sneak out some of his off-the-record remarks into *EG*'s diary column (and later receive a rueful reprimand in consequence). By 2007, Slough Estates had altered enough to enable Coull to rebrand the company as Segro, which suffered £1.2 billion of losses in the following two years. Coull knew what needed changing.

IAN COULL, CHIEF EXECUTIVE OF SEGRO 2003–2011:

The thing that I found extraordinary when I came across from Sainsbury's in 2003 was how unsophisticated the industry was in financial matters; how narrow-minded it was in relation to its business profile – but most of all, the complete absence of any customer focus in the industry. When I joined Slough it felt like we had "bloody tenants" instead of customers. That got changed.

What we saw in the five or six years leading up to 2007 is PLC boards responding to shareholder demands for less volatility in performance. That impacted on the business model. But it has also impacted on the type of people selected to run listed property companies. Over that period, virtually every CEO was replaced.

More traditional managers have replaced Sir John Ritblat at British Land, Ian Henderson at Land Securities, and others. Most new CEOs have come from property, but they have more rounded leadership skills, although less entrepreneurial flair. Those with real entrepreneurial flair tend to work in the unlisted sector.

Coull handed over to his chosen successor in April 2011. This was Segro finance director David Sleath, a down-to-earth Midlander entirely devoid of airs and graces. I spent a morning with Sleath in April 2012 driving around the original estate to hear of a fifteen-year modernisation plan budgeted between £400 million and £500 million. Its objective was to double the value of the estate to £2 billion. Sleath was as unlike Sir Nigel as it is possible to be – except perhaps in breeding, as I discovered the next day when researching an article for the *Evening Standard* to be published that Friday, 27th April:

All Eyes on Segro's Sleath as He Looks to Build Up Empire

David John Rivers Sleath, 51, chief executive of £5.2 billion property company Segro, is perhaps the poshest boss in the listed property sector.

The man who stood up before shareholders yesterday to defend his record after one year in the job is a descendant of the earls Rivers. The first earl was Edward IV's father-in-law and his granddaughter married Henry VII.

The extremely likeable Midlander is no toff, unlike his predecessor-but-one, Sir Nigel Mobbs. The AGM at what was Slough Estates used to be held at Claridge's, followed by a heavy lunch. Yesterday shareholders were treated to tea and biscuits at the TUC offices in Holborn. Here Sleath admitted the company has "underperformed over the past decade". But he added: "We have a clear strategy to transform performance for the future."

The former Arthur Andersen accountant says Segro will concentrate on assets which produce rents rather than on assets which might produce rents. Has this pleased the City? Not yet. Segro's shares languish 30% below last April's price, valuing the company at £1.7 billion, well short of the NAV of £2.2 billion.

But Sleath does have City supporters. "He is a good man, very intelligent, highly approachable, well-liked," says one analyst. "He has come up with an easily understood and coherent plan to increase margins."

He was brought in by his predecessor, Ian Coull, as finance director in 2006 from engineering group, Wagon. Coull spent most of his seven-year reign from 2003 reshaping the sprawling empire. The pair successfully negotiated the biggest property crash in history, repairing the balance sheet in 2009 with a rights issue and buying stricken rival Brixton for a song.

THE CRASH

Segro was able to buy Brixton for a song because the latter was either unwilling or unable to sell shares at a discount to repair its balance sheet. But the "big four" did. The biggest giveaway sale in property history took place in early 2009. Land Securities, British Land and Hammerson, as well as Segro, raised more than £2.5 billion in deeply discounted "rights issues" of new shares. If the shares could have been magically sold at the same price as the existing shares, a total of £8 billion could have been raised – as suggested in chapter one of this volume. The effect of adding all these cheap shares to the register caused "the biggest dilution in history" for existing shareholders, according to Alan Carter of Investec.

Considering the gross assets, net debt and net assets of Land Securities, British Land and Hammerson combined provides a rough measure of how the UK's biggest listed property companies performed between 2003 and 2012. The trio's assets rose by eighty percent over four years, up from £22 billion in 2003 to £40 billion at the start of 2007. Over the following two years, their total asset value fell by £17 billion, collapsing from £40 billion down to £23 billion. Debt was cut by a quarter, to £11.5 billion, but this was not enough to prevent net assets falling in 2009 to a level at which they were equalled by the level of debt.

LAND SECURITIES, BRITISH LAND AND HAMMERSON: COMBINED ASSETS AND DEBT

Gross assets rose by eighty percent before nearly halving in the crash, then slowly recovered from 2009 – the point when net assets and net debt equalled one another

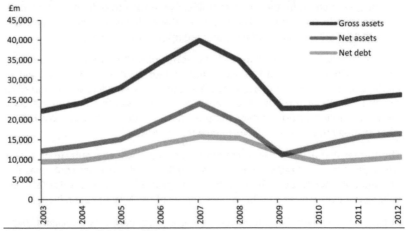

Source: Land Securities/British Land/Hammerson

During the boom, so-called "balance-sheet profits" played a starring role. Headlines such as "Mega Property Makes £1.5bn Profit" were common. These profits showed on the balance sheet largely because the value of a company's assets was rising with the tide. When the tide fell, the headlines became "Mega Property Makes £1.5bn Loss." Collapsing values forced Land Securities to post losses of £830 million in 2008 and a record £5.2 billion in 2009. The figures for British Land were £1.6 billion and £3.9 billion; those for Hammerson, £1.6 billion and £344 million. Between 2008 and 2009, the trio posted total losses of £13.5 billion. Dreadful numbers, enough to sting directors into change. The emphasis switched to highlighting trading profits.

The trio's aggregated rental income moved up by twenty-seven percent between 2003 and 2007, while trading profits rose by a touch under thirty percent. Income and profit both fell back between 2008 and 2012. But the point to note is that the line shows the big three produced pretty steady "real" profits right through the crash.

LAND SECURITIES, BRITISH LAND AND HAMMERSON: RENTAL INCOME AND PROFIT

While rental income took a hit during the crash, trading profits remained fairly steady

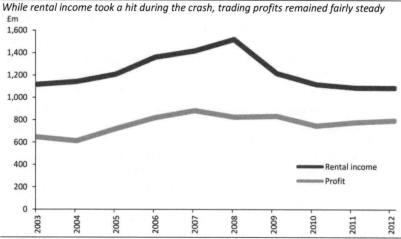

Source: Land Securities/British Land/Hammerson

HAMMERSON

The so far unexamined member of the trio of UK property giants is Hammerson, the most open and friendly of the three towards the press during my time at *EG*. We were invited each year to drinks with board members and staff. These were served on the balcony at 100 Park Lane, Hammerson's palatial headquarters, until the building was sold to the Qatari royal family in 2006 and the firm moved to 10 Grosvenor Street. I can remember looking out over Hyde Park, downing my third glass of champagne, and thinking, "This is the life" – only to have my reverie broken by the loud Devon burr of chief executive John Richards, a man who loved to tell stories.

Richards became chief executive in 1999 at the age of forty-three, taking over from Ron Spinney, who shifted up to chairman. Spinney, then in his late fifties, would occasionally pop in to these media sessions. I'd look at him and think, "This man has everything. He is cultured, companionable, good-looking, and, on top of all that, he has a fine head of grey hair!" But as many Hammerson staff testified, "Ron could be a ball-breaker" whenever he felt it necessary to get things done. "When he lost his temper, you wanted to hide under the table," said one.

Spinney joined from Greycoat in 1993, to rescue the firm from what is referred to as the "Sydney Mason era". Mason had been with Hammerson since way back in 1944, just two years after it was founded by Lew Hammerson, on whose death in 1958 he took over the reins. Pressure was put on Mason to depart after Hammerson beat off a hostile bid from Dutch developer Rodamco in 1989. Bid rumours persisted in the early Nineties, by which time the chairman was into his seventies and under growing pressure from institutional shareholders such as Standard Life to leave. This event finally happened in June 1993, whereupon Spinney took over.

ALAN CARTER, INVESTEC:

When he came in, Ron rationalised Hammerson. Initially he did a rights issue and invested the cash in secondary offices, mainly. The capital performance was not great, but the company desperately needed to buy income. Hammerson had been doing lots of things adequately but not many things well. The key thing that Ron did was to run that business in a way the management wasn't used to.

He was a very hard taskmaster. Latterly he rationalised the portfolio, selling most of the overseas assets in Australia and Canada, and then expanded the UK development portfolio in prime retail. He also got "the monkey off the back" – that was the twenty percent shareholding held by Standard Life. In 2004, when I was at Citi, we sold those seventy million shares: they were worth £350 million. It was the single biggest sale of property equity ever seen in the UK.

By 2003, Spinney was in his fourth year as chairman. I met him that June for lunch at The Greenhouse in Mayfair. I remember him telling me about the work he was doing raising money for the Unicorn children's theatre on the South Bank, which he chaired, and how he was looking forward to a weekend away at his house in France. Again, I thought, "This man has everything." He stepped down as chairman two years later, in 2005.

But this was a retirement that would be only three years' long. Spinney, who had previously lost his first wife to cancer, succumbed to the same disease on 13th July 2008, at the age of sixty-seven. The memorial service was held in Southwark Cathedral four months later, on a cold, bright November morning. The pews were packed, and such was the catholic nature of Spinney's interests that at least half of those present were from outside the property sector. Many came from the nearby Unicorn theatre.

Actress Joanna David gave the most accurate assessment of Spinney: "He had the selflessness and lack of pomposity of a man who never felt he had anything to prove. Ron was a marvel," she said. Sir Stuart Lipton, who had worked with Spinney at Greycoat, said: "He was one of the leading property figures of the last half-century. But more than that, he was a good man." "He was a top, top man, much missed," agrees analyst Alan Carter.

In Carter's estimation, "Hammerson were the best of the three companies in reading the boom. They geared up quite aggressively. The reward was turbo-charged returns as yields fell and rental values rose. It is worth bearing in mind that it's one of the very, very few periods I've ever known where you've actually had the two key dynamics working positively together. This happened from 2005 onwards. At one stage, Hammerson had about a third of its market capitalisation in speculative developments. The level of risk involved was significant. That has played a part in forming a corporate philosophy at Hammerson never to put themselves in that position again."

John Richards did a great job as chief executive at Hammerson, according to Carter. But as the analysts hints, the crash left the board more nervous of risk. Richards retired at the age of fifty-three in September 2009, after ten years in the top job and three decades with the company.

His leaving had been announced in early August. No one at his well-attended party at the Plaisterers Hall in the City on 1st October was under any illusion that Richards had retired happily. He'd gone because he was at odds with new chairman John Nelson (brother of Phillip Nelson, the founder of Nelson Bakewell). But the proprieties were kept: Richards gave a warm and jolly account of his thirty years at Hammerson, and new chief executive David Atkins also spoke. The forty-three-year-old former DTZ surveyor – nicknamed by his colleagues there "Chippy" (as in argumentative) – gave his maiden speech to a doubtful audience, many of whom felt affection towards Richards and annoyance towards Nelson.

The atmosphere in the room was uneasy, but the consensus was that Atkins spoke well under the circumstances. He had joined Hammerson some years earlier in 1998, after advising the company on an aborted takeover of MEPC – something Spinney had been very anxious to complete. "Ron Spinney took me and Robert Peto of DTZ out to lunch to say thank you," said Atkins later. "When Robert went to the loo, Ron leaned across the table and said, 'If you ever fancy working for Hammerson, come and see me.' I said, 'What about tomorrow?'"

The new man steadied and readied the ship as the market recovered. A great deal of internal restructuring took place, and clearly a great deal of thinking about the future too. In February 2012, Atkins told the world that Hammerson was no longer interested in offices; the owner of Brent Cross was to become a retail-only REIT. Crikey! The share price promptly rose; the City clearly approved of the move.

By then, only eleven percent of the Hammerson portfolio comprised offices. What remained was investment stock such as the Bishopsgate Tower, a half-interest in 100 Bishopsgate (a site with consent for an eight-hundred-thousand-square-foot tower), another big development site on London Wall, and yet another at Principal Place, north of Broadgate. These and others were sold to Canadian giant Brookfield Office Properties in June 2012, for £518 million. Hammerson's agreeable office development boss, Martin Jepson, had left to join the company himself the year before. The deal catapulted Brookfield into the position of number one developer in the City of London.

The sale also left Atkins free to concentrate on another surprise: signing a joint venture with Australian retail giant Westfield to build a shopping centre of two million square feet in Croydon on the site of the Whitgift Centre. Earlier in the year, the pair had been sworn enemies: Westfield had reached agreement with the freeholder to build a new shopping centre, while Hammerson had reached agreement with some of the long leaseholders to do just the same. I'd had a chat with John Burton of Westfield as the spat was warming up, coming to this conclusion in my 7th April *EG* column:

Only Westfield Can Provide Croydon Facelift

Who would you trust to whistle up a mega-mall in London? British Hammerson, or Aussie Westfield? Both are vying to rebuild the Whitgift Centre. Long leaseholder, Royal London, came out in favour of Hammerson this week. Freeholder, The Whitgift Foundation, says no, no, we want Westfield.

That leaves Croydon council two choices: back Royal London and Hammerson; or back the Whitgift and Westfield. Hold the threat of a CPO over either. There is, maybe, a third option. Grab every party's ear and bang heads together till the promise to construct a loose JV to rebuild the town centre is extracted.

At this point it would be fair to judiciously weigh up the pros and cons of either party. Blow that. The need for a swift decision followed by an emergency operation draws close for ailing Croydon. Hammerson's last mega-mall in London was Brent Cross, which first opened in 1976. Westfield has built two in ten years. No contest.

This view resulted in an invitation from Hammerson's chief executive. I'd not met Atkins one-to-one before, and came away impressed with his calm and rational explanation of why Hammerson was perhaps best for Croydon after all – as you can tell from this volte-face in *EG* on 21st April:

Why Hammerson Bested Hard-driving Aussies

David Atkins is either a persuader par excellence, or yours truly is very suggestible. I had a cup of tea and a tuna roll with the boss of Hammerson Monday lunchtime in his Grosvenor Street office. Why? Two weeks ago I strongly suggested here that Westfield would be a better bet than Hammerson to build a mall in Croydon. Atkins naturally disagrees. Er... maybe he is right.

If Croydon wants certainty, there certainly is no firm more certain of itself than Westfield. The hard-driving leviathan seized the White City and Stratford projects and finished them with minimum fuss and maximum efficiency.

But who wants another Stratford? Croydon has suffered more than its fair share of boxy developments on steroids over the years. They will want to build a huge enclosed mall. Westfield is not into fine grain urban master planning. They own none of the land. They've simply managed, somehow, to seduce the freeholder – who only holds 25% of the leasehold interest.

By the end of 2012, the pair had kissed and made up, entering into a joint venture that promises Croydon a £2 billion heart transplant.

INSECURITIES AT LAND SECURITIES

We left Land Securities nearing the millennium, with boss Ian Henderson under attack at the British Property Federation's annual conference for being Old Property. The assault clearly wounded, and just a few months later change was clearly signalled by the hiring of Peter Walicknowski in May 2000. The formidable Australian from Lend Lease, who had impressed the property world with the development of the Bluewater shopping centre in Kent, was immediately dubbed the heir apparent.

In the autumn of 2000, *EG* was invited to a boardroom lunch with the directors of Land Securities at their headquarters on the Strand. The invitation came days before the deal to buy property services company Trillium was announced. One moment lives in the memory: a black-jacketed butler padded round the boardroom table offering cigars and port, which was then a dying practice in the City. Something suggested that this was merely an old ritual being played out; that actually ordering port and lighting up a cigar would not be a good idea. I desisted, as did everyone else. But there was a Bateman cartoon moment when the butler asked Walicknowski if he'd like coffee. "No... do you have camomile tea?" The butler stiffened; the atmosphere cooled. Then, "Of course, sir," separated by a fractional pause from: "I'll see if I can find some." It was hard not to burst out laughing.

Walicknowski helped persuade Land Securities to buy a huge chalk pit next to Bluewater. The Ebbsfleet site became a money pit after he left and Land Securities dithered. A decade later, just a few hundred of the thousands of promised homes had been built. The £96 million cost of filling the pit was written off.

As Walicknowski sipped his camomile tea, you felt the cultural gap between the old guard and the new meant a split was likely. By autumn 2001, there were published rumours of fallings-out between the two. The hard-driving Manish Chande of Trillium had joined the year before, when his facilities management business was bought. The more sedate Francis Salway of Standard Life had also joined in 2000, charged with managing the Land Securities portfolio. The split rumours centred on which one of these three different characters was going to get Henderson's job when he retired.

Salway, it turned out. Walicknowski and Chande both resigned in the week before Christmas 2001. The City was not pleased with Ian Henderson's "It's all going to be fine" response to the resignations. Miranda Cockburn, at Credit Suisse, said: "It is not enough to be reassured about the general running of the group. We need to know who is running the different divisions." This was City-speak for "What the bloody hell is going on – is anyone actually managing this company?" The answer turned out to be that Henderson was, for slightly longer than planned, and then Salway, who took over in 2004. The levelheaded pair steadied the ship. So it seemed fair to say just that, in an *EG* leader April 2004, when Henderson announced his departure.

A Great Deal Was Done by This Retiring Man

Atop the twin peaks of UK Property sit characters of a completely different stripe. Metropolitan sophisticate John Ritblat presides over the £9.6bn British Land as the forceful ruler of his self-built empire. Country gentleman Ian Henderson runs an already built £8bn estate at Land Securities in a more lord of the manor style.

Or so it would appear. Looking back at Henderson's seven-year reign, the thing that strikes is the profound change for the better that has taken place.

There have been mistakes: appointing forceful Australian Peter Walicknowski in 2000 as heir apparent was a disaster. But since 1997 LandSec has turned from somnolent rent collector and fitful developer into an active portfolio manager and energetic builder – at the same time adding an increasingly successful FM business in Trillium. The board and senior management have also almost completely changed. Those now running what was described here three weeks ago as NewLandSecurities are the pick of their generation.

They are to be led by the calm and cerebral Francis Salway, a welcome appointment. There is clearly more of the John Ritblat in Ian Henderson than meets the eye. But as his rolling gait carries him away, it is worth pausing to salute this deceptive man who embraced and then enforced the changes needed to transform the company he has worked for since 1971.

BUYING AND SELLING TRILLIUM

Trillium certainly was, as this leader suggested, an "increasingly successful" part of the business. The purchase was part of a long-term plan to turn Land Secs into "Land Secs-ier" in the eyes of the City, which was now demanding that property companies focus on generating stable income, as Richard Cotton – then a close adviser to Ian Henderson – explains.

RICHARD COTTON, FORUM PARTNERS:

I remember a lot of conversations with Land Securities at the time of the dot-com boom, in 2000, when listed companies were expected to produce annual returns of ten to fifteen percent. Finance director Jim Murray was very exercised, because he couldn't see how a large company financed in the way Land Secs was could produce high enough returns to satisfy the markets.

Jim's point was that unless you put in huge amounts of leverage there was no way that a normally financed property company could really earn more than about eight to ten percent per annum on a consistent basis. And he was a very old-fashioned finance director. So Ian Henderson and I spent a lot of time in the summer of 2000 discussing how you might put a bit of sex and violence into Land Secs. We landed on Trillium.

On 3rd November 2000, Land Securities announced that it was paying £165 million in cash and assuming £165 million of debt to invest in Trillium, a business started up three years before by Manish Chande and Martin Myers to act as a property services manager, initially for the Department of Work and Pensions. The Goldman Sachs Whitehall fund received £135 million in the deal, Chande and Myers £15 million each. Trillium had signed a twenty-year contract with the government department in 1998.

IAN HENDERSON, CHIEF EXECUTIVE OF LAND SECURITIES 1997–2004:

At the end of the Nineties, the strategy was to reduce the number of properties held by at least two-thirds and focus on enhancing the returns from those we retained or from new acquisitions. In furtherance of this strategy we acquired Trillium from the Whitehall fund, which had been ably organised by Manish Chande. This fresh expertise enabled us to obtain much better returns from existing assets. The strategy was very successful: very significant returns were extracted. But the City never really understood Trillium. So it was decided to sell.

It was the Pears family, led by Mark and Trevor Pears, who bought Trillium from Land Securities in January 2009 for £750 million. This generated a £306 million loss on the book value. The division had been put up for sale in the autumn of 2007. Why? After all, three months before, Land Securities chairman Paul Myners had hailed Trillium as "one of the key drivers of future value". Answer: because Land Securities boss Francis Salway and his new chairman Myners wanted to split up the entire company.

THE SPLIT

Richard Cotton of Forum Partners was part of the team advising Land Securities in 2007–2008 on the plan to split the company up into three parts – Trillium, offices and retail. He says: "I think Francis Salway genuinely took the view that having smaller, focused businesses would provide greater shareholder returns. I think he really believed that intellectually, and I wouldn't be surprised if he continues to believe that to this day. One of the first things Land Securities chairman Paul Myners said to me was he wanted to 'put the alpha back' into the stock. What he wanted to do was to do something different to achieve that."

The news broke in the first week of September 2007. The market at that time was weakening. Land Securities revealed that business consultants had been hired to conduct a "strategic review" – a review prejudged with the announcement that this was likely to lead to the sale of Trillium and the splitting of retail and offices into two separate companies. This news fed a rumour that Mike Hussey, who controlled the offices part of the business, wanted his own empire, well away from Francis Salway, who would get to look after retail.

It was one of those moments when you don't know whether to laugh or cry. Anger and shock rippled across the sector: What on earth is going on? Has Francis Salway been bounced into this by Paul Myners? (No.) Is this all about offices director Mike Hussey getting to run his own company? (Hmm...) The financial reasons put forward to justify the split seemed sound – they had to know what they were talking about, surely? Even so, the plan felt crazy. I took a deep breath and wrote this *EG* leader, published on 8th September 2007:

Calm Head Required in Financial Storm

This is precisely the wrong time for Land Securities to appoint a group of self-interested outsiders to "conduct a review of its business structure", as chief executive Francis Salway puts it delicately this week. Are the financiers that LandSec chairman Paul Myners has bullied the rest of the board into hiring really fit to make a level-headed decision? After all, the summer stock market shocks seem to have left most of them either semi-hysterical or catatonic.

Myners obviously wants to make his mark. He is clearly worried that the negative gap between the share price of LandSec and the net value of the assets leaves them prey to the wolves of private equity. In all this he is right. Where he is wrong is in the panicky and semi-public manner of hauling on board new PR and financial advisers in the midst of a wider financial storm.

Should the Trillium FM business be hived off one day? Perhaps – but hardly to-day. Should the £14.8bn worth of assets be split into specialist REITs? Maybe, but they can still be run by one business. LandSec is running along well. De-stroying the 63-year-old firm would be an act of corporate vandalism.

Each Friday brought my least-pleasant task of the week as editor of *EG*: looking through rival paper *Property Week* to see what we'd missed. In the late Nineties, I had to watch out for one former colleague from *Building* magazine: Penny Guest, the founding editor of *Property Week*. Her irrever-ence and intelligence set the sharp and breezy tone of the large-format title that replaced the dull *Chartered Surveyor Weekly*. But for most of my time at *EG* it was Giles Barrie who needed watching – another former *Building* colleague, he was a terrific news journalist and a hard-working editor who surrounded himself with great reporters. So the Friday read of *Property Week* could be a glum affair, with much quiet cursing. But Friday 7th Sep-tember 2007 was different. Barrie also thought the idea of splitting up Land Securities was crazy; we were marching in step. Phew!

Six months after the split was announced, Bear Stearns collapsed and the credit markets began to freeze over. Merrill Lynch published a report in March 2008 that concluded the refinancing of Land Securities' £5 billion of debt to enable the split would cost £280 million. I was once again rude about the whole idea. This led to lunch with Myners in May 2008 at Tate Modern – where he was chairman of the trustees – at which he went through the gene-sis of the plan and the rationale for the split, which was still to take place. Myners, who had been a highly successful fund manager at Gartmore, was appointed six months later as financial services secretary to the Treasury, a role in which he became a key figure in helping save RBS and Lloyds. After lunch at the Tate, he gave me a lift back over the river on his way to chair a board meeting of the Guardian Media Group. I sat in the car thinking, "Well, he must be right. They must know what they are doing."

But he was wrong, and Merrill Lynch was right. The cost of splitting up Land Securities became too much. The collapse of Lehman Brothers in September 2008 was presumably the final straw, because just two months later defeat was admitted, with the cost of restructuring the debt blamed. Myners went off to Whitehall, and was replaced by Alison Carnwath. Land Securities produced a gloomy set of results that November and admitted the aborted exercise had cost £16 million. Salway said, "We will be focusing on managing the business, and will come back to it if the time is right."

The time never proved right during Salway's tenure, which ended in the spring of 2012 with his retirement at the age of fifty-four. Back in May 2009, the Land Securities chief executive had been given six months to save his job, according to undenied City rumours. The ultimatum was supposedly delivered by Land Securities' formidable new chairman (sic). The rumoured threat put the entire industry firmly against Alison Carnwath and resolutely for Francis Salway, who remained highly regarded, despite acknowledging the split having been his idea.

Land Securities steadied and recovered well under Salway, and began to develop big projects like the Walkie Talkie. So news of Salway's retirement in 2012 came as a bit of a shock. I asked him what he was going to do next: "Climb Mont Blanc," was the deadpan reply – and he did. He also joined the board of property data service IPD, knowing full well the business was up for sale (see chapter two). Later that year, Salway joined the board of Cadogan Estates as a non-executive director and a still much-admired man.

THE NEW MEN

RICHARD COTTON, FORUM PARTNERS:

The biggest change I've noticed is that we have moved from the old-fashioned property entrepreneurs like John Ritblat, Donny Gordon at Liberty and Sidney Mason at Hammerson. Today's leaders are much more like professional managers. The companies are run very much as you would expect any large company to be run. It's become a more professional, but probably a less fun place.

There is an incessant demand for transparency from the stock market and for more and more information. You used to just get a simple report and accounts, now pages of analysis need to be put in. Investor meetings are now huge shows in big auditoria – plus webcasting. It means all the formerly irreverent analysts keep their irreverent comments and questions to themselves now. It means that, over time, listed companies will become increasingly income focused, rather than buccaneering developers or corporate raiders.

The new man at Land Securities is Rob Noel, who took firm charge in April 2012 and is definitely not a dull numbers man. I had the embarrassing task during a results call that May of asking him if he had a tattoo on his, er, "lower back". One of his former colleagues at agent Nelson Bakewell, who had seen Noel in the showers, had ratted on him. "Yes," he barked. I hastily turned to the results and then listened to the forty-seven-year-old's very clear vision for boosting a business that his staff feared he was overenthusiastically shaking up.

I wondered if he'd ever speak to me again, especially after my leading on the tattoo tale in that week's *Evening Standard* column. Not the case: we had lunch at Wilton's that October. He was great; open, chatty, clear-minded – a bit scary, but obviously the right man for the job. Lettings were beginning to happen on the Walkie Talkie tower in Fenchurch Street, and Noel was about to embark on a series of new ventures. Two days later, he announced a £350 million speculative development on the site of the old Land Securities offices in Victoria Street. He even succeeded in getting prime minister David Cameron to visit the site of the newly billed Zig Zag building.

What was more interesting was the view that new man Noel took on persuading occupiers to take space – fresh and interesting enough to write up for *EG* on 27th October 2012:

Developers Need to Rethink Their Pitch

"The rent is far less important than the total cost. The cost per workstation is the story." Developers should rethink the way new space is pitched to occupiers. What appeals more? "Land Securities to build 190,000 sq ft Zig Zag building in Victoria as part of £350m development," or, "Land Securities to develop 2,400 new workplaces in Victoria that will cost no more than existing office space in the area"?

The former is what the company said last Thursday. The latter is what chief executive Rob Noel said over lunch two days before. Moving can cost no more than staying, even if the rent is 30% higher, he says. "The rent is far less important than the total cost. The cost per workstation is the story. We feel that if we produce buildings that give tenants the chance to move to better buildings with no real differential in cost, they will move."

An obvious argument, but one rarely put. Noel began putting the case by drawing a graph in my notebook. It showed how the cost of putting a bum on an office seat had fallen from 30% of the tenant's salary bill in 1974 to 8% today. Salaries have risen seven-fold over 38 years. But one bum took up 150 sq ft in the 1970s. Today, almost two bums can be squeezed into the same space.

Rents have declined – according to CBRE, by 41% between 1975 and 2010, if adjusted for inflation. "New space is cheap today, cheaper than yesterday." But not even José Carreras singing these lyrics to the tune of La Donna e Mobile will convince a single occupier to move. Shouting "not a penny more" more loudly might, says Noel.

Over coffee, I asked if he could give a live example – perhaps one of those insurance companies that have taken 25% of the space in the 690,000 sq ft Walkie Talkie? He declined. Instead we took a theoretical tenant employing 100 staff in 12,000 sq ft of clapped-out space nearby – one paying a base rent of £50 per sq ft plus £31 per sq ft in rates and service charges. Total: £81 per sq ft x 12,000 sq ft equals £972,000 pa.

Move them to the Walkie Talkie? Charge £65 per sq ft in rent and £31 per sq ft in rates and service charges. Total: £96 per sq ft. The 100 staff now need 8,000 sq ft, because this tower has been designed to fit one bum into every 80 sq ft. Total cost: £768,000 pa. Result? Let's move!

GREAT PORTLAND ESTATES

Rob Noel had come to Land Securities in 2010 from Great Portland Estates, where another new(-ish) man had been quietly making his mark since April 2002. That was when Toby Courtauld became chief executive of the central London office specialist. John Burns of Derwent did beat the Old Etonian member of the textile dynasty to the draw in late 2006, when he merged Derwent Valley with London & Merchant Securities to form Derwent London. Great Portland Estates had made a 240p per share offer, but this was topped by Derwent. Apart from that, Courtauld's record is spotless.

The company is a bit media shy, though. I had lunch with Courtauld in 2003, and once again in 2007; both occasions were at my own request. His chairman Richard Peskin was rather less shy: Peskin remains a legendary luncher. I can see him now, across the room in Wilton's, peering over his half-glasses at the mandatory bottle of champagne; then comes the laying-on of hands to test its temperature. Peskin ferries vintage reds and whites from his own cellar to restaurants – not something you see done often.

I have experienced such a thing only twice myself: once at *Building* magazine long ago, when having lunch at the Garrick Club with one of the magazine's columnists, Lord Alistair McAlpine. The former Conservative Party treasurer ordered "a bottle of my brother's claret" – his brother being David McAlpine, the chairman of the club's wine committee. Then Alistair said that his doctor forbade him to drink red wine at lunchtime. Happy days: I enjoyed the whole bottle. The second time was with Paul White of Frogmore at Alfred's club in Mayfair. After we'd chosen a bottle from his private stash, I began to relate the tale of Lord McAlpine ordering his brother's claret – whereupon in walked David McAlpine, so Paul hailed him over that I might tell the brother in question the tale.

Peskin's leaving party took place in March 2009. In front of about four hundred guests packed into Claridge's ballroom, the man put on quite a performance, opening with a rumination on the world forty years earlier: "When I started at GPE, a Big Mac was a large raincoat and a Brazilian was someone who came from Brazil." At the end of a funny and provocative speech, Peskin broke into song – hesitantly at first, but with gathering conviction: "Lunches, I've had a few; a glass or two, was my convention. I've lived, I've laughed, I've cried; I've done my share of corporate schmoozing..." and so on, to an ovation from guests agape.

QUINTAIN

Peskin's not-quite-so-outrageous kindred spirit is Adrian Wyatt. We'll finish the list of developers with the story of this irrepressible character, who became the victim of a City wanting predictable income rather than unpredictable profits. Wyatt founded Quintain in 1992, aged forty-four, after twenty-one years at Jones Lang Wootton. The only way to start this tale is in a final lunch story, with my apologies: I met Wyatt for the first time in May 1999 at The Greenhouse restaurant in Mayfair. He had arrived before me and was sitting at the bar with a cheeky grin, part-way through a kir royale. He insisted I have one, and it proved impossible to resist the kir, or the fine wine that followed – not to mention a final large Armagnac.

Wyatt was in the middle of two complicated deals, I seem to remember. I also remember his warmth, wittiness and dazzling ability with numbers. The last lunch we had was in September 2011 at Patterson's in Mayfair, at which we got through two bottles of Meursault – with only limited help from fellow diner Becky Worthington, Wyatt's finance director– who later left Quintain to set up Lodestone Capital after a brief spell as deputy managing director. Wyatt was in fine form; Worthington was, as ever, supportive.

But one point of the lunch was to counter a negative article I'd written in the *Evening Standard* four months earlier, on 27th May 2011:

Key Project for Quintain Is to Build Up Investor Confidence

Two weeks ago, Quintain Estates chief executive Adrian Wyatt was in northern Portugal, speaking at the launch of a partnership between Cisco Systems and Living PlanIT, a loose-fit organisation encouraging the building of a fully wired community of 250,000, 15 kilometres north of Oporto.

One week ago, the ebullient 61-year-old was enthusing about "syntonic cities" to a pre-lunch crowd at the Dorchester. He says the world needs 10,000 new cities that, according to the dictionary definition of syntonic, "have a high degree of emotional responsiveness to their environment".

This week, Wyatt, in a natty wide-check suit, faced an emotionally unresponsive City audience to present results for a company with a slight problem. The present stock-market valuation of £271 million is miles below the £648 million net asset value at the end of March....

A series of milestones set last year by chairman William Rucker of Lazards have almost all been met – and more have been set for this year. Analysts at Liberium Capital are guardedly optimistic that Quintain can extract value from the 22 million square feet of granted planning permissions and from projects at Wembley and on the Greenwich Peninsula, where Georgian Squares will not be built in the place of blocks of flats....

What analysts say, but won't write, is this: "Okay, the crash delayed development profits. You are a great bloke, Adrian – funny, fluent, with wide interests, and extraordinarily clever. But we don't want to be sitting here in 2012 and be told that the jam is not being delivered until 2014."

In July 2011, Max James of Lazard, a former head of global real estate at HSBC Investment Bank, was appointed to the board of Quintain. In May 2012, Quintain declared net assets of £572 million. The share price had been languishing all year at around 35p, valuing the company at £180 million – still way below the net asset value. Forty-four-year-old James replaced sixty-two-year-old Wyatt as chief executive that same month: New Property replacing Old. The cycle continues.

CHAPTER EIGHT
BIG THINKERS

You have to think anyway, so why not think big?
Donald Trump

Here are the stories of nine of property's biggest thinkers. Apologies to the other eight for including Achilleas Kallakis, but the man who conned Allied Irish Bank out of £740 million certainly did think big. Simon Halabi thought big too, although this Syrian-born investor who built up a £2 billion real estate empire was reduced in size by the crash. Robert and Vincent Tchenguiz are financiers who thought big and differently about how to multiply property income, while Mark Dixon thought of a new way to make money from property by saving big landlords the trouble of dealing with small occupiers.

Mike Slade is a mid-sized mainstream developer but one with a big heart. Irvine Sellar thought big for over a decade on how to produce the Shard, London's tallest tower, while Gerald Ronson always thinks big – the Heron Tower and its residential sister in the City are a marker of his tenacity. Sir Stuart Lipton is Britain's most widely known developer, a man who has thought big since conceiving Broadgate in the Eighties. Last, but not least, is Sir George Iacobescu, the father of Canary Wharf, the biggest commercial development of them all. Here they are, in reverse order of the above list:

SIR GEORGE IACOBESCU

I met George Iacobescu on 28th May 1998, just three weeks after I'd settled into the editor's chair at *EG*. The Romanian-born civil engineer, then in his early fifties, had been chief executive of Canary Wharf for a year. He'd been construction boss since 1988, when Olympia & York began to build London's "second City", but work on the project, which was driven by Paul Reichmann of O&Y, came to a temporary halt four years later. Olympia & York Canary Wharf went into administration in May 1992. Iacobescu remembers it well:

SIR GEORGE IACOBESCU:

By then, about 4.5 million square feet of space was built. We had spent £2 billion on infrastructure. We practically put the services in for the whole of the Isle of Dogs. The lesson we learned is that on all very large projects that require infrastructure, it will be tough. You need to assume it will take ten years to get off the ground.

In 1991, the Jubilee Line had not even got royal assent. I remember taking the chairman of Barclays bank around, in 1991. He looked at one building and said, "I'll take it tomorrow. Just get the DLR running properly." There was obviously no Jubilee Line; there was no Limehouse Link. An enormous amount of area was open to development, but with no transport links.

The first wave of development was forced: something we decided to do in order to create a critical mass. The government had done a great thing by creating an enterprise zone. The London Docklands Development Corporation was practically a mini-government. That really helped. The second wave came in 1997, when the economy started moving.

In 1998, we met at Canary Wharf Group headquarters, near the top of One Canada Square, the first and sleekest tower on the Wharf. A model the size of four snooker tables was on display. It included miniatures of the existing buildings, mostly to the west of One Canada Square. In addition, a series of transparent boxes delineated the shapes of unbuilt towers that were planned to rise to the east: over the course of the next ten years, these were gradually built. Iacobescu again...

SIR GEORGE IACOBESCU:

That was the start of a fantastic boom period. Two years before, Paul Reichmann came back with a group of investors, mostly American. Not a single British investor put money in it. In 1997, Citibank signed a lease to come to the Wharf. They had trawled the whole market looking for six hundred thousand square feet with big floorplates to allow trading space.

Very large importance was placed on our ability to deliver robust services. Every single street had services for the next hundred years, and the capacity of every service was doubled up. That made the difference. Immediately after Citibank came HSBC. The bank said, "This is where we want to be. We want to do a tower, and if we cannot do a tower here we're going to move back to Hong Kong."

We built HSBC a million-square-foot tower. There was a second tower for Citibank, when they became Citigroup. Clifford Chance took a million square feet, then so did Lehman Brothers. This all happened between 1997 and 2004. The estate grew from 4.5 million to twelve million square feet. It was a very intense process. We offered them something they could not get elsewhere for the price.

We make buildings look elegant and simple on the outside but sophisticated on the inside. We don't build offices of a certain shape and then say, "This is the building you're getting, like it or not." Take Clifford Chance: we said, "You tell us how you operate, the technology you need, what works for you, and we'll transform that into brick, glass and stainless steel."

The most important lesson that I learned is that you're in the service business. You need to deliver what the tenant wants. It's one thing to try to do sculptures and call them buildings, then by hook or by crook you make the tenant fit. It's totally different to say: "Tell me what you need and I'll do it."

You would occasionally meet Iacobescu on the cocktail circuit, but not often – even though he lives in Mayfair. He had more "hinterland" than most, being a member of the British Museum's board of trustees as well as a patron of Jewish Care. His knighthood, awarded in December 2011, was for "charity and community" work as well as financial services.

We had lunch in June 2008; Bear Stearns had collapsed in March of that year and the financial world was teetering. I was late. Iacobescu was entirely composed. Canary Wharf was reliant on banking tenants – including Lehman Brothers, which was renting a million square feet. On 15th September, the bank collapsed and consequently stopped paying the rent on its offices at 25 Bank Street. On the same day, the US government was forced to bail out AIG – the world's biggest insurer – with an $85 billion injection. But Iacobescu had both bases covered.

He explains: "The rent insurance deal we had with AIG was not linked to the banking collapse. It was linked to a downgrade of AIG. The deal was that if AIG's rating fell, they would have to post collateral with us. AIG posted about £220 million, four years' rent on the Lehman and Citigroup buildings. This was deposited and we had the right to draw against that money when there was a shortfall of rent."

September to December 2008 was the blackest period of the crash. But one banker held his nerve: Jamie Dimon of US investment bank JP Morgan had been looking for a new site to build a European headquarters, either in the City or at Canary Wharf, since mid 2007. The City won out on price in early 2008, and the selected site was on London Wall. The City Corporation owned the land. Hammerson was to be the developer. But JP Morgan began to realise there was little chance of the project being delivered on time, partly due to opposition from the residents of the nearby Barbican estate.

So the bank came back to Canary Wharf. JP Morgan agreed to pay £237 million in December 2008 for a plot next door to Lehman Brothers:

this was quite a call for Dimon, given what had happened to Lehman and the world financial system just three months earlier. Canary Wharf Group was paid £80 million to put in the foundations for a headquarters building of some 1.9 million square feet. But in early 2010, Dimon finally lost his nerve and the project was put on hold. Meanwhile, next door stood 25 Bank Street, a million-square-foot tower owned by Lehman Brothers' administrators: a building that was sure to become empty.

On 12th April 2010, I interviewed Iacobescu in his office, high up in One Canada Square. Afterwards, we looked down at JP Morgan's £80 million hole in the ground next to the River Thames. I ventured that Dimon might take the Lehman Brothers' space. He smiled: Iacobescu had clearly figured that out long before. JP Morgan paid £495 million for 25 Bank Street in September 2010 and moved in during 2012, taking the population of the Wharf to a hundred thousand for the first time.

Our next meeting was in October 2011. Lunch was at Roka, a pricey Japanese restaurant in the Wharf where you get to sit at embarrassingly low tables. At the time, Canary Wharf Group, with a staff nine hundred strong, managed an estate of ninety-seven acres, containing fifteen million square feet of space. It was also collecting rents of £230 million on the 6.4 million square feet of directly owned real estate.

Iacobescu talked about how the new £500 million Crossrail station was way ahead of programme. Of how the population of Canary Wharf might double to two hundred thousand over the next twenty years, helped by the building of fifteen hundred homes to the east on Wood Wharf, along with another five million square feet of office and retail space.

Canary Wharf Group was by then building well away from the Isle of Dogs. Iacobescu had levered the group's construction expertise into joint ventures, including one to rationalise and then build the Walkie Talkie tower in Fenchurch Street in a joint venture with Land Securities. Another was to redevelop the huge Shell Centre site on the South Bank with Qatari Diar, the oil state's property company.

The company was flourishing in late 2012, Iacobescu having survived two crashes. But in 2008, he had sometimes wondered if the game was up.

SIR GEORGE IACOBESCU:

There were times when it was eerie; times you didn't know what the next day would bring. But we were sitting on about £1 billion of cash, money accumulated over the previous three to four years. Some shareholders did wonder why we didn't pay dividends. Our idea was that it was going to be money for future development – but also money to protect us from accidents. And Lehman was an accident. You cannot take three or four accidents like that; one accident was enough. Luckily we had insurance, but two more accidents like that could have been lethal.

SIR STUART LIPTON

At 5pm on 26th March 2012, I went to see Sir Stuart Lipton of Chelsfield at his company offices in Brook Street, Mayfair, just to the west of Claridge's. We were both going on to the Connaught at 6.30pm to toast the retirement of Land Securities chief executive Francis Salway. A rather awkward moment would occur that evening at the party: an incident that helps explain the motivations of this tall and portly knight who became Britain's most long-serving and distinguished developer.

At the meeting, Sir Stuart explained in his soft voice the concept for a series of branded corporate "pavilions" on a fifty-acre site at Silvertown in London's Docklands. What he was describing was a new genus of real estate: not the out-of-town office campus he had pioneered at Stockley Park and Chiswick Park, nor a replica of the groundbreaking inner-city office campus at Broadgate.

Each of the Silvertown pavilions, fifty to a hundred thousand square foot in size, would feature corporate office space integrated with a research centre and visitor centre. The site would be a concentrated collection of "brand statements" – like the Docklands Siemens Centre that was nearing completion at the foot of the new Emirates Air Line cable-car crossing between Greenwich Peninsula and the Royal Docks.

Sir Stuart said Chelsfield had received promises from a number of global corporates to take space. "Oh," I said grandly, "you mean like 'brand embassies'?" He looked briefly impressed, until I told him the term was pinched from architect Lee Polisano, who had just hooked a job in the Chinese city of Ningbo to design a "fashion city" filled with such objects.

The losing bidders on the Silvertown site were furious with the London Development Agency for choosing the Chelsfield submission to build up to forty of these corporate embassies on publicly owned land. The Wellcome Trust and the Berkeley Group had interpreted the brief to mean lots of homes and shops. Sir Stuart concentrated instead on the words "high-tech sectors and the visitor and tourist economy" – and came up with his unique idea. Chelsfield was named as the preferred bidder, and given until 2013 to sign up half-a-dozen global brands. If it failed to do so, the site would go for housing and shops.

Why was Chelsfield chosen? Because the pavilions would bring lots of jobs, explained Sir Stuart at our meeting, which was prompted by my expression of scepticism at the whole idea in the *Evening Standard*. "I think we produced an original idea which will really add value to the site, to the neighbourhood, to east London and to London." He made the point that there was going to be a glut of new homes in the East End. Permission had already been granted for fifty thousand, and no more were needed, he said.

Stuart Anthony Lipton was born on 9th November 1942. After skipping university to become an estate agent, he turned developer at the age of twenty-nine – founding Sterling Land in 1971, then Greycoat in 1976, then Stanhope in 1983. There he stayed until 2006, before joining Chelsfield at the age of sixty-four, alongside veteran developer and friend Elliott Bernerd. In late 2012 came a switch into another guise as a partner in Lipton Rogers, a development company he set up with Peter Rogers, a former colleague from Stanhope and brother of architect Lord Rogers.

But that's only part of the CV. Sir Stuart built a strong bridge between the development and design communities early in his career, then another into Whitehall. He was knighted in 2000. His interest in architecture got him elected to honorary membership of the Royal Institute of British Architects and into the job of chairman of the government design watchdog, the Commission for the Built Environment, between 1999 and 2004.

But he was forced to resign the chairmanship of CABE in 2004 after accusations of conflicts of interest made by rival developers. One came from Arrowcroft, which had permission to build a stadium and offices on land adjacent to Croydon East station. The designs were criticised by CABE. Meanwhile Sir Stuart's company, Stanhope, was promoting a rival scheme.

How can you have a developer chairing a public body that is supposed to vet schemes by rival developers? That was the tricky question. There were also accusations from traditional "brick and wood" architects that CABE favoured a clique of the "glass and steel" modern brigade. Whatever the reasons, his treatment seemed shabby and unfair.

Sir Stuart was the ultimate establishment developer: a board member of the National Theatre for ten years, he also served on the board of the Royal Opera House and gave advice to the National Gallery. In addition, he was a willing helper to the British Property Federation on tricky political issues that needed someone of gravitas to get everyone round the table to sort them out. In all, the industry's most eminent *homme d'affaires* – but not just for property; for architecture as well.

I had first come across plain Stuart Lipton in a previous life. I joined *Building* magazine in 1985, getting to edit the building industry equivalent of *EG* from 1990 to 1996. My first assignment, in the late summer of 1985, was to visit Broadgate. "Beat this" were the first words of a story on the astonishing rate of progress on this three-million-square-foot project. Having just come from working for twenty years in the building trade, I'd never seen anything like it. A few weeks earlier, prime minister Margaret Thatcher had climbed into a JCB and performed the groundbreaking ceremony. "Here, in a way, we are drawing back the curtain of the future," said Mrs T presciently.

The future arrived on 5th December 1991, but at the wrong moment. The Eighties property boom was over. Nevertheless, Sir Stuart and his partner in Broadgate, Godfrey Bradman, did not stint on the official opening ceremony. The band of the Household Cavalry announced at 3.45pm the arrival of the Queen, who declared the project finished.

Hundreds of guests came to lunch beforehand, accommodated on a bare floor finished just to shell and core. The late Alastair Ross Goobey, author of *Bricks and Mortar*, was there. He wrote later of entertainer Roy Castle compering a rendition of *The Twelve Days of Christmas*, complete with can-can dancers and pearly queens.

The next day, Bradman's company, Rosehaugh, reported a £227 million loss. In the end, both men lost control of Broadgate. But in Sir Stuart's case, emotional investment in the scheme was not relinquished: more than twenty years later, it led to that uncomfortable incident at the Connaught. British Land had control of the estate, which had risen in size to four million square feet. British Land boss Stephen Hester announced plans in October 2006 to add 1.2 million feet by enlarging between five and sixteen of the blocks before 2020.

This eventually led to architect Ken Shuttleworth of Make designing an enormous silver block for Swiss bank UBS to replace 4 and 6 Broadgate Circle. The designs were released in 2011. Sir Stuart was deeply unhappy: he called the seven-hundred-thousand-square-foot, silver-clad "engine block" Shuttleworth had designed "the worst large building we have seen in the City for twenty years".

British Land's normally equable boss, Chris Grigg, was angry with Sir Stuart. He'd asked for immunity from listing for the two blocks as a precaution against English Heritage springing a surprise listing before work started in early 2012. Sir Stuart's remarks encouraged the Twentieth Century Society to cause a fuss, and English Heritage subsequently recommended listing. But the City and the Treasury were determined that the UBS scheme would be built. Chancellor George Osborne became involved.

The immunity from listing was granted, and the two blocks were torn down. On 1st March 2012, Osborne came along to the groundbreaking ceremony. Three-and-a-half weeks later, I absent-mindedly made the mistake of trying to engage Sir Stuart Lipton in conversation with Chris Grigg at Francis Salway's retirement party at the Connaught. If air could freeze...

GERALD RONSON

It took several weeks to set up an interview with Gerald Ronson, which eventually took place on 31st March 1999. His elegant daughter, Lisa, looked after these things at Heron House, the modest headquarters of Ronson's property business on the Marylebone Road. Ronson looked tense and wary.

The man had been punished in the press during the Guinness share scandal. He'd served a six-month prison sentence in 1990. Two years later, his company was slowly and painfully taken apart by the banks, leaving him with just a five percent share, but with the crucial support of a group of US investors. Nine years later, Heron International was on the up again. Ronson clearly wanted to talk. But was I going to take liberties by raking up the past?

Ronson's top-floor office was cluttered with memorabilia, along with pictures of his vivacious wife, Gail, and their four daughters. The man himself, then aged sixty, sat behind a large, wooden desk. Lisa and I sat on a low couch, yards away. The tape recorder on the low table in front of me could not pick up his voice. I asked if he could come closer. Without getting out of his wheeled chair, he crabbed slowly out from behind his desk and edged warily in our direction, before creaking to a halt.

I began with a few anodyne questions, and the tension eased. Gerald Ronson simply can't help speaking his mind. He began to do so after a few minutes, and the interview went well. I did mention the jail sentence and banking problems in the resulting story. But the article was largely affirmative, concentrating on his plans to open a series of thirteen Heron City developments across Europe. His long-time lieutenant, Peter Ferrari, told me later that the boss had given him a rare Sunday morning call after the article appeared in *EG* on the Saturday and asked him gruffly, "It's all right – isn't it?" Ferrari assured Ronson that it was.

Each spring would bring an invitation to the annual Heron lunch, originally at the Savoy, then later at the Dorchester. Guests wait in line to be announced by a man in a red tailcoat, then after a quick shake of Ronson's hand emerge into a room filled with perhaps the most eclectic mix of guests ever likely to be encountered. It is a bit old-fashioned in the sense that there is a huge, elongated top table containing the seventy or eighty guests designated as most important from among the three hundred attendees. I stood, one year, watching the then owner of the Telegraph Group, Conrad Black, poking his cigar in a threatening manner at publisher Richard Desmond, owner of Express Newspapers. I think the row was over a printworks.

The top table contained politicians, captains of other industries, bankers, and even ambassadors to the countries in which Heron International was developing. Ronson does not do light, or witty, so his annual lunch speeches tended to be rather doom-laden. The structure was along the lines of: "Watch out – X is going to happen. Heron is going to avoid X, of course. But there are many fools who won't."

Ronson can be thin-skinned. I once published a diary story in *EG* suggesting he had some lesser mortal carrying his bags around for him at MIPIM. His anger was so hot that the letter of reproof almost self-ignited in my hands. I briefly considered publishing it – but didn't dare. Those who deal with Ronson are slightly afraid of him. "You don't want to come to a meeting with Gerald without having all the answers," said one agent, "or you get a rollocking."

But the same source also said what many others echo: "Ronson is a man of transparent honour. If Gerald agrees a deal, he never reneges. If he promises to do something, he does it." Millions of pounds each year are donated to mainly Jewish charities; his reward for that was a CBE in 2012. The occasion, however, generated hostile press stories under the "fraudster" tag, suggesting Ronson was unworthy of such an honour.

The coverage verged on anti-Semitic. If just some of those millions had gone to the Tory party, a knighthood would have been in the post. Ronson himself feels he remains the outsider, betrayed by the Gentile establishment over the Guinness affair – as the account of his own life, *Leading from the Front*, makes clear. As far as the property world is concerned, however, Ronson is firmly part of the establishment.

IRVINE SELLAR

I met Irvine Sellar at the Dorchester for lunch on 10th April 2002. He fussed over the suitability of the table; we were moved. The Shard of Glass, as it was then called, was on the discussion menu. Italian architect Renzo Piano had been appointed in July 2000 to "work with" the already assigned British firm Broadway Malyan. By 2002, the UK architects were no longer involved in the project: Sellar had signed an agreement with Piano giving the Italian the final say-so on design issues. The plans, which had been approved by Southwark council the previous month, had since been called in by the secretary of state, John Prescott.

A public inquiry was inevitable; English Heritage objected to the thousand-foot spike into the London sky. So Sellar needed to harden up the concept designs. A discussion on suitable cost consultants, project managers and engineers followed; I suggested a few that I thought operated in a higher league than those Sellar was already using. He was clearly asking around.

In March 2003, new designs were unveiled for the tower. A public inquiry into the proposed scheme took place during April and May; Prescott granted approval in November. But that's just a précis of what happened over nineteen months in the fourteen-year development saga of the Shard. It had all begun back in 1998 with Sellar buying the twenty-four-storey offices occupied by PricewaterhouseCoopers.

Sellar paid £71 million to buy out the occupant's long lease, and the accountants finally moved out of the building in 2007. Before this happened, however, there was a nasty legal battle with Simon Halabi, one of the original partners in the scheme. The venture nearly collapsed in 2008 and was saved only by the Qatari government taking a ninety-five percent stake. This left Sellar with just five percent of the equity, but ninety-five percent of the glory. He also ended up with a twenty percent stake in the company that will run the £2 billion London Bridge Quarter, which includes the development of six hundred thousand square feet at the base of The Shard. In 2012, the tower was completed amid much glory, but by the year's end none of the five hundred and seventy-five thousand square feet of office space had been let.

Short and stocky, Irvine Sellar comes from the school of rough and tumble: a background conveyed by his cockney accent and reputation. He started work in 1955 with a firm of accountants, before moving into the fresh air to sell clothes from market stalls. His dealer's instinct quickly moved him up the ladder in the rag trade. Sellar founded Mates, the first chain to sell both men's and women's clothes in the same store. He ended up as one of the kings of Carnaby Street in the Sixties, eventually owning a chain of ninety shops   before moving his cash into property.

The early Nineties crash took him back down to the bottom of the ladder. His property company, Ford Sellar Morris, went bust in 1991 with losses of £132 million. But he began climbing again, building up the Sellar Property Group. On the way, he did the deal that will bring him immortality, buying the Shard site for £37.4 million in 1998.

I would see Sellar regularly at property events, and once or twice for dinner at Le Gavroche in Mayfair. He was always solicitous and listened more than he talked, both uncommon attributes among developers. Sellar arranged for me to visit Renzo Piano in Genoa in July 2008, after the Qataris had rescued the project. We met in Piano's wonderful design studio, built like a large greenhouse on a steep slope overlooking the sea. What intrigued me was how the elegant and cultured architect got on with the former market trader. "I found him very interesting," said Piano of Sellar.

"He is a big character. I know him now for nine years. He has never betrayed me. We always talk very frankly. If I have to tell him something, I tell him. If he has to tell me something, he does. And even in the difficult moments – and we did have difficult moments – he was very loyal. He has a desire to build this tower. You need that kind of desire."

MIKE SLADE

"A real estate developer was not like an industrial CEO or an investment banker. No, you either had THE AURA, the aura of magic, fireproof confidence and invincibility, or you had nothing." Tom Wolfe's description of Charlie Croker, fictional Atlanta developer and central character in his 1998 novel, *A Man in Full*, is one that fits precisely Mike Slade of Helical Bar.

Steely faced bankers stripped Croker of his private jet and repossessed his empire when the market crashed in Wolfe's novel. Read the chapter headed *Saddlebags* – it's a wonderful evocation of how a bank's lavish treatment of a big borrower becomes a bread-and-water grilling when they want the money back. The title of the chapter comes from the shape of the slowly spreading sweat stains under Charlie Croker's armpits as it sinks in that the game is up.

There was no such grilling for Slade. The boss of Helical Bar informed the world in November 2008 that it was a great time to start buying again, before flying off to board his thirty-metre yacht, *Leopard*, in Capetown. In January 2009, aged sixty-one, he broke records sailing across the southern Atlantic to Brazil as the market plunged. Slade was right: late 2008 did turn out to be the perfect time to buy.

Slade is a man who enjoys life to the full, funded by an eye-popping salary and hefty bonuses. But what you actually feel, when his arm goes around your shoulder, is glad to see him. I'd guiltily accept an invitation each summer to take a trip on the *Leopard* from Southampton down the Solent along with ten to a dozen City folk and press. We sailed to the Isle of Wight, for a bibulous lunch, usually at the George in Yarmouth. Guiltily, because Helical Bar's results would be looming: fortunately the figures were mostly fine. But that's not much of an excuse for having your journalistic edge blunted by such hospitality. My excuse was: "Bugger it, don't be so pious."

Slade's intelligence was in evidence even as a student at Reading's College of Estate Management. He graduated in 1968, winning the *EG* top student prize. After an early career developing on the continent, he took control of loss-making Helical Bar in July 1984. (The name comes from the raised spirals on steel reinforcement bars.) The rise of Helical Bar began with Slade charming Sam Whitbread into allowing him to develop the brewer's Chiswell Street site. "We laid out £50,000 and took out £11 million," said Slade in 1998 when I first interviewed him.

By then, turnover was up tenfold to £214 million. Happy shareholders were content for Slade to draw his £1 million salary and additional bonuses for almost the next decade. Why? Because between 1998 and 2008 Helical Bar gave shareholders annualised returns of 18.3 percent, compared with an average among the listed property sector of just seven percent. The crash brought losses, but by 2012 Helical Bar was investing in new projects again – including one to build a couple of hundred new apartments next door to my flat near St Bartholomew's Hospital in the City.

Slade remains the man you most want to talk to at a party. He was at the Portman Estate cocktails in Manchester Square on 1st November 2012; on this occasion, however, I was wary of talking to him. Aged sixty-five, the Helical Bar chief executive had that summer announced his intention to carry on for another five years, after a modest boardroom reshuffle. The City had been clearly unimpressed with this news. And a week or so before in my *EG* column, comparing the share price performances of the listed real estate companies, I'd noted that Helical Bar was bottom of the class – a ranking that Slade was sure to dispute.

He grabbed me round the shoulder and pulled me into a hug. "Dear boy! I see you are a bit worried about our share price! I think we should have lunch. How about that Club Gascon place near your flat?"

MARK DIXON

Multimillionaires don't often man stands at the annual MIPIM property show in Cannes. But Mark Dixon can regularly be seen fronting for Regus, the world's largest serviced-offices supplier, which the former sandwich salesman founded in 1989. The life story of this son of a Ford worker could be entitled, *How to Make a Billion, Lose a Billion, Then Make Half a Billion Again While Remaining Grounded.*

"I met Mark first when he came over from Belgium and no one had heard of Regus," says former Credit Suisse banker Ian Marcus. "He'd just bought into the business via a bust Scandinavian firm called Reinhold. Mark had this vision of creating a brand as recognisable as Hoover. Well, everyone knows of Regus now. I think he is one of those who has changed the mould of how property is utilised."

By 2012, that vision had been turned into a company employing seven thousand staff in fourteen hundred centres across a hundred countries – Cambodia, Rwanda and Madagascar being the latest. Regus revenues that year were £1.2 billion, with profits of £90 million. Dixon himself, who owns thirty-four percent of the company, saw his own wealth put at £527 million in 2012. Ten years before, he was down to his last £80 million.

Regus was laid low in January 2003 in America, when it was forced into chapter 11 bankruptcy for a year. The business lost over £100 million in 2001 and again in 2002, after the dot-com bubble popped, leaving many centres half-empty and landlords baying for rent. Dixon had to seek protection from his US creditors because landlords refused to lower fixed rental bills.

As Regus grew during the Nineties, so did Dixon's personal wealth. He became a paper billionaire in 2000 at the age of forty, soon after the company floated, and his sixty percent stake was valued at £1.2 billion in early 2001. Dixon was seen by the City and the media as a Midas, a man who invented a new way to make money from property. This was true enough, thanks to his exploitation of landlords' distaste for dealing with the masses.

But those same landlords kept pointing out to me the flaw in Dixon's business model: Regus had signed long leases saddling the company with fixed long-term expenditure in a market where income was uncertain and the occupier market fickle. I'd mentioned this flaw several times in *EG*. That may partly explain this dyspeptic comment on 7th July 2001, just after the Regus bubble burst.

Regus Now Wears a Tarnished Crown

It is hard to know which is the more nauseating: the ramping of Regus by the City and media alike over the past few years that helped to drive the share price up to 392p by this February; or the rubbishing that the same folk are now dishing out to founder Mark Dixon after this week's profit warning that sent the share price tumbling this week to 50-odd pence by Thursday.

The truth about the serviced office supplier has always been apparent: Regus is an unsafe bet... Long-lease liabilities will one day sink the supplier of short-lease serviced offices... What cannot be shrugged off are long-lease liabilities... Three-quarters of rents payable are on conventional leases... Icarus's iron rule dictates that the higher a market flies in good times the faster it will fall in bad... If a downturn comes, and tenants flee, Regus will unglue.

Three of these six sentences appeared here on 4 September 1999, two weeks before Regus aborted a £250m float. The other three appeared on 30 September 2000, just before 23% of the firm was floated successfully at 260p a share. There was nothing particularly clever about what was said. It was a simple summing-up of the view held then (and now) by the property sector.

These truths are now, of course, being rediscovered by the City and commentators alike. But for three or four years it was all very different. There is none so blind as an analyst whose corporate finance team is chasing flotation fees. There is no-one so gullible as a profile writer with rags-to-riches cuttings faced with a salesman of genius. All should look back and blush.

The truth is that 41-year-old Dixon has done a fantastic job in building up a company to service a need that most property owners were too snooty to bother with. At an operating level, Regus provides a smilingly efficient service that is greatly appreciated by a customer base that may shrink, but won't go away. For that, he does deserve great praise – and the money he has made.

That lack of snootiness is one of Dixon's greatest assets. But he can be a bugger to work for, as a couple of his lieutenants testified. In 2002, Regus sponsored the Ryder Cup, and I remember sitting in the firm's tent on the eighteenth green watching Dixon acting more as maître d' than as master of the universe – unsnootily making sure everyone was being looked after.

But I also remember sitting with two of his recent senior hires, both of whom appeared shell shocked by his hard-driving work ethic. Neither of them lasted long at the company. But Regus flourished after what Dixon called in 2003 a "near-death experience".

In February 2009, I wrote something fairly positive in the *Evening Standard* ahead of a set of results that showed Regus had largely resolved its lease liability issues. Dixon dropped me a note, which ended "if you are ever down on the Côte D'Azur…". My wife, Lizzie, and I had booked a trip to Cannes in April 2009, so we took up an invitation to Sunday lunch at Dixon's fifteen-hundred-acre estate, Chateau Berne, high in the hills above St Tropez. A people carrier with the chateau's brand carried us to his weekend retreat.

You'd think a man with a global business run from his office in Monaco would want to put his feet up at the weekend. No: he bounded up from the garden in jumper and jeans, then took us on a tour of what in effect is a mid-sized business comprising hotel, cookery school, olive press and a huge vineyard. Dixon said he was determined to lift production from six hundred thousand to five million bottles a year.

ROBBIE AND VINCENT TCHENGUIZ

"I am Britain's biggest landlord," boasted Robbie Tchenguiz from the deck of his huge boat at MIPIM in 1999. Asked to explain his remark, he told me: "Because we are the freeholders of a hundred and seventy thousand residential properties." Technically, that was correct. What he and his brother Vincent owned of value was an income stream from the ground rents on these properties. The Iranian-born brothers had figured out something that others who trade ground rents hadn't seen before: you can sell the income stream.

Richard Cotton was at merchant bank JP Morgan Cazenove when he first came across the brothers, long before they became "property tycoons". (He later left the bank, in 2009, to work for fund manager Forum Partners.) At the time, he was struck by the brothers' inventiveness.

RICHARD COTTON, THEN PARTNER AT JP MORGAN CAZENOVE:

I first came across Robbie and Vincent Tchenguiz in 1991 or 1992, right in the middle of the previous downturn. James Tuckey of MEPC was selling them a couple of buildings in Croydon: Apollo and Lunar House. I remember having a conversation with them, then another on the same day with James Tuckey. They were talking completely different languages.

MEPC felt they were selling tired buildings with no potential for rental growth. The Tchenguizes didn't see it that way at all. What they saw was a twenty-year income stream from a government tenant that could be financially exploited. They weren't buying a building; they were buying an income stream with a government covenant.

That, to my mind, was a crucial point at which property moved from being an old-fashioned, rather traditional business, into an era where the financial engineers took over. The whole private equity boom that began in the late Nineties and peaked in 2007 was really modelled on the same theme: how you secure and exploit the cash flows from property.

It was the foundation of a fortune. The walls were built with debt between 2000 and 2006. In those happy days, "debt buyers" could invest £1, borrow £99, buy an office block for £100 and sell two years later for £130 – making thirty times the original stake. From here came an awful lot of capital. By 2006, the sons of the jeweller to the Shah of Iran were judged to be worth £1 billion and were being hailed as property tycoons.

It was impossible to tell what they were actually worth. But their conspicuous expenditure on cars, boats and entertaining suggested it was a very great deal. I did not board a Tchenguiz boat again until 2011 – but that's another story. In 2005, the Tchenguiz brothers were clearly flying along, but in a multitude of vehicles without windows. This leader from *EG* on 28th May gives a flavour:

Tchenguizes Should Offer a Clearer Vision

The accounts of companies controlled by Robert and Vincent Tchenguiz are as opaque as those controlled by British Land are transparent. Does this matter? In one sense, no, of course not. The brothers do not operate a public company. They are not using shareholders' money. Those that do lend are grown-ups. Those that have dared, and borrowed to the hilt, over the past seven years have won handsomely, cashing in on rising values and stable or sometimes falling interest rates. Good luck to them.

One day that luck will run out. Nobody knows when. British Land has properties worth £12.5bn and fixed debt of about £6bn. A 20% fall in prices and a 2% increase in interest rates would wound, but not kill. The brothers Tchenguiz own, at a guess, £4bn worth of assets – of which £3.6bn is debt and £400m is their own money. A similar shift in values and interest rates would see them crucified.

Or would it? The point is, nobody knows. The figures are, to repeat, simply a guess. The brothers' defence is that they operate on a different philosophy to the rest of the property industry. That their buying appraisals are based on income, not assets; that they assess value according to rents, not capital values; that each business is ring-fenced; that they are, in fact, more hedge fund than property company.

The scepticism that this defence elicits is understandable. But the fact is that there is no sign or suggestion that the brothers' archipelago of companies is badly run, or is in any sort of trouble. So they have the chance, if they wish to take it, to convince the sceptics, confound the critics and enjoy a more enduring fame than that conferred by the celebrity press. There is no need to be as transparent as BL. But published accounts with an external valuation of the assets would be nice.

On 9th November 2007, I met Vincent Tchenguiz in the light-filled boardroom of his Consensus Business Group offices, on the corner of Park Lane and Curzon Street. The lunch had been arranged following an article in the *Evening Standard* that I'd written, showing he had been forced to reduce the management charges on one of the seven hundred blocks managed by a subsidiary of Consensus. Poached salmon and tinned Diet Coke were served up, along with a most baffling presentation.

The property world was on the downward turn by November 2007. But the Tchenguizes had a new global strategy, and it was all explained in a series of PowerPoint printouts that were slid across the table. Vincent Tchenguiz talked of "green" technology transfer funds in South Africa and Abu Dhabi. He mentioned a neat way of linking military sales to green technology in Libya, which I failed to grasp. The two final slides were about leveraging the huge Consensus block management business. They were covered with a hundred and fifty or so well-known brand names.

The first, headed "Consensus Residential Estates" showed an ambition to link the company's interests in both housing and technology funds to bring "green" power and other utilities to both their own tenants and house builders at large. The second slide suggested doing much the same across the rest of world. Logos of big-name firms, ranging from British Gas via Shell and BP to the Clinton Foundation, were on display. The slide was bewildering: except to Vincent Tchenguiz.

On 9th March 2011, both brothers were arrested. More than a hundred and thirty police were involved in what was literally a dawn swoop on their homes and offices in Mayfair, ordered by the Serious Fraud Office. On 10th March, Vincent was due to turn up in Cannes to host a MIPIM party on his forty-metre yacht, *Veni Vidi Vici*. I felt it was worth going to a Tchenguiz party again. Sadly, Vincent failed to come, see and conquer the media – understandably, perhaps. The party was a lot flatter than the one I'd attended twelve years before.

The Serious Fraud Office appeared convinced of wrongdoing relating to the Tchenguizes' relationship with Kaupthing, the bust Icelandic bank. The brothers protested their innocence and began a fight-back that raised real questions over the competence and judgement of the SFO. On 31st July 2012, they had something to celebrate: a judge condemned the raids as unlawful – opening the way for Robbie and Vincent to sue the pants off the Serious Farce Office for £200 million.

SIMON HALABI

Simon Halabi's first name is apparently pronounced like the surname of the singer Nina Simone. The Syrian-born developer first came to public attention in 1997, when he bought Mentmore Towers. Halabi promised to develop a six-star hotel within this Buckinghamshire mansion, built by Baron de Rothschild in the middle of the nineteenth century.

Then in late 2002, *EG* reported that unnamed Russians had bought the premises of the In and Out Club, which was moving from Piccadilly to St James's Square. No, no, responded Halabi, in a letter on yellow paper headed "Buckingham Securities". "I have bought the building on behalf of my family trusts," he explained. The letter is as close as I ever got to Halabi. From 2000 until 2007, he flourished.

One of his first big moves was to take a stake in the Shard. This led, however, to a bitter falling-out with Halabi's two partners on the scheme,

Swedish developer CLS and Irvine Sellar. A long legal fight over the relative size of each partner's stake finally ended in December 2005, with an out-of-court settlement whereby each party agreed to take an equal one-third share. Halabi eventually sold his.

This row did not affect his reputation. Halabi built up a portfolio of London office blocks that was worth over £2 billion at its peak in early 2007. The feeling in the property market at the time was roughly this: "Okay, he is very secretive. Yes, he can be a tricky customer. But the man can lay his hands on vast sums of money and he has done some very astute deals."

This reputation allowed Halabi to do his best deal yet. In 2006, he refinanced his London office portfolio, which by then included the Aviva Tower in the City and the JP Morgan headquarters on London Wall. Prices had soared, allowing him to take out a new loan of £1.45 billion, which left plenty of spare change after paying off existing loans of around £1 billon.

But the purchase of the Esporta Health Club chain for £475 million in late 2006 proved a deal too far. In August 2007, the banks called in the administrators to run the chain. Halabi's plans for a luxury hotel on the In and Out Club site on Piccadilly also stalled. In 2008, architects Auckett Fitzroy Robinson sued for the recovery of £1.5 million in fees. Halabi countersued and won, but the dominoes had begun to fall. In the summer of 2009, Buckingham Securities went bust. That autumn, the banks took back the City properties and sold them to US Carlyle Group at a huge loss. In April 2010, Halabi was declared personally bankrupt after failing to pay back a £56 million loan to Icelandic bank Kaupthing, which had asked for a personal guarantee. Halabi was later discharged from bankruptcy,

Postscript: A French baroness of mature years once contacted me wanting to talk about Halabi. We met on a park bench in Berkeley Square, where she expounded at length on a dispute over fees she was claiming for introducing possible partners in his new nightclub venture on the Embankment to be called the Budda Bar. Could I print the story? No, but I knew a man who might. (He didn't.) The tale gave a rare glimpse into a world where people who know people get paid thousands just to connect people.

STEFANOS KOLLAKIS, AKA ACHILLEAS KALLAKIS

The man who perpetrated the biggest fraud in property history is short, portly and balding. Achilleas Kallakis, then aged forty-four, was wearing a well-cut dark suit, red tie and plain white shirt one fine day in October 2011, when I popped into Court 14 at Southwark Crown Court to see him in the flesh. I was writing a story about the man who had conned Allied Irish Bank into lending him £740 million. This money was used to buy sixteen commercial properties, including the Telegraph Group headquarters, a glassy block adjacent to Victoria Station purchased for £225 million in August 2007. This is a story of guile, greed and gullibility: the first and second sins being committed by Kallakis, the second and third by Allied Irish Bank.

Kallakis bustled around the court during the break, retreating to a private room to consult with his solicitors. He padded back in with an armful of papers to chat with his QC, George Carter-Stephenson. Then Judge Andrew Goymer appeared, and silence descended. Kallakis sat in open court looking like a helpful solicitor's clerk; alongside him sat his co-defendant, Alexander Williams, who was also aged forty-four. The pair were accused by the Serious Fraud Office of carrying out "an audacious, persistent fraud that enabled these defendants, Mr Kallakis in particular, to lead the lifestyle of the super-rich".

Prosecuting barrister Victor Temple QC then questioned an Allied Irish employee. The following exchange tells much. Victor Temple: "Tell me, Mr Banker, did you take a three-day trip to Mauritius with Mr Kallakis?" Mr Banker: "Er... yes." Victor Temple: "Tell me, Mr Banker, did that have any influence on your judgement when it came to granting loans to Mr Kallakis?" Mr Banker: "Er... no." Jury members smiled. But that jury had to be dismissed and a trial of three months collapsed, when Williams fell ill. It began again almost a year later, in September 2012. The pair were found guilty and sentenced to seven (later increased to eleven) years in the case of Kallakis and five (later increased to eight) years in the case of Williams.

Who were they? Alexander Williams (then Martin Lewis) and Achilleas Kallakis (then Stefanos Kollakis) were convicted in 1995 for selling fake "Lord of the Manor" titles to Americans. Eight years later, the artfully renamed pair made a £141 million offer for the Mayfair InterContinental Hotel and bid £57 million for an office block in Mayfair. Both deals collapsed. By 2003 (mea culpa), *EG* and others in the media were writing of the "secretive Greek millionaire" Kallakis, or, worse, the "Greek tycoon". But if *EG* wrote that Kallakis was acting as the principal, a call would come from his Mayfair office insisting we say it was for a "family trust".

Things appeared to go quiet until July 2006. Then Kallakis did three deals with three sets of brothers. He first paid Robert and Vincent Tchenguiz £100 million for Apollo House and Lunar House in Croydon, netting the pair a handsome profit. Then £75 million was paid to David and Simon Reuben in January 2007 for a twenty-three-storey tower in Vauxhall. Then came the biggie: David and Frederick Barclay sold him the Telegraph headquarters for £225 million. These three added up to a total of £400 million, spent in the final year of the boom. So why did Allied Irish Bank fund these purchases – and clearly many others that went unreported – to the tune of £740 million?

Because the man who played grandmaster-class poker under the nickname "The Don" – and who claimed to have won a million dollars at one sitting – was a world-class conman. The con worked only because bankers were both greedy for fees and gullible enough not to check carefully the credentials of a fraudster who entertained them rather too handsomely. The con was complex in execution, relying on hundreds of forged documents, at least one impersonation, and industrial-scale lying by Williams and Kallakis over at least five years.

A third person, Michael Becker, was alleged to have conspired with the defendants. The Swiss-based lawyer "was closely involved in the fraud and was director of companies presented to the banks in the loan agreements as 'borrowing companies'", said the Serious Fraud Office. "He is a Swiss national who has not been charged due to his absence from this jurisdiction."

The principle behind the fraud was fairly simple. In Hong Kong sits a large, respectable company called Sun Hung Kai Properties. It purportedly guaranteed to pay the current or an even higher rent if the occupier defaulted, thus guaranteeing or even enhancing the capital value. The firm's Walter Kwok appeared by video link from Hong Kong during the trial. Needless to say, he claimed never to have met with the defendants and said his signature on the purported guarantees had been forged.

The fraud began to unravel at the same time as the market was collapsing. German bank Helaba approached AIB in mid 2008, drawing its attention to Kallakis's conviction under another name. What?! The Irish bank hurriedly hired a private detective to investigate. On 5th September 2008 in Hong Kong, the detective discovered that the supposed guarantees from Sun Hung Kai Properties were false. By December 2008, Allied Irish Bank had seized the entire portfolio and quietly sold it off-market to Green Properties, an Irish property company run by Stephen Vernon.

The off-market deal with Vernon's firm crystallised a loss of some £60 million for Allied Irish Bank on £740 million of original loans. Bank of Scotland also lost £5.8 million: Kallakis almost persuaded the latter to lend him £29 million to convert a rust-bucket ferry into a luxury yacht, and had already filched £5.8 million before the bank realised it was a con. The final word on this case lies with the judge, Andrew Goymer, in his summing-up of the trial of Kallakis and Williams – which also sums up how things can go criminally wrong during a boom:

ANDREW GOYMER, TRIAL JUDGE:

AIB and BoS have undoubtedly acted carelessly and imprudently by failing to make full inquiries before advancing the money. Indeed, the latter bank was given clear and precise warnings by its lawyers about the risks of accepting assurances in a letter from an alleged co-conspirator, a Swiss lawyer. It almost beggars belief senior management chose to disregard that warning and rushed to complete the deal at all costs. It is apparent... both the defendants took full advantage of the prevailing banking culture in which corners are cut, and checks on them superficial and cursory...

CHAPTER NINE
AGENTS OF TRADE

*The propensity to truck, barter and exchange one thing for another
is common to all men, and to be found in no other race of animals*
Adam Smith

Agents are like regiments. They are all members of the same army. But Knight Frank is as dissimilar to CBRE as the Life Guards are to the Royal Marines, while Savills is the Queen's Royal Lancers to Jones Lang LaSalle's Dragoon Guards. Each has its own feel and traditions.

The very largest firms employ tens of thousands of people around the globe, and their roots run deep: ten can trace ancestry back to the eighteenth century; another dozen to the nineteenth. Agents are the centre of gravity of the sector: a centre that altered more in the fifteen years leading to 2012 than it had over the preceding one hundred and fifty.

Globalisation, consolidation, and boom and bust each played a part in this restructuring. *EG* published the first ever table of the top one hundred British brokers in April 1997, just six months before the agents' world began its transformation. Chesterton stood at the top of the table, ranked in terms of UK turnover. By 2012, the list would have reduced to just fifty and looked very different.

UK TURNOVER OF TOP TEN AGENTS IN 1997

The transformation of the agent community began six months after this table was first published. At the top stood Chesterton, which would later collapse in March 2005

Rank	Name	UK turnover (£m)
1	Chesterton International	75
2	DTZ Debenham Thorpe	66
3	Jones Lang Wootton	62
4	Savills	55
5	Knight Frank	42
6	Hillier Parker	40
7	Lambert Smith Hampton	38
8	Richard Ellis	34
9	Grimley	33
10	Conrad Ritblat/Colliers Erdman Lewis	28
	Total UK turnover of top ten	**473**

Source: *Estates Gazette*

MERGERS AND CONFUSING ACQUISITIONS

First off the mark was Savills, which formed an alliance with an Asian firm, First Pacific Davies, in September 1997. FPD took a twenty percent stake in Savills, which was then rebranded as FPD Savills. In April 2000, the stake was raised to thirty percent when FPD subsidiaries were fully subsumed into the UK listed company. A couple of months later, First Pacific Davies sold a third of its stake to US property management company Trammel Crow, then in December of that year sold the remainder to institutional investors.

Savills dropped the FPD brand in January 2005. An unfulfilling relationship with Trammel Crow lasted until September 2006, when CB Richard Ellis bought the property manager. Savills somehow remained Savills from beginning to end of this period: a time of extraordinary growth, during which the business multiplied fivefold in size – faster than any other firm.

The first really significant change in the market occurred in October 1997, with the first transatlantic takeover: US agent Insignia's purchase of oh-so-British Richard Ellis. What became Insignia Richard Ellis went on to absorb City firm St Quintin in 1999.

In the run-up to Christmas 1997, another American agent, CB, which had an alliance with DTZ, bid for Richard Ellis International. No, not the overseas arm of the British firm Insignia Richard Ellis, but rather its continental namesake. An entirely separate firm called CB Richard Ellis operating on the continent was born, confusing the pan-European market.

Now there were two different firms using the "Richard Ellis" tag: CB Richard Ellis and Insignia Richard Ellis. Then it gets more confusing. In July 1998, CB Richard Ellis (the overseas lot) bought Hillier Parker, an even more British business. This meant that the continental CB Richard Ellis now had a British brother called CB Hillier Parker. Hang on to that thought: it does become important.

A few months later, a third US agent entered the arena: Cushman & Wakefield took a controlling stake in its long-time associate, Healey & Baker. In the UK and on the continent, the names were merged into a mouth-filling Cushman & Wakefield Healey & Baker.

Jones Lang Wootton then stunned the agency world with the biggest deal so far. In October 1998, the world's number one agent linked up with LaSalle & Partners, a blue-blooded American real estate fund manager from Chicago. Jones Lang LaSalle was launched as an elegant new brand at the MIPIM property fair in Cannes in March 1999.

The following year the French became active, as the Vendome group, which owned agents in both France and Germany, bought Weatherall Green & Smith. Its name changed to Atis Real Weatheralls in 2001. Then everything calmed down a bit on the mergers and acquisitions front, as the market quietened after the dot-com bubble burst and the global shock of 9/11 hit.

LOCATION, LOCATION

London's Hanover Square was once to agents what Savile Row is to tailors. In 1998, Jones Lang Wootton, Knight Frank and Healey & Baker all had offices on the square, which is positioned west of Regent Street and south of Oxford Street. Nearby in Grosvenor Street stood Hillier Parker, behind stone pillars with affixed bronze nameplates still displaying its former, fuller name of Hillier Parker May & Rowden. On nearby Berkeley Square stood Richard Ellis in a brash brick block, while Savills operated from an ugly concrete building up on nearby Grosvenor Hill.

By 2012, only Jones Lang remained in Hanover Square. Healey & Baker chief Paul Orchard-Lisle said presciently in April 1999, "We've been here since 1935; I doubt whether we'll be here in 2035." Healey & Baker subsequently ended up on Portman Square as plain Cushman & Wakefield. Knight Frank meanwhile moved to Baker Street, after being priced out of an attempt to relocate to Berkeley Square. North of Oxford Street had been forbidden territory back in 1998, but times had changed.

CB Hillier Parker leased offices in Paternoster Square in the City, while Insignia Richard Ellis moved to Wimpole Street. When the two merged into CB Richard Ellis, both offices were kept. Ever-expanding CBRE moved its West End operations in 2011 to new offices behind Debenhams. Slowest to move was Savills, which had spilled over from Grosvenor Hill into marbled offices at the bottom of Berkeley Square; the entire firm was due to move into a single headquarters north of Oxford Circus in summer 2013.

Why the move away from the Mayfair heartland? "Simple, really," says John Stephen, Jones Lang LaSalle director and chairman of the England division between 2006 and 2010. "Most were operating from antiquated premises in knackered buildings unfit for use. Overseas clients in particular, used to modern, open-plan offices, could not believe how some firms occupied rabbit warrens with rows of partner offices by the windows."

So why didn't Jones Lang LaSalle move? "Hanover Square suited us for size and floor layout," says Stephen. "The twenty-five-year lease JLW signed had an upward or downward rent review clause after ten years: no one can recall why. But it proved a financial godsend when the market turned down. In the early 2000s, there were no other self-contained eighty-thousand-square-foot buildings near the Central Line at a similar rent. It wasn't perfect. But rent was a big factor, and so the firm stayed put."

JUST THE ONE SCOOP, THANKS, ARTHUR

By early 2003, the UK economy was recovering from a mild bout of depression. I was in the offices of Cushman & Wakefield Healey & Baker near the beginning of February, having a cup of tea with senior partner John Travers. (Four years later, in August 2007, the hardworking, unpretentious Welshman would suffer a fatal collapse on Ascot racecourse at the age of sixty, just weeks into his retirement.)

Into Travers' office walked his American boss, Arthur Mirante. He asked if I knew that CB Richard Ellis was about to take over Insignia Richard Ellis. Eh? Even then, I still mixed up the Ellises. Mirante said the deal was just days from being signed. It sank in that the merger would create a $2 billion business employing sixteen-and-a-half thousand staff: an enterprise that would usurp Jones Lang LaSalle at the top of the table.

This was a global merger. But from a UK perspective, the Americans who owned Hillier Parker (CB) were taking over the Americans who owned Richard Ellis (Insignia). This felt like the Queen's Royal Hussars absorbing the Royal Marines. Could the genteel folk at Hillier Parker control the less refined folk at Richard Ellis, always the more aggressive business?

The Americans running CB had anticipated this issue. Mike Strong of Insignia Richard Ellis was put in charge after a short, face-saving interlude. His compatriot Alan Froggatt had deftly absorbed St Quintin into Richard Ellis with little fuss four years earlier, and now he and Strong managed the same trick again. The combined business, CB Richard Ellis, soon took on the stronger coloration of Richard Ellis; by 2005, you could barely see the join.

I called Mike Strong after Mirante's tip-off, saying news of the takeover would be posted on the EGi website – unless he could tell me it was not true. There was no denial. A few minutes later, his media consigliore, Tony Danaher of PR firm Tamesis, confirmed the report. I wrote a few lines and pressed the button: up went the only decent scoop I ever got. And that was the last of the big transatlantic mergers.

JONES LANG LASALLE ADJUSTS, PAINFULLY AT FIRST

News of the merger between CB and Insignia hit like a thunderbolt at Jones Lang LaSalle, whose "number one" brand tag line had to be dropped. "Imagine joining the number one firm," said one Jones Lang LaSalle director. "Imagine spending your working life at the number one firm. Then along comes Richard Ellis to usurp your position. It hurt."

CB Richard Ellis staff could barely contain their delight. One senior director confided to me at the time: "I cannot tell you how wonderful this feels. I've spent my whole career so far being looked down on by those guys at Jones Lang. Now I can look down on them." Over at Jones Lang LaSalle, there was gain as well as pain, though, as the firm's John Stephen explains: "It proved to be a blessing for us. It brought about a change of culture, as we sharpened up the business and finished up being better rather than bigger than the competition."

Confidence recovered, and a period of rapid expansion followed. The firm's revenues nearly doubled in the UK between 1999 and 2003. But costs were rising faster than income, as Jones Lang LaSalle scrambled to counter CB Richard Ellis around the world. When I suggested in an *EG* leader that this was a flawed approach, a stern reprimand followed. This was delivered with style in the private dining room of a Mayfair restaurant by four senior directors, including global chief executive officer Chris Peacock.

But things still felt wobbly in early 2004. I wondered aloud whether (following Peacock's departure, for genuinely personal reasons) Jones Lang LaSalle was "having a bit of a Manchester United moment" – the football club was at the time suffering a temporary bad run of games. Some clients had begun quietly to suggest to me that the shine was coming off, resulting in this not exactly loving leader in *EG* on 14th February 2004:

Global Game Set to Cause Local Casualties

There are currently seven teams in the premier league; the top three are: CB Richard Ellis (Arsenal perhaps?), Jones Lang LaSalle (maybe Manchester United?), C&W (resurgent Chelsea?). The next four, in order, are (pick your own team) Knight Frank, ATIS REAL Weatheralls, FPDSavills and DTZ. In turnover terms, the top three have a wide lead over the next four.

CBRE is burdened with debt, but it has firmly secured the number one position and looks determined to exploit that great advantage. Jones Lang LaSalle is having a bit of a Manchester United moment. Worse, the manager's gone and the shock at not being number one has yet to wear off, but the pedigree remains and JLL will surely return to form. Cushman & Wakefield is third out of three, a weak spot but it has no debt...

At Jones Lang LaSalle, the remark stung. Director John Stephen recalls: "When I read this, I walked into [EMEA chief] Alastair Hughes' office and discussed what we needed to do. It resulted in me becoming chairman for the next six years."

UK TURNOVER OF TOP TEN AGENTS IN 2004

By 2004, the agency world had effectively globalised. UK turnover among the top ten had more than doubled in five years. But Chesterton had fallen from first to last place...

Rank	Name	UK turnover (£m)
1	FPD Savills	207
2	CB Richard Ellis	151
3	Jones Lang LaSalle	120
4	DTZ Debenham Tie Leung	118
5	Knight Frank	95
6	King Sturge	86
7	GVA Grimley	80
8	Lambert Smith Hampton	65
9	Colliers CRE	60
10	Chesterton	56
	Total UK turnover of top ten	**1,038**

Source: Estates Gazette

THE FALL OF CHESTERTON

One way or another, the agency world effectively globalised between 1997 and 2003. DTZ bought out subsidiaries in Asia, adding the names of Edmund Tie in Singapore and CY Leung in Hong Kong to the brand. Knight Frank made a loose alliance with Grubb & Ellis from America, although it fell apart later – inevitably, because the Life Guards were never going to get along with the US Marines.

Grimley joined the GVA global alliance after a merger with Donaldsons was abandoned in the summer of 2002. Lambert Smith Hampton was bought in 1999 by engineering group WS Atkins (Lord knows why) and eventually sold back to its management in 2007 for £46 million of fettering debt. By 2004, only two in the class of '97 remained corporately unaltered: Colliers and Chesterton. The latter had by this point slipped from number one to number ten in the table, but worse was to come.

I was in Cannes on 8th March 2005, the day the banks called in the receivers at Chesterton. Word flashed round the MIPIM property show. The market was on the up, and although Chesterton had long been in trouble, all had been quiet for about a year. So the collapse came as something of a surprise. Why did the agent topping the *EG* list in 1997 collapse just eight years later? The tale is long, convoluted and tragic – and could form a chapter of its own. I spent that evening in my room at the Majestic hotel boiling down a summary of the story, for a leader published on 12th March 2005:

Chesterton: A Double Century and Then Out

Believe it or not, in 1997 Chesterton topped Estates Gazette's agents league table with a UK turnover of [£75m] – [£9m] more than DTZ and [£13m] more than third-placed Jones Lang Wootton. Today, the firm lies in ruins, following eight years of poor management bordering on farce – if it were not so tragic for the hundreds of staff thrown out on the street with no pay.

On Tuesday, the 200-year-old business was hanged by its bank, RBS, and drawn by the receiver, Grant Thornton, which is now busy quartering the body and selling off choice cuts. The residential business, along with the name, is being parcelled out to an agent eager to expand its network. Five of the regional offices have gone to Atisreal. The asset management team will survive in another form. But the head and the heart have been destroyed along with 300 jobs.

Former chairman Sir William Wells must bear much responsibility for the incautious rise and start of the fall of the house of Chesterton. It was he who was the architect of the expansion that peaked with the firm's flotation in 1994, valuing the company at £51m. It was he who was in the chair in 1996 when profits collapsed and chief executive Giles Ballantine was forced to resign. It was he who brought in Michael Holmes from Rentokil.

Wells retired in 1998 after a £7m loss was posted. Holmes steadied the ship, but failed to expunge crippling lease liabilities. He left in 2001 after a profits warning. Ex-Pru executive Lorraine Baldry joined in January 2002. She had to rebuff several takeover bids and failed to bring off an MBO. A year later, she left, also defeated.

In 2003, the pace quickened. Chairman Peter Brooks – who bears responsibility for the final tangled chapter – brought in one Neil List and his partner Mike Backs. They sacked MD Tony McKay. Soon after, Mohammed Jafari-Fini, who owned 10 percent of the firm, made a bid. He was backed by a firm called Skillglass, which lent him £12.9m under stiff terms.

In September, the facilities management business was sold for £20.4m – nearly twice the price paid for the whole business. Then, in January 2004, everybody started suing everybody else. There is no space to detail this descent into farce... the brutal truth is that RBS has chosen receivership now, rather than administration, to minimise its losses... this benign time was as good as any to stop paying the bills and sell off the bits of the business worth anything.

THE SQUEEZED MIDDLE

Middle-ranking firms were feeling the squeeze by the mid Noughties. Growing optimism sparked a new round of consolidation. In late 2004, Atis Real tried to buy Nelson Bakewell. Phillip Nelson and Simon Bakewell had created the five-hundred-strong property management specialist from scratch in 1982. Atis Real wanted to pull together Nelson Bakewell staff with those from Weatherall Green & Smith, bought three years earlier.

CB Richard Ellis stepped in and spoiled the party with a counterbid of £22 million, chipped later to £18 million – then pulled the offer at the very last minute. "We were literally waiting for the money to arrive in the bank the day exchange was supposed to happen," said a Nelson Bakewell partner. "Then a call came to say CBRE had changed its mind. It was bloody infuriating. We cursed them."

The firm continued to operate successfully enough under Mike Hatt and David King until 2010, when a £10 million deal was agreed with government outsourcing giant Capita: Nelson Bakewell was no more. Hatt, King and many others subsequently left the firm; King ended up at CB Richard Ellis, Hatt at DTZ.

THE HEDGEHOG'S TALE

In 2004, the boom was gathering strength. A tale that typifies the times began with the purchase late that year of Manchester agent Dunlop Hayward by the oddly named Erinaceous. The company, whose name means "like or pertaining to a hedgehog", began life as a property management and insurance business. The hedgehog had been busy gorging on a series of acquisitions during the boom. By early 2007, it was to become a five-thousand-strong "one-stop property shop".

In April 2005, I met for lunch with Neil Bellis and his sister-in-law, Lucy Cummings, who together ran the listed company. Joining us was Bob Dyson, the gregarious boss of Dunlop Hayward, which had recently become the hedgehog's latest meal. It was a "chalk and cheese" occasion, with the real cheese being accompanied by far too much port. Cummings and Bellis were watchful, Dyson loquacious. The best-known agent in the North West chatted away about his plans, while Bellis silently swallowed port and Cummings looked from one to the other and said very little.

The relationship was never going to work. I met Dyson for a drink a couple of times the next year: he was keen to get out. In October 2007, Jones Lang LaSalle offered an exit, and Dyson became its North West chairman. Erinaceous began to breach banking covenants in late 2007; the business finally collapsed in 2008. Why? This leader from *EG* on 19th April 2008:

Hedgehog Was Always on Wrong Road

Why did Neil Bellis and his sister-in-law Lucy Cummings try to expand a sleepy but solid insurer and residential management business into a one-stop-property-shop — with the disastrous example of Chesterton smouldering in the background? Why did the Hercules-controlled firms like Dunlop Heywood Lorenz and Harman Healy, plus Millar Kitching and Egan Lawson, sell into this patently unrealisable dream?

The small battalions brought together by Bellis and Cummings to form an army with the risible aim of becoming a "top-five" property adviser have been scattered by the KPMG administrators. They are now busy clearing the Piccadilly HQ by selling these businesses for a song and bayoneting unwanted survivors.

Bellis and Cummings thought that bolting on a few advisers and then floating the boat would make them millions. "Never mind the clashing cultures. Let's get on! Build a single brand, and sell that brand. Never mind the staff, forget the moaners, think of the money we'll make, quick, quick, quick... Damn."

Money is, of course, what those who sold to Erinaceous made — at the expense of their own staff and brands. There is a great deal of sympathy for those stranded in the wreckage. In the case of those who benefited, that sympathy should be tempered by an amount proportionate to the cash they got from selling up.

Postscript: The Easter 2012 issue of *Country Life* carried a rapturous article on Isfield Place, a listed manor house north of Lewes in East Sussex. The owners were not mentioned. But the house belonged to Neil Bellis and Lucy Cummings, along with Bellis's wife, Julia. They had bought the place in 2004 for around £5 million, shouldering aside footballer Vinnie Jones in the process. Savills was instructed to sell for £9.5 million.

THE OLD SURRENDER

Other mid-ground firms enjoyed happier fates. Drivers Jonas, the world's oldest agent — formed by Samuel and Charles Driver way back in 1725 — grew rapidly during the Noughties under its thoughtful boss, the lanky Nick Shepherd. Revenues more than quadrupled between 2000 and 2009, reaching £92 million. The partners nonetheless grew apprehensive about the future, despite Drivers Jonas' profitability.

The firm freely surrendered two hundred and eighty-five years of independence in 2010 to become Drivers Jonas Deloitte, after transferring its equity to the eponymous global consultants. The Drivers Jonas tag was eliminated from the name in late 2012, giving rise to Deloitte Real Estate.

The second most venerable agent, King Sturge, was founded in 1760 as JP Sturge in Bristol. After merging with King & Co in 1992, it grew rapidly and profitably between 1997 and 2010 under Malcolm King, tireless grandson of King & Co founder Herbert King, then under his equally tireless joint heirs, ex-army officer Richard Batten and investment agent Chris Ireland.

Income rose from £24 million in 1997 to £136 million by 2010. In May 2011, Jones Lang LaSalle (which harks back to 1783) announced it was to buy King Sturge for £197 million – a scoop I fumbled and dropped. News of the deal was circulating in February, but (unlike CB Richard Ellis in 2003) Jones Lang LaSalle would not confirm. So I just stuck a couple of lines in my *Evening Standard* column on 4th February revealing the pair were "in serious talks". Both sides white-lied away until the day the deal was announced.

BIGGER WAS GENERALLY BETTER AT HOME
In 2012, it was possible to look back to 1997 and examine the UK growth of the biggest seventeen surviving agents. Some licence has been used to combine the turnover of Hillier Parker and Richard Ellis, which became CB Richard Ellis upon their 2003 merger. The figures show two things. First, the group grew more than four hundred percent over a fifteen-year period during which inflation rose by only fifty percent. Second, the bigger firms in the group generally grew faster than the smaller firms. But, for all seventeen, the property boom supercharged growth.

COMBINED UK TURNOVER OF TOP SEVENTEEN AGENTS 1997–2012

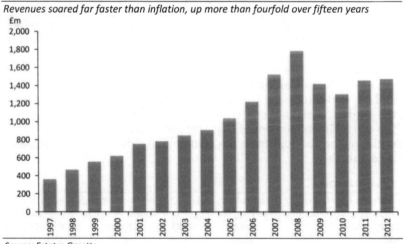

Revenues soared far faster than inflation, up more than fourfold over fifteen years

Source: Estates Gazette

Seven firms (eight, if King Sturge is considered separately from Jones Lang LaSalle) emerged in 2012 with UK turnovers over £100 million: Savills (£352 million); Jones Lang LaSalle, including King Sturge (£335 million);

CBRE (£235 million); Knight Frank (£192 million); DTZ (£134 million); GVA (£117 million); and Cushman & Wakefield (£109 million).

The average revenue growth of four hundred and twenty percent among this premier league of agents over fifteen years was skewed by the extraordinary growth of Savills, whose turnover multiplied more than sixfold between 1997 and 2012. Jones Lang LaSalle also grew sixfold in terms of revenue, but that included £135 million from King Sturge, bought in 2011. Cut Savills, and growth in this group averaged three hundred and eighty percent.

The four mid-table firms, with income of £50 million to £100 million in 2012, grew more slowly. Lambert Smith Hampton, Colliers, Strutt & Parker and Drivers Jonas Deloitte grew, on average, three hundred and twenty-five percent. Again the figure is skewed by the outperformance of one firm, Drivers Jonas, whose increase was almost sixfold. Ignoring Drivers Jonas, the growth of the remaining trio was two hundred and forty-five percent.

The final five are Cluttons, Gerald Eve, Allsop, Montagu Evans and Bidwells, the East Anglian agent. In this £25 million to £50 million bracket, turnover rose by an average two hundred and fifty percent over those fifteen years. This time the figures are skewed by Allsop, whose number one position in the auction market boosted its fifteen-year growth to three hundred and thirty percent. Remove Allsop from the table and the average fifteen-year growth of the remaining quartet is two hundred and thirty-eight percent –about the same as for the mid-league teams.

BIGGER WAS DEFINITELY BEST ABROAD

Global consolidation was over by 2005. Biggest by far was CB Richard Ellis; firmly second Jones Lang LaSalle. The top four boosted revenues by between a hundred and ninety-eight percent (Savills) and two hundred and thirty-two percent (CB Richard Ellis) in 2005–2008. The crash crimped growth. But by 2012, all four had higher revenues than in 2008: Jones Lang LaSalle outpacing the others, presumably in its determination to pursue CB Richard Ellis.

Ultimate control of Cushman & Wakefield passed in December 2006 from the Mitsubishi Corporation of Japan to Italy's Agnelli family. Savills powered on, boosted by the UK housing market and expansion in Asia. Outside the quartet, Knight Frank cruised along debt-free, making £95 million profit in 2011. Ninety percent of that was generated in the UK: half from the residential sector and half from the commercial side of the seven-thousand-strong partnership.

GLOBAL TURNOVER

These four agents more or less doubled turnover in the boom. The next four years saw variable growth rates, and Jones Lang LaSalle got a late boost from buying King Sturge

Rank 2005	Name	2005 (£m)	2008 (£m)	Change (+/- %)	2012 (£m)	Change (+/- %)
1	CBRE	1,292	3,000	(+232)	4,200	(+40)
2	Jones Lang LaSalle	637	1,365	(+214)	2,320	(+70)
3	Cushman & Wakefield	533	1,100	(+206)	1,300	(+18)
4	Savills	328	651	(+198)	806	(+23)

Source: Estates Gazette

DEBENHAM, TEWSON... ZONKED

It was a very different story at DTZ, however: the UK listed company faltered during the boom and went bust in the downturn. Shareholders lost everything, but Australian engineering services group UGL rescued the company in December 2011. Here's how it happened...

What drove one of the strongest global brands to the precipice is worthy of study by Harvard Business School. The title would be *How to Mismanage a Business Without Screwing up the Brand*. In the late Nineties, DTZ was flourishing under chairman Richard Lay, aided by his trusty lieutenant, Mark Struckett, who had been doing a good job as chief executive since being appointed in 1995. Lay retired as chairman in 2000, endorsing Struckett to his chosen successor, Tim Melville-Ross.

This tall, good-natured high-flyer had risen to become chief executive of the Nationwide in 1985, aged just forty. He left nine years later, in 1994, to run the Institute of Directors, a job he held until 1999. Who better connected to take up the chairmanship of DTZ in September 2000? All went well to start with. The numbers looked good in both 2000 and 2001. Profits were rising and confidence was high. Melville-Ross said in the summer of 2001 that DTZ had "not been affected by the downturn". What could go wrong?

Almost everything. Lay's legacy allowed DTZ to ride out the early Noughties dot-com downturn, but his departure left a visible leadership gap unfilled by the more reticent Struckett or Melville-Ross, who was part-time. Unease over the top management had begun to affect morale by 2004. Shareholders called for Melville-Ross to resign in 2005, when corporate governance adviser PIRC drew attention to his multiple chairmanships, and questioned his ability to fulfil all these roles effectively. He refused. The upturn then helped ease the strains, allowing DTZ to pursue expansion.

In 2006, $45 million was spent buying fifty percent of American investment firm Rockwood. The stake was eventually sold for cents in 2009. The high-water-mark error, however, was the purchase of Donaldsons for almost £50 million in July 2007, when unease had already begun to pervade the market.

It certainly pervaded breakfast at the Ritz on 11th July, when *EG* was invited along to meet the newly married couple. An uncomfortable occasion with little eye contact, what made it even more uncomfortable for me was the dawning sensation that what I'd said in *EG* on the previous Saturday was way off the mark:

DTZ/Donaldsons: A Good Deal, So Do It

DTZ this week posted a fine set of results – and finally confirmed that it was in talks to buy Donaldsons. The results show the somewhat reticent DTZ business is doing as well or better than its more outgoing peers. If the [£50m] deal to purchase the 700-strong retail specialist is signed, it will push DTZ pretty close to being the number one agent in the UK.... The only danger now is that this deal – said to be 99% done – won't be done quickly. But with some luck it will have gone through by the time EG is printed. With good fortune it will be done by the end of next week.

The marriage took place on the following Tuesday. The honeymoon lasted just a few months: by early 2008, the deal and the downturn was aggravating DTZ's internal divisions. A key group of staff badgered Melville-Ross with requests for Struckett to go. In June, DTZ lost its American affiliate Staubach, grabbed by Jones Lang LaSalle. I wrote a less accommodating comment on 21st June 2008:

Time, Perhaps, for DTZ to Change Its Management Style

Should DTZ group chief executive Mark Struckett consider new pastures? Maybe. Not because the business has done that badly under the tenure of the 50-year-old chief executive. Quite the opposite: Struckett has built DTZ up into a fine and solid business since he took the helm in 1995.

Between 2003 and 2007, turnover in the 11,000-strong firm doubled to £310m ... in the same five years, profits have jumped fivefold to £42m, garnered from a network of offices in 140 cities. The figures for the 12 months to April 2008 will not be so good when revealed next month. But that will hardly be Struckett's fault. Every large agent is trying to grapple with an economy that seems to take a turn for the worse on a weekly basis.

The problem is more of style than substance. While his fellow directors and counterparts at rival agents are happiest working a noisy cocktail room, Struckett prefers to work quietly in the backroom. Fine during the long boom: but in today's more challenging times there are internal worries that his style is beginning to affect DTZ's substance. Would US affiliate Staubach have defected to Jones Lang LaSalle if different personalities had been involved? Would the somewhat confusing DTZ hierarchy be this way under another chief?

Not exactly "In the name of God, go!". Struckett had apparently decided to resign weeks earlier; the *EG* comment simply brought forward the date. His departure was announced on the following Monday. There was then a brief flowering of the idea of letting DTZ's suffocated "stars" take control. But the crash was making that idea redundant: the firm needed fresh capital, way ahead of nurturing the talent.

Millions had been spent in shares and cash buying full control of the Asian businesses, run by CY Leung, who resigned in 2012 after being appointed chief executive of Hong Kong. Talks with the City on raising fresh capital were under way.

What Melville-Ross needed in 2008 was a banker: someone with City credentials; someone who would be able to repair the balance sheet and restore the profit and loss account by cutting costs. Barclays former chief operating officer Paul Idzik was given the job in November 2008. The forthright American became cordially disliked at DTZ, especially after his Barclayisation of top management.

The period between Idzik's appointment in November 2008 and his resignation in August 2011 were dark times for DTZ staff. But without Idzik, DTZ would not have been able to raise £48.7 million in January 2009 to repair the sins of past profligacy. He also turned a loss of £35 million in 2009 into a slim profit in 2010 through savage cost-cutting.

The French Mathy family had built up a fifty-five percent stake in DTZ by 2008 through Saint Georges Participations, a subsidiary of their construction and investment business. Why the Mathys chose to buy into DTZ remains a mystery. They were French; BNP Paribas owned what was once Weatherall Green & Smith – perhaps the French bank and the Mathys were hoping to form a countervailing Gallic force against the growing dominance of Anglo-American agents. That was the rumour. Who knows? The Mathys' loss – estimated at between £150 million and £180 million – was crystallised in December 2011, when Australian engineering group UGL paid £94 million to rescue DTZ.

All that money went to pay off bank debts. The shareholders, including many staff and former staff, got nothing. By the autumn of 2012, the company had been integrated into UGL. Happily, the clients had remained largely loyal – to the staff. Although many of the staff had gone, those that stayed had preserved the good name of the company. UGL found the DTZ brand was far stronger than its own brand. (Add a Y and you'll see why.) So much so, that twenty thousand, five hundred UGL employees were folded in with the remaining five-and-a-half thousand DTZ staff to form "DTZ – a UGL group company" under a cool blue logo. A much larger DTZ was reborn.

"I am delighted that DTZ found such a satisfactory home," says former chairman Richard Lay. "But I was greatly saddened by the preceding events. The board failed to exercise proper control of the business." Lay says that Struckett should not take all the blame: "It is too simplistic to put the whole responsibility for the decline onto one man's shoulders." He faults the directors for the appointment of Struckett's successor, saying, "Whether the board was then right to appoint a total outsider such as Paul Idzik must be a matter for debate."

PAY – THE BOSSES

At 4.30pm on a Thursday in late April 2007, an hour before *EG*'s final pages were due to go to press, our lead news story fell apart. We urgently needed a replacement. Poking around a website called Edgar, belonging to the US Securities and Exchange Commission, I discovered that Jones Lang LaSalle had just filed its compensation statement for 2006. The earnings of six senior directors were there, down to the last dollar. We cut and pasted the table into the page, added a few words and whipped the story off to the printers.

On the Monday I got a call from the firm's EMEA boss, Alastair Hughes, who had featured in the list. His proud mother had rung from Scotland after being alerted by a neighbour to the story. This showed that her son's total compensation was $2,224,247. Peanuts compared with Lynn Thurber, the chief executive of the LaSalle division ($6,406,801) or the group's quietly effective English chief executive, Colin Dyer, whose pay and bonus totalled $4,636,165. Their basic salaries ranged from $325,000 to $750,000; the rest was made up from stock awards and bonus plans. Not quite so eye-watering as Alastair's mum might have thought.

CBRE bosses are equally well rewarded. In 2011, global chief executive Brett White received total remuneration of $11.1 million, and EMEA chairman Mike Strong $1.8 million. The ebullient chief executive of Savills, Jeremy Helsby, earned £1.6 million in 2012.

The rewards from running listed companies are clear to see. The pay and rations of those holding equity in partnerships used to be a mystery. But by the mid Noughties, all the big property partnerships had converted to limited liability partnership status, which brings the obligation of publishing financial reports. In 2007, *EG* asked accountants BDO Stoy Hayward to draw up a table of earnings. They produced figures in terms of "operating profit per member" – for member, read equity partner, but either way the figure is more akin to "average dividend per shareholder".

LIMITED LIABILITY PARTNERSHIP EARNINGS 2006

Partners' take-home pay is not quite the same as 'operating profit per member', but those holding equity in the top firms earn between £200,000 and £700,000 a year

	Year-end 2006	Operating profit per member (£)	Number of members	Total operating profit (£m)	Highest salary paid to a single member (£)
Knight Frank	30 Apr	1,280,500	32	40.98	1,212,000
King Sturge	30 Apr	659,175	57	37.57	2,200,000
GVA Grimley	30 Apr	656,426	68	44.64	867,000
Allsop	30 Apr	375,545	34	12.58	845,040
Montagu Evans	31 Mar	295,417	56	16.54	1,221,000

Source: Estates Gazette/BDO Stoy Hayward

What gets transferred into the member's bank account can be very different. The single "member" with the highest salary tends to be the senior partner, but not necessarily – the £2.2 million paid at King Sturge went to head of investment Philip Marsden. In 2011, the average pay of an equity partner at Knight Frank was £500,000, but in 2010 its highest-paid member received £1.48 million. Partners' pay tends to track earnings in the "thinking professions" such as accounting and law. A quiet chat with one senior partner revealed the pay band for partners in a typical large firm in 2012 as £200,000 to £700,000 – about the same as for lawyers or accountants.

PAY – THE WORKERS

Working as a commercial agent pays twice the average wage in bad times and close to three times during a boom. In 2005, the average wage in Britain was £381 per week, while average weekly pay in commercial property firms was £1,082, or almost three times as much. In 2012, average pay in Britain was £469 per week, while the average agent earned almost exactly twice this, at £936. This slipping-back from three times to twice the average wage is partly accounted for by post-boom salary cuts.

These figures are derived from government statistics and twenty years of salary surveys carried out by *EG*. Mr Average puts in regular appearances in the property salary surveys, Mrs Average less so. But in 2005, the pair appeared together as amalgams of the two thousand or so agents who responded to the survey.

EARNINGS BY MR AND MRS AVERAGE PROPERTY IN 2005
- The average man is thirty-nine and has annual earnings of £56,300.
- He'll get a bonus of £11,450 on fee income of £184,950.
- The average woman is thirty-four and has annual earnings of £35,760.
- She'll get a bonus of £4,140 on fee income of £132,970.

Mr Average suffered a series of pay cuts after 2008. By 2010, he was earning a basic salary of £48,721 a year – a thirteen percent decrease over five years. His bonus had halved to £5,884. He took a further four percent cut in 2011, down to £46,738. But that's only the average; the table from the 2012 survey gives a more detailed picture of falling pay.

And there is one notable oddity in the 2012 figures: investment agents were earning less than development agents at this time. That is not normally the case, and may have happened simply because there was little investment activity – while development activity was just starting to take off. Either way, the figures show the continuing squeeze on pay in a flat market, with both average pay and bonuses well down.

AVERAGE PROPERTY SALARIES IN 2012

Almost everyone in commercial property was earning less, on average, than in 2011

Job type	Pay (£)	(vs 2011, £)	Bonus (£)	(vs 2011, £)
Asset manager	51,772	(58,090)	6,314	(7,694)
Corporate	51,270	(64,650)	4,531	(10,570)
Development	48,228	(51,670)	7,616	(6,782)
Investment	46,530	(47,280)	10,861	(15,992)
Valuation	37,420	(36,580)	2,983	(2,205)
Management	37,380	(44,480)	2,098	(4,198)
General practice	35,100	(38,650)	1,668	(2,821)

Source: Estates Gazette/Foundation Recruitment

Many toil on less, while a few of those at the top earn a great deal more. I've no idea how much, beyond suggesting that remuneration of top agents in London will be comfortably into six figures, or seven figures in a handful of cases. In niche practices, the partners *are* the brand. But even in the biggest firms, some individuals hold strong sway over clients that would follow them rather than stick with the brand.

I don't know with how much remuneration Jones Lang LaSalle's then EMEA boss, Alastair Hughes, tempted Neil Prime to defect from rival Knight Frank. All I know is that Hughes was at Wimbledon when he got a text from Prime turning down an offer, whereupon Hughes immediately left the tennis. He took a taxi to Prime's home and persuaded him to change his mind.

I have no idea how much Digby Flower of CBRE was earning before he was wooed away by Cushman & Wakefield in 2012. But his value to C&W can be judged by the fact that the wooing was done by Carlo Sant'Albano, the chairman of the board of the world's biggest privately held agent. When I had breakfast with the quietly spoken Italian in late 2012, he told me he regarded the plucking of Flower as being highly significant for C&W, because it was seen as being a bit weak in central London. So much so that Flower reported directly to Sant'Albano.

AND SO TO LUNCH...

I'd met a couple of senior partners from the big agents soon after joining *EG* in September 1997 as editorial director: coffee with the reserved and kindly Don Newell of Hillier Parker in his wood-panelled office in Grosvenor Street; lunch with ramrod-backed disciplinarian Paul Orchard-Lisle of Healey & Baker. I'd invited the latter to the Reform Club for 12.30pm, and he strode in looking at his watch as the clock chimed the half-hour. Fifteen years later, in 2012, I was having lunch in Wiltons with Land Securities chief executive Rob Noel. In the corner, aged seventy-four, sat the still ramrod-backed – and still influential – Orchard-Lisle.

A jarring early encounter was with Michael Holmes of Chesterton. This occurred in May 1998, during my first week of editing the magazine after seven months as editorial director. Chesterton was in trouble. A profit warning had been issued the previous November, and merger talks with support services group Summit had just collapsed.

The outgoing *EG* editor, Helen Pearce, had speculated in her final leader on the magazine that the deal with Summit had collapsed because the buyer had found an "almighty skeleton" in Chesterton's financial cupboard. She left the day before the magazine appeared on the Saturday; I dropped into her job on the Monday.

That very day I was commanded to appear before Holmes, threatened with the Press Complaints Commission – and, far, far worse, libel lawyers. Not a good start. I'd attracted five libel writs while editing *Building* magazine; I didn't want another. Fortunately, Britain's biggest agent at the time had a levelheaded press officer by the name of Graham Downie, who brokered a settlement: I would grovel in my first leader for *EG*, and Chesterton would not sue. I grovelled.

It got easier. There was lunch at the Ritz with Arthur Mirante of Cushman & Wakefield. Baroness Thatcher sat nearby, at a corner window table. As she rose from her table and began to leave the room, other diners broke out in spontaneous applause. Heady stuff. I'd been used to plainer fare in plainer surroundings during my ten years at *Building* magazine between 1985 and 1996.

Between editing *Building* magazine and *EG*, I spent what turned out to be a difficult "gap year" working in the City. This was at Flemings, then a family-owned merchant bank. My boss was wonderful. Tom Hughes-Hallett was head of broking, with so large a remuneration that he was nicknamed Tom Huge-Wallet. He left to become head of the Marie Curie cancer charity and was knighted in 2012: one of the truly great and good. But I had a truly bad below-stairs job at Flemings: trying to persuade cleverer-than-me analysts to write notes that not-so-clever-as-them fund managers could understand. I failed.

I was therefore very grateful to return to journalism, especially to the warm embrace of the property sector. And so it went on, over those first few years: lunches with John Martin, the ironic and humorous senior partner at Knight Frank; with Johnny Nettleton, the roly-poly boss of Donaldsons, a genuine English eccentric with a liking for claret who collected lawnmowers;

and with opera buff Alistair Voaden of Grimley – a man of great civility who invited my wife Lizzie and me to Glyndebourne. He continued to do so for many years. There was also Aubrey Adams, the perma-tanned chief executive of Savills, perhaps the most successful agency boss of his generation. Utterly charming, Adams moved the business up into the premier league with seeming lack of effort.

There was one lunch with Tim Melville-Ross of DTZ, but many more with director Robert Peto, the public face of DTZ for many of the Struckett years: an open and cultured character, given to wearing a bow tie when happy and a normal tie when not. I even had a kiss-and-make-up lunch with Chesterton's Michael Holmes in 1999. Six months later came a letter from the Press Complaints Commission rejecting Chesterton's complaint. I assume Holmes had forgotten to withdraw the grievance.

There were many meetings with Malcolm King of King Sturge, but one that I missed. He'd promised to fly me back to England from MIPIM in his own (small) plane, but I'd grandly assumed a car would roll up at the Majestic hotel in Cannes to whisk me to Nice airport. No such luck, and I missed the plane, which took off from Cannes airport.

But later came a trip to Islay, where Malcolm owned a (small) hotel and tufty golf course. I ended up in the foetal position after a rather heavy night and eighteen wind-blown holes the following morning. He went out and played another nine. There were regular lunches for *EG* in the dining room at Knight Frank's offices, and many across the road at Jones Lang LaSalle in Hanover Square...

The agency world felt open, welcoming and friendly. It seemed to me I'd landed the best job ever. The only thing I had to watch out for was becoming sucked in by the welcome, and turning into a cheerleader rather than a cool-eyed spectator. It was never easy.

Sometimes I went too far one way and was too nice. More often I'd go the other way, being overcritical. An example involves the Windsor Club, a group to which the top dozen individual agents belong and which takes its name from the town where meetings were first held. The official agenda includes items of innocent mutual concern, such as training and education. It would be a mistake to conclude there is much collusion. I put it to one member that it would be easy to fix pay and divide up work. He snorted: "It would be easier to herd a group of stray cats."

"The Windsor Group isn't perfect," says former Jones Lang LaSalle UK chairman John Stephen. "But it allows senior folk at the big firms to have a decent working relationship with their counterparts. One aspect of the UK agents' world is that despite intense competition there remains a special camaraderie, unlike any other profession."

The group certainly reached a friendly accord on one point in the autumn of 2008: *EG*, they all agreed, was being extremely critical. True, the world economy was in a state of collapse; nevertheless, it was not sporting of *EG* to attack the suffering. So Robert Peto of DTZ was deputed to deliver a reprimand. It was deserved: I knew that I was going to retire in early 2009, even if no one else did, and I'd begun to freewheel. We'd made some stupid reporting errors at the magazine, I had to admit. Peto was an ideal choice as messenger, for he is impossible to take against. I paid for lunch; then passed on the pain to the news desk.

To the enduring credit of the agency community, I was never threatened with any commercial consequences from causing them grief on a fair number of occasions during my eleven years in the job. How easy it would have been for someone to say, "Now look here, you: we spend a lot of money advertising with *EG*. I think you should be more careful what you say." But such a thing was never said, even during the crash, when negative stories were appearing weekly.

CRASH, BANG AND BACK AGAIN

MIKE STRONG, EMEA CHAIRMAN AT CBRE:

We felt that the market was completely overheated by July 2007. We were getting feedback from the US that the capital markets in the US had all but stopped operating. The first warning signs on sub-prime had come prior to that. Nobody really knew what sub-prime was all about. But we knew from experience that if it stops in the US, it stops in the UK, maybe six months later.

We had a management meeting in late July 2007, which we picked up again early in September, at which it was decided to produce a contingency plan to start reducing the costs. When we produced this plan we were actually still on track for a record year. Then very early in 2008 I called a European board meeting at which the continental businesses said they were still doing fine. I said: "Look, it will not be fine for very much longer."

The view round the table was, "This is a US/UK problem, an Anglo-Saxon problem." I said: "I'm sorry, there is no outcome that leaves the continent unscathed." We took action to reduce our costs. But we didn't know how bad it was going to get. In the event, we didn't do enough, because it simply went on getting worse.

But by the time of Lehman Brothers in September 2008, we had implemented plans to take the cost of the business right down. We took out huge amounts of discretionary spending. Unfortunately, this is a business where the biggest cost is people; regrettably, a lot had to go. Between 2008 and 2009, CB Richard Ellis reduced operating costs in the EMEA region by $230 million: that's a total reduction of some thirty-five to thirty-eight percent. You name it, it was cut.

JEREMY HELSBY, CHIEF EXECUTIVE OF SAVILLS:

We started to dramatically cut costs at the end of 2007. So by the first half of 2008, we were right into it. As a result, we took out £37 million of costs that year, and another £40 million or so in 2009. You knew things were going wrong when Irish investors be-

*gan buying secondary shopping centres at yields as low as five per-
cent: in other words, the yield gap between prime and secondary
had vanished. That was at a time when you felt the banks were
simply going to wake up one day and realise this couldn't go on.*

SILENCE OF THE RESEARCH LAMBS

The picture began to darken in the summer of 2007. But it took twelve
months for many agents to admit this in public. Part of the problem was that
revenues were still rising. In November 2007, both CB Richard Ellis and
Jones Lang LaSalle produced strong figures for the July-to-September quarter. The latter's UK revenues were up by twenty-three percent over the same
period a year earlier. Across the globe, the figure was thirty-five percent.

Between July and December 2007 , the IPD all-property capital value
index fell twelve percent. The man in the street was beginning to panic and
take money out of property unit trusts. Early 2008 was an odd time, a false
dawn. While the index continued to fall, losing a further nine percent of its
value in the first half of 2008, there was a general feeling the worst was over
– although that didn't last much beyond the spring, when US bank Bear
Stearns went under. Fund managers were buying in the market; sentiment
brightened. But none of that excuses what happened next – or, to be more
accurate, what didn't happen.

Agents employ large teams of forecasters. During 2008, most refused
to forecast. "Nobody wants to go first, and nobody wants to spook the clients" was how it was put to me time and again between the spring and autumn of 2008. We'd sit there at lunch, agreeing that the market was going to
hell in a handcart. But would their research departments say so in public?
No. It was shameful. In 2007, values fell twelve percent. In 2008, they lost
twenty-seven percent. In 2009, they decreased by a further thirteen percent.
Between June 2007 and June 2009, the average capital value of property fell
forty-five percent. Yet during the critical period of spring to autumn 2008,
there was a resounding public silence from the big agents, who were supposed to be taking the pulse of the market.

The big lesson for the next downturn is: don't rely on the big agents
to publicly call the market. They have far too much to lose. (Tip: ask them
over lunch instead.) It took the smaller firms to blow the whistle. "Big agents
have gone very quiet on the rental outlook for the square mile" was how,
in an *EG* leader on 26th April 2008, I expressed mild frustration at this
omerta, continuing: "But that has not stopped Drivers Jonas and NB Real
Estate from issuing some really horrible numbers on the amount of unlet
space now hitting the market."

Lambert Smith Hampton recorded the largest outward shift in property yields a week or so later. The last week in April was also the week in
which the first redundancies among agents were announced; "the air quivers
with rumours of mass layoffs" was my overcoloured view. In mid June of
2008, DTZ fired fifty of its eighteen hundred UK staff.

Its rivals were still half-heartedly denying any cutbacks, when asked
by *EG* to respond to the flood of rumours. "We will carefully control costs,"

said Alastair Hughes of Jones Lang LaSalle. "We have looked into all areas in terms of costs," said Jeremy Helsby of Savills, "as you would expect in a challenging market." CB Richard Ellis's Martin Samworth responded: "We have no redundancy programmes in place," while Alistair Elliott of Knight Frank said he was "not anticipating" sweeping redundancies at the firm.

At the time, *EG* was preparing to celebrate its hundred-and-fiftieth anniversary. To mark this momentous event, a special supplement (a whole year in the making) was to be published, and a dinner for three hundred at St James's Palace was scheduled for 29th May 2008. The Duke of Edinburgh was to come as guest of honour, and we were aiming to raise well over £100,000 for the Duke of Edinburgh's Award charity.

The money was to come from selling twenty-eight of the thirty tables of ten for £7,000 each. In 2006, we would have sold the lot in a week. The first invitations went out just before Christmas of 2007, and it was not until a week before the event, five months later, that the last table sold. It was scary. The slow takeup was an unmistakeable marker of a slowing market.

It turned out to be a wonderful night. Prince Philip was on fine form; so much so that it took forty minutes rather than the scheduled twenty to chaperon him around the reception. The world-class josher was halted only at the end by solicitor Susan Freeman, of Mishcon de Reya – the firm that arranged Princess Diana's divorce from Prince Charles. Freeman stepped in front of us, and I gave an introduction. Prince Philip replied, without missing a beat. "Ah, you do property *as well*, do you?"

The dinner was spread through three rooms, ten tables in each. Who got the best and who got the worst tables? In the end, it was easy to decide: we allocated them by the date on the cheques that oh-so-slowly arrived. Land Securities got the best table, closest to the duke. I think it's now safe to name Alistair Subba Row of Farebrother as getting the furthermost table.

THEN, THE GREAT, BIG BANG...

When Lehman Brothers collapsed on 15th September 2008, agents finally stopped pretending. Many had been making cutbacks for months, but now deeper cuts requiring general redundancy warning notices to be issued began to happen. On 19th September, up to a hundred DTZ staff received notices. CB Richard Ellis also began to issue notices.

The *EG* league tables for 2008 had been published two months earlier. They showed revenues had risen eleven percent to £2.8 billion among the top sixty-nine firms since 2007. Yes, *risen*: for two reasons. First, the year-ends of many in the table were between December 2007 and April 2008 – too soon to catch the big downturn. Second, many customers were busy buying and selling right up to the day Lehman Brothers collapsed.

The broking market virtually froze in the last three months of 2008. I asked one City agent how on earth he was occupying his time. He replied as follows: "I stay out of the bloody office as much as possible and hope nobody notices I've got nothing to do except drink coffee with rival agents who also have nothing to do."

During the first quarter of 2009, almost every top-twenty agent – including DTZ, Cushman & Wakefield, Colliers CRE, Strutt & Parker, Drivers Jonas and Savills – announced formal redundancy programmes. Some imposed salary cuts averaging ten percent. Montagu Evans was brave enough to spell out why. "These measures are aimed at managing our cash flow, so we are not reliant on an overdraft facility," said managing partner Clive Riding. "The intention is to keep the teams together."

The extent of the damage was exposed in the 2009 *EG* league tables, published that September. Revenues were down by seventeen percent, or £500 million, to £2.3 billion among the sixty-six firms listed. The number of fee earners fell by eighteen hundred, down to fourteen thousand, six hundred. These falls ended twelve years of uninterrupted growth. Eighty percent of the agents admitted to making redundancies, while a third said more staff would go in 2010. Savills took sixteen fresh graduates that year, down from sixty-five; Knight Frank took nine instead of forty.

AND BACK AGAIN

A further fifteen hundred job losses were recorded in *EG*'s 2010 survey, again published in the September, taking the total number of fee-earner jobs lost over two years to three thousand, three hundred – a decrease of around twenty percent. But total revenues fell far less steeply in 2010, by just 6.5 percent. Respondents thought the worst might be over, and half said they hoped for higher revenues in 2011. This hope was fulfilled when a year later the top ten firms reported a rise of ten percent in revenues, with five hundred new jobs being created. But the recovery proved to be what the City calls a "dead cat bounce" – in other words, not much of a bounce.

In 2012, revenues among the UK's top ten property firms rose a tiny 1.2 percent. The mood again turned cautious, although not all that cautious. "You could argue this industry is ripe for consolidation," said CBRE's UK managing director, Martin Samworth, who was promoted to run the firm's European business that October. CBRE had just snapped up niche agent Franc Warwick, along with partner Franco Sidoli – about the best investment agent of his generation.

In September 2012, the top ten list of UK agents looked very different from its appearance in 1997. Capita Symonds had joined the list, after absorbing Nelson Bakewell. Only three others had survived since 1997 untouched by takeover, merger, partial sale or receivership. All three have strong residential brands: Savills and Knight Frank arguably the strongest in the world; the third is Strutt & Parker.

Strutt & Parker had stood just outside the table, at number eleven, back in 1997. It bought agent Lane Fox in 2007 – not great timing, but the deal did help promote the firm to number nine in the table. Rising house prices in London tempted both CBRE and Jones Lang LaSalle to set up residential divisions by 2012 – not for trading secondhand homes; Lord, no! – rather, to use their global connections to sell off-plan flats in the booming London market.

UK TURNOVER OF TOP TEN AGENTS IN 2012

Since 1997, only three among the original top ten had escaped takeover, merger, partial sale or receivership: Savills, Knight Frank, and new entrant Strutt & Parker

Rank	Name	UK turnover (£m)
1	Savills	352
2	Jones Lang LaSalle	336
3	CBRE	236
4	Knight Frank	192
5	DTZ	135
6	GVA	117
7	Cushman & Wakefield	109
8	Drivers Jonas Deloitte	86
9	Strutt & Parker	81
10	Capita Symonds	72
	Total UK turnover of top ten	**1,716**

Source: Estates Gazette

Many firms have survived happily since 1997 outside the top ten. Niche practices in particular flourished, many of their partners earning way more than their counterparts at larger rivals. Tony Gibbon, Tony McCurley and Neil Scambler at GM Real Estate in the City of London are good examples; another was Franco Sidoli at Franc Warwick, until he succumbed to CBRE in 2012. John Stephen describes Sidoli as "a real force, taking many of the sales big agents would have previously secured".

Consolidation was the theme of those fifteen years to 2012. The theme of the last five years was recovery, as illustrated by this final table. In 2007, the firms listed here were at their peak in terms of revenue. Then the crash hit. But come 2012, the quintet had recovered pretty well. The collective number of fee earners had grown by nearly five hundred to reach six thousand, three hundred – an eight percent rise – although the average fee per fee earner was down by £9,000 to £201,000.

AVERAGE FEE PER FEE EARNER, 2007 AND 2012

By 2012, the number of fee earners was up. But for all except Cushman & Wakefield, the average fee per fee earner was down

Company	2012		2007	
	Fee earners	Average fee (£)	Fee earners	Average fee (£)
Savills	1,814	194,000	1,691	198,000
CBRE	1,137	207,000	1,073	230,000
JLL/King Sturge	2,003	168,000	1,728	202,000
Knight Frank	821	234,000	807	249,000
Cushman & Wakefield	527	204,000	529	170,000
Total/average fee	**6,302**	**201,000**	**5,828**	**210,000**

Source: Estates Gazette

REFLECTIONS

MIKE STRONG, EMEA CHAIRMAN AT CBRE:

In 1997, there were ten of us doing much the same thing. But a small number of firms had international aspirations. We did, at Richard Ellis; so did JLW, Healey & Baker and DTZ. Big corporates were globalising; the banks were globalising. The real estate industry wasn't globalising, because developers were inherently local. But we could see the big funds, the global banks and international occupiers wanted a single service provider in one region, or globally.

Richard Ellis had built a business in Europe; it wasn't too bad. We had built a business in Asia, which wasn't too bad either. We had those markets covered. But we didn't have America. We had tried and failed on our own in the US. So in 1997 we made a conscious decision to seek a US partner. JLW were doing exactly the same thing. They ended up joining LaSalle; we joined Insignia. European aspirations met US aspirations, and new global firms were born.

There was also investment capital going all round the world needing advice. And it really did look possible to connect up all these markets horizontally through clients. That's what it was all about. The Americans brought to the party ability and capital to complete the global expansion. They also brought access to a huge depth of American clients. Many have now become clients of the rest of the organisation in Europe and Asia. We didn't have this before.

NICK THOMLINSON, SENIOR PARTNER AT KNIGHT FRANK SINCE 2004:

We quadrupled turnover at Knight Frank between 1997 and 2009. I think there was a general push for growth – partly driven by events, shall we say, because everyone was growing, weren't they? I mean not just our industry but the whole world was growing. But we'd also perhaps been a bit slow in the Nineties.

A lot of the growth came from opening more residential offices, which we needed to do. We also became a bit braver than we had been in the past on the commercial side of things. We felt that we were slightly a slumbering giant – "giant" may not be the right word; a slumbering animal perhaps – and actually we needed to pick up our game and go for it a bit more, be braver.

Becoming a limited liability partnership in 2003 helped. It made us act slightly more corporately in running ourselves. But it can be interesting having sixty-one shareholders, all wanting a say in how the business is run. There is a very strong feeling against selling the partnership and turning corporate. We have looked at it from time to time. But the thing is with selling: you just get one shot at it.

The guys in their thirties have the possibility of equity taken away forever. One has to be careful not to sound pious, but I think there is a feeling that you hold the partnership in trust for future genera-tions. You can't blame those who have sold: the lure of the mighty greenback or the pound is strong. To be fair, if you're a partner aged fifty-nine and you're having to retire in a year's time and someone says you can either have a million pounds or nothing, I think most people would take the million.

JEREMY HELSBY, CHIEF EXECUTIVE OF SAVILLS SINCE 2008:

We focused on profit. We were never trying to be big. Our turnover had grown, but the strategy was to grow the bottom line. We weren't chasing turnover; we were chasing profitable growth... and we've been very, very strong in following the capital. What we've been consistently good at is working out who's got the money and where they're going to spend it, and then helping them spend it. One of the good things about Savills, as most people will tell you, is that it's got a unique culture. It has been very strong, very performance-driven. I would say we are a collection of like-minded entrepre-neurs. So we try and give everyone the benefits of running their own businesses – which everyone wants – but overlaying that with the Savills brand and the global platform.

ALASTAIR HUGHES, HEAD OF EMEA AND THEN ASIA AT JONES LANG LASALLE:

I joined Jones Lang Wootton in 1988, and worked for ten or eleven years in various departments. Then our merger with LaSalle was announced in 1999. I was a salaried partner at the time. It was quite a change to be told that you'll leap from a partnership to a public company overnight. To merge two businesses is also a really difficult thing. JLW was a very kind of "British Empire" sort of firm, sending English chaps off abroad to build businesses. It's not quite like that now, but there is still a deep culture at the firm.

LaSalle was not materially different. The good thing about LaSalle is that they are a Chicago-based practice. This might be a massive generalisation, but Chicago people (to me) are about as close to a British type of culture as you get in America. They are not out-and-out New York-style brokers, nor are they touchy-feely West Coast types. They're just Midwestern, earnest guys trying to do the right thing. That helped a lot.

They were nice people to deal with from day one. They didn't do much broking – mostly investment management and corporate out-sourcing. What was also different was that JLW was a landlord-facing business; LaSalle looked at the world more through an occu-pier lens. Then we were Europe and Asia, and they were America. It took time to get to the point where we all acted as one business.

We also had to adjust from being the largest firm to the second-largest, with the formation of CBRE. There's one word that we used to suffer from – and we don't suffer from it anymore – which is a very insidious word in our industry: "arrogance". In the late Eighties we had that – and I don't say that with any pride; it's not a good thing to have. Now we've got used to having to prove to everybody that we are worthy of each job.

DTZ had an aspiration to be the third global player and were quite strong in the UK, Europe and Asia but had no presence in the world's biggest market, the USA. Then they used around £50 million – a lot of money – to buy Donaldsons, which was eighty percent UK. I could never understand that.

I think Savills has a unique way of looking at the world. I've got a lot of respect for them. They don't aspire to be like us; we don't aspire to be like them. So there's not really any angst between us. I often think that if JLW had not gone public and gone global we might have ended up a little bit like a middle-class Knight Frank. That's not particularly where we want to be.

Being run by partners is not easy. I remember we had a post-merger meeting of the old equity partners: we spent ages talking about what the agenda should be, and then two of them had to leave to see clients, so that set us back; then others arrived late and started arguing the toss about the agenda! Being a corporate entity is not perfect, but at least decision-making is well defined, with less competing personal agendas and politics than in a partnership.

RICHARD LAY, FORMER CHAIRMAN OF DTZ:

When Blair came in in 1997, it was after a period of political inaction and ineptitude. But I don't think the year was particularly important from our point of view, other than the fact that we were able to continue to grow DTZ in an economic climate that appeared fairly secure. Our board recognised that we needed to develop our UK business by forming a linkage with an American company in order to have access to American investment funds and corporates.

Amongst those we talked to was LaSalle, while they were in final negotiations with Jones Lang. We decided not to do a deal with them, and probably couldn't have done so anyway. We were also talking to CB at the time and didn't particularly want to complicate those discussions. It was not clear to us that there would be a direct benefit of being owned and run by an American organisation, and we thought we could do it on our own, and create a UK-based global business, bringing in America on the sideline rather than being totally dominated by them.

We spread our international influence by linking with CY Leung in Hong Kong and Edmund Tie in Singapore. CY had one of the few operating licences in China. With these two moves, we had successfully built an international business. I also remember talking to Andrew Farkas of Insignia, who was staying at Claridge's. He got into a chauffeur-driven car and said, "Take me to 46 Brook Street." After a few seconds, Farkas asked, "Why have we stopped?" "You're here, sir," said the chauffeur, opening the door outside our offices. Farkas was a very personable guy, charming and very amusing. The meeting was just before he did a deal with Richard Ellis.

That was a good deal for Richard Ellis, because they had difficulty staying where they were. He was clearly just checking the market with us, so he could say to his board, "I've talked to DTZ." CB then decided to take over Hillier Parker. I must confess we didn't lose a great deal when CB detached themselves from us. All that we had had was a joint venture, which had worked reasonably, but not spectacularly well. But our critical Far Eastern contacts were secure, and we looked upon these as vital to our future development.

We did need to have access to American capital and also be a point in Europe to which American corporates would come. We then found other ways to achieve it. We asked ourselves whether we actually needed to be taken over to achieve that objective. And we decided that no, we didn't need that. What we did do was to seek to develop our Asian connections by building on our relationship with CY Leung in Asia. He was clearly going to go places, and so we cemented our link with him, seeing that as being the key area for long-term growth for the company, which it plainly still is today. That proved to be the right long-term move.

AND FINALLY...

ANDY MARTIN, SENIOR PARTNER AT STRUTT & PARKER SINCE 2009:

The quantum leap for agents in the Seventies and Eighties was when pension funds entered the property market and demand for investment advisory services grew. Every firm of any size had retained clients among pension and life funds; for instance, when I was at Bernard Thorpe it was the Post Office Staff Superannuation Fund (Possfund) and the Co-operative Insurance Society.

Property started to become a more important direct investment class in that era, and demand to invest overseas helped grow huge international businesses. In the early stages of this new investment era, Richard Ellis was the biggest in this area and had an important influence on the institutional investment market. When I spent some time there, they probably had the best systems in the market.

Agents grew, and we began then to see the emergence of the listed entity: Fletcher King, Wright Oliphant, Debenham Tewson Chinnocks, Chesterton's and, probably the most successful private-to-public entrant, Savills. Following this, the insurance sector started to consolidate in the early Nineties recession and started to create their own fund management businesses.

All of a sudden, from Strutt & Parker's point of view, General Accident, who were our big investment client, were merged with Commercial Union Properties, who then merged into Norwich Union. Investment agents began to lose a lot of these retained mandates, as the management of the property funds internalised.

Hermes was created out of the Post Office and British Telecom pension funds. Prudential merged with Scottish Amicable; AMP entered the market from Australia and acquired Pearl Assurance and later Henderson. This meant that the whole advisory world changed, because we now became brokers rather than retained advisers. A strong part of our business had gone, and we had to change our spots. You had to become more entrepreneurial.

Clients said to us quite clearly: "If you stick with broking, then obviously we don't see you as a competitor." So we focused on building up strong brokerage links to the likes of Standard Life and Henderson, as well as maintaining relationships with the merged Norwich Union Funds.

Those like JLW, Richard Ellis, DTZ and Healey & Baker were going global through mergers and acquisitions in the same way that the big four accountancy firms did. Below that, there was a "keeping up with the Jones Lang" scramble to form associations or affiliations with smaller overseas brokers.

We became associate members of the Commercial Network. This tied us in with some good brokers in Germany and Spain and a whole plethora of strong businesses in local markets in the States. The problem was that these links kept breaking. Just as you got things settled, one of the bigger consolidators would buy one of the key members. We realised it was basically a game with no winners and decided that we would just stick to what we saw as core, recognising that this may not be as adventurous, or maybe as desirable, as being multinational, but it meant we could live within our skin.

CHAPTER TEN
HOMES PLANET

Business is a combination of war and sport
André Maurois

Planet Property is perhaps best imagined not as a single body but as a twin planetary system, comprising a commercial sphere and a (far bigger) residential sphere. Trading in secondhand homes is carried out by estate agents generally operating in a world apart from those who broker commercial property. But these two worlds do have overlapping orbits, and the area of overlap is residential development. Operating in this space are not only said agents but also volume house builders, specialist fund managers, buy-to-let investors and the builders of luxury flats. Between 1997 and 2012, this market was distorted by boom then reshaped by bust, emerging chastened and changed. The change occurred as a result of the following:

- **A mergers and acquisitions frenzy**, which led to near-death experiences for volume house builders like Barratt and Wimpey, who then eschewed volume in favour of profit.
- **A failure to develop an institutional rental market** during the buy-to-let boom, although the appearance of half a million or more renters very slowly began to change attitudes.
- **A surge of overseas buyers in London**, which drove residential values skywards and led to the development of flats for the super-rich in Mayfair and Knightsbridge.

HOUSE BUILDERS: VOLUME INSANITY TO PROFIT SANITY

Barratt shares were worth 1,260p in January 2007; by July 2008, they had crashed to 16p. Taylor Wimpey shares were 518p in April 2007 and 9p in December 2008. Both house builders plunged close to corporate death and were kept from drowning in debt only by obliging banks – which had problems enough of their own to manage, without having to manage bust house builders as well.

At the end of December 2012, Barratt shares had revived to reach 200p and Taylor Wimpey's to 60p. This was well short of their 2007 peak, but at least they had survived. Many did not. Volume builders found themselves hit by a double whammy in the crash: sales slowed dramatically, choking off cash flowing into the profit and loss account, while balance sheets were wrecked by asset values that shrunk and liabilities that did not. Land prices increased by fifty percent between 2004 and 2007, before tumbling by a third between 2007 and 2008. Many developers had borrowed heavily in order to buy land.

At the peak of the boom, there was unprecedented mergers and acquisitions activity. HBOS entered the market in March 2007, first partnering with Sir Tom Hunter to buy into Crest Nicholson for £1 billion, then taking a share in retirement home specialist McCarthy & Stone. Both deals went sour.

But a look at Barratt and Wimpey is example enough. Barratt had a stock market capitalisation of £3.2 billion in February 2007. That month, the company paid £2.2 billion to acquire the Leicester-based house builder Wilson Bowden. The purchase was masterminded by chief executive Mark Clare, an approachable accountant who had joined Barratt from British Gas in the summer of 2006.

Wilson Bowden co-founder David Wilson and his family were fortunate enough to take £198 million in cash as part of the acquisition deal – but unfortunate enough to take £271 million in Barratt shares too, then valued at over £12.50 each. Within six months, the market and share price were tumbling. The house builder declared a loss of £485 million for the year to June 2009. When Barratt got itself back into the black again in 2010, Clare resolved to do things differently: profit first, and scale second by a long way.

In the spring of 2007, Wimpey and Taylor Woodrow merged. The new, £5 billion business boasted fourteen thousand staff, then employed in building twenty-two thousand homes a year. A substantial part of Taylor Woodrow's operations were in the US. At the time, new home sales in America were falling, and the word "sub-prime" was already in the air. But no matter: the "underlying" market was reportedly stable in both the UK and the US and there was "a steady demand for new houses", said Taylor Woodrow at the time.

Wimpey boss Pete Redfern, then thirty-six, got to run the combined company. Only seven hundred job losses were expected as a result of the merger. Then: crash, bang! A loss of £1.8 billion was declared for 2008, followed by another of £503 million in 2009. Endless discussions with the banks took place. The US business was sold. Staff numbers were cut to three-and-a-half thousand. The company emerged slimmer, chastened but profitable, with Redfern resolved to do things differently, like Barratt's Clare. He too promised the City a profit-first, volume-second policy – which is one reason why construction starts for housing remained stubbornly low in 2012.

One house builder had a boss with experience of several downturns. The Berkeley Group, founded by Tony Pidgley in 1976, survived the great crash with only a few bruises. In April 2008, Berkeley reported pre-tax profit amounting to £194 million on revenue of £991 million, gained from selling three thousand, two hundred homes. The crash did hit Berkeley, whose founder appears later in this chapter. Turnover fell by a third to £615 million in 2010, while profit almost halved to £110 million and home sales fell by a thousand. But recovery was fast: by 2012, revenues topped £1 billion, while sales had climbed to three thousand, six hundred, generating £214 million in profit. So, why no near-death experience for Berkeley?

TONY PIDGLEY, FOUNDER AND CHAIRMAN OF BERKELEY GROUP:

The coming-together of Taylor Woodrow and Wimpey, and Barratt taking over Wilson Bowden – they nearly destroyed themselves. If you start to believe your own growth hype, you're in trouble. You have to establish a culture of common sense. There is only one king – and it's called cash. We've always had a fear of borrowing money. We kept our balance sheet under control. Once you have set limits, there is nothing great about the rest of it. When house prices go up, you have to tell yourself the truth. You say thanks for that extra twenty percent, but you mustn't start believing it will go on.

THE COALITION TRIES TO BOOST NUMBERS
In 2010, the new Conservative-led coalition government faced a looming shortage of new homes. Not only had mortgage finance all but dried up, but also the big house builders had switched their focus from volume to profit and the number of new housing construction starts of all types in Great Britain collapsed from *two* hundred and nineteen thousand in 2007/08 to just *one* hundred and nineteen thousand in 2008/09. Incoming housing minister Grant Shapps turned out to be an unusually accessible and pretty successful minister in his short time in the job. (He was promoted to run the Conservative Party in 2012.) But he proved unable to push up the numbers. By the year ending March 2012, starts had only recovered to the level of a hundred and thirty thousand. This vignette from 2010 gives a glimpse of how Shapps was searching for solutions after taking on the housing job.

Ping! An email arrives one Saturday morning in June 2010 from the man himself. I'd written about the new housing minister, but had only met him briefly. Why on earth would he email me directly rather than get a press officer to call? But all he wanted was contact details for housing and regeneration expert Jackie Sadek. I pinged them back, adding as an afterthought something along the lines of "I know your job is a bugger and your diary a nightmare. But if you want to have a relaxing and highly amusing long lunch, invite Jackie." Ping! "I will – and will you come as well?"

I gave little thought to the exchange, assuming it was a promise that would never be kept. But come October, Sadek and I found ourselves sitting down to lunch with Shapps. No press officers, no aides, nothing off the record – a highly unusual event, be assured. Jackie Sadek is a "tell it like it is" woman, in possession of a highly developed comedic sense of the absurd aligned with a strong social conscience. The lunch went well.

Nine months later, in early 2011, an article in *EG* revealed Shapps was endorsing a £3 billion plan to build twenty thousand homes for rent by Sadek's company, UK Regeneration, backed by Barclays. At the end of 2012, work was under way on a site in Nottingham, although no one was likely to move in before 2014. Other sites – all outside London – were also in the pipeline. Building homes outside the capital was still a slow and bloody business, four years on from the crash. But politicians must be seen to be trying.

RENTAL SECTOR: LONG, SLOW START, THEN START-UP

On 23rd August 2012, the president of the Royal Institution of Chartered Surveyors rang me, sounding pleased. Former Allsop senior partner Alan Collett remarked on a government report published that morning. This had picked up on an idea he had dreamed up six years earlier for having a separate planning use class to encourage the development of homes for rent.

The twenty-eight-page report produced by Sir Adrian Montague did not go so far as to recommend a complete new planning class. Not quite. Instead, the government adviser-for-all-seasons suggested that local authorities mark out land on local development plans suitable for private rented homes, then allow only homes for rent to be built on the land. That, he argued, would reduce the price of the land to well below the amount a rival build-for-sale buyer could afford to pay.

The individual sale of those homes would then be disallowed for ten to fifteen years by way of restrictive covenants. Abracadabra! The foundations for a large-scale build-to-rent sector supplying tens of thousands of new homes would thus be laid: rented homes that could be financed or bought by institutions looking for long-term reliable income from the rents, without relying on capital appreciation. Once again.

MISSED OPPORTUNITIES

Rising house prices pushed up the number of those choosing to rent – or, rather, of those with no choice but to do so – by half a million in the first half of the Noughties. That ignited a buy-to-let investment boom between 2000 and 2007. Hundreds of thousands of individuals invested, in many cases off-plan, long before the homes were even built. A new generation of small landlords was born. Richard Donnell of Hometrack estimates buy-to-let investors bought homes worth £300 billion between 2000 and 2012: "It dwarfed institutional investment."

Pension and life funds can't say they weren't alerted. In 1999, Savills produced what turned out to be an under-forecast of the growth in renters. The agent predicted that they would increase by a million in number, to reach 3.2 million by 2016; Sir Adrian Montague found the market contained

3.6 million renters already in 2012. Alan Collett had said back in 1999: "This year will definitely see more institutional money coming into the private rented sector." These early forecasts did help Schroders and Charterhouse Bank set up funds to buy rented property. But it didn't happen on a large scale. Legal & General Property managing director Stuart Beevor, who went on to run fund operations at Grosvenor, was probably speaking for most fund managers when he said: "The principles are attractive. It's a question of being convinced that net returns remain attractive after all the deductions."

Hometrack's Donnell explains why individuals rushed in where institutions failed to tread: "Funds have to rely upon making a return on income, not capital. The big issue is the mindset of the small landlord world, which largely revolves around house price growth driving returns. They are far less concerned about the rental returns. It is the exact opposite for funds." The reluctance of the big funds to bet on rising prices left the field clear for individual investors to buy up the flats that began springing up like toadstools, particularly in Northern cities such as Leeds and Manchester.

Enter Jim Moore of Inside Track. The former sunbed salesman set up the business in 2001 to sell courses at £2,500 a pop to couples wanting to become property millionaires. He then founded Instant Access Properties, a bulk-buying operation that negotiated discounts on off-plan properties. It worked, wonderfully well. During the boom, dinner party conversation was dominated by the rising price of property and the desirability of buying "a little flat somewhere" to rent out.

By 2005, Moore's operations were booming. That year, his business employed three hundred and fifty staff and turned a profit of £9 million. You could hardly open a newspaper without seeing an Inside Track advert, and there was even talk of a £150 million flotation on the stock market. By 2007, Moore had made the *EG* rich list, with a fortune calculated at £40 million. But the market was turning against him – as was his wife, who extracted a £16 million divorce settlement.

Inside Track went bust in May 2008 and Instant Access four months later, leaving four-and-a-half thousand buyers in limbo. But was Moore deterred? No. Just before Christmas 2008, invitations were issued to the press for dinner at the Lanesborough hotel. Over turkey and sprouts, Moore announced he was setting up again: he had bought the Inside Track mailing list from the administrators and set up Instant Access Properties Global.

Former Chesterton boss Tony McKay, a burly and charming Australian accountant who had been running Inside Track for a year or so, was to run the new company. IAP Global went bust in 2010.

TRY AND TRY AGAIN...
Back in 2006, the then chancellor, Gordon Brown, tried indirectly to stimulate a debate on the rental sector. The great concern at the time was that house builders were either unwilling or unable to build enough new rental homes to fulfil demand. Housing minister Yvette Cooper called for a "step change" in provision.

One way of airing the arguments was by using what was sometimes described as "Gordon Brown's think tank" (see chapter six). Smith Institute breakfast presentations took place in a bare-boarded room on the first floor of 11 Downing Street, overlooking the garden of the neighbours at No 10, wherein stood a trampoline. At breakfast on 17th May 2006, Yvette Cooper and a group of senior civil servants gathered there to listen attentively to the experts who had contributed to *More Homes for Rent*, a Smith Institute publication I'd edited.

The central recommendation made was the introduction of a separate planning use class for rented homes – a proposal put forward by Alan Collett of Allsop and William Hill of Schroders. The planning restriction would depress the land value for rented homes below the open market price, making it more attractive for funds to invest. But the proposal came to nothing – because the civil service killed the idea, as I later discovered.

By 2008, household formation projections estimated that two hundred and twenty-three thousand new homes a year were needed, up from an earlier estimate of two hundred and nine thousand. By then sales were collapsing amid the economic crash. Private rental demand was rising as those who could not afford to buy a home grew more numerous. Institutional interest perked up again. Aviva became keen. Meanwhile, US investors such as Alliance Holdings were scouting the market.

The Smith Institute then had another go. *The Future of the Private Rented Sector*, in 2008, included a recommendation from Mark Long of fund manager Invista. He repeated the proposal for a separate use class, suggesting as a better alternative a form of licensing scheme that would oblige developers to rent the homes for a fixed number of years. Again, no take-up.

... AND FINALLY

After the 2010 election, the coalition government discovered for itself the pressing need for homes to rent. Housing minister Grant Shapps then asked Sir Adrian Montague to look into the matter, and in 2012 he came up with the idea that pleased the president of the Royal Institution of Chartered Surveyors, Alan Collett. Sir Adrian added a cautionary note, however: that no one wanted to be "the first mover, especially overseas investors, who see UK institutions holding back".

Yet in Olympic year, something did move: Qatari Diar and Delancey bought over fourteen hundred new homes in the athletes' village on the Olympic Park in 2012 and pledged to make nearly all of them available for rent. Barratt also dipped a toe into the Olympic rental pool, as chief executive Mark Clare announced a link-up with giant US rental company LeFrak to build eight hundred new homes close to the athletes' village.

In September 2012, the coalition government pledged to back the Montague reforms and gave debt guarantees to the funding of £10 billion worth of homes to rent. Bovis and Barratt began to take seriously the idea of building for rent. Funds such as Aviva and Legal & General, which had been contemplating investment in the rented sector for at least a dozen years, began at last to sound more interested.

LOSS OF PROFESSIONAL VALUES
The great buy-to-let boom that came with the rise of the rental market had an unfortunate effect on Planet Property: it all but bust the valuation system. Lenders agree to advance a percentage of the amount they think a property is worth, not a percentage of the amount the buyer has agreed to pay. And the worth of a property – its valuation – is supposedly based upon the price paid for similar properties. It all sounds pretty straightforward.

But builders have a whole bag of tricks up their sleeves. The most common is for the first flat or two in a new development to be bought by "friends and family". An employee or director of the company buys the property at an inflated price. That then "fixes" the value of the other properties – in more ways than one. All this – and more – was going on during the buy-to-let boom. There were suspicions that "friendly" valuers were complicit with both lenders and developers in order to retain lucrative business.

ROBERT PETO, VALUER AND FORMER RICS PRESIDENT:

> *Part of the problem was that quite a lot of money was being lent by building societies in a ferociously competitive marketplace. People weren't actually trained sufficiently to see what the problems would be. I don't think the right checks and balances and risk controls were in place. The lenders were motivated by short-term profits rather than long-term caution. So they said to their staff, "Please can you go out and lend."*

> *The system was built on paying commission. People were encouraged and paid commission. Structures were in place that encouraged people to turn a blind eye to abuses. The cost of administering a full and proper system of control in a competitive market was just too great. I think the societies accepted that a percentage of the advances would default.*

The biggest buy-to-let mortgage lender at that time was Paragon. In early summer 2005, Paragon director John Heron was so concerned at what was going on that he approached the Royal Institution of Chartered Surveyors as an official representative of the Council of Mortgage Lenders. Lenders are required to use RICS qualified valuers, who follow the surveyors body's big Red Book of rules governing valuations. But the valuation division of the institution didn't take Heron terribly seriously, and nothing much happened. Six months later, Heron requested lunch. I related his tale of frustration in *EG* on 3rd December 2005:

Valuing to Get a Sale at Any Price Is Not Right

It is hard to know where to start apportioning blame for the scandal that will surely afflict the new-build flats market; a market where prices have already started to fall and where some very questionable valuations have led the Council of Mortgage Lenders to blow the whistle. This market has ballooned and now accounts for 46% of all new starts in Britain.

It has been fuelled by the scramble of individuals desperate to make a buck or have a buy-to-let pension. The aggressive tactics of the property investment clubs, who, for large fees, offer the promise of riches and discounts, has goaded investors....

The Royal Institution of Chartered Surveyors often talks loftily about its role as a protector of the public interest. Well, for the past six months it has turned a deaf ear to the concerns voiced by the Council of Mortgage Lenders that RICS members may be negligently valuing or, worse, colluding with the developer or mortgage broker to get the deal done. This is very definitely not in the interests of the flat-buying public.

It is simply not good enough for the RICS to say that the rules laid down in the valuers' Red Book have been agreed by the CML. Neither does it go far enough to say, in response to prodding from EG, that "this puts chartered surveyors on notice of the potential issues". What about the public? No warning to them? The RICS needs to sit down very soon with the CML to deal with an issue that, in a falling market, needs treating with some urgency.

The issue was subsequently tackled, although hardly with urgency. New rules that obliged valuers to take account of prices of secondhand properties outside the development in question were introduced nearly four years later, on 1st May 2009 – a whole two years after the market collapsed.

LOUIS ARMSTRONG, THEN RICS CHIEF EXECUTIVE:

I think it's fair to say that in an ideal world we should have given more detailed additional guidance to those valuers about the pitfalls and the poo traps and the scams earlier than we did. We had rather assumed that anyone in that market would know that there was a whole range of hidden mathematics going on behind the scenes to create artificial values for some new off-plan flats.

Clearly, there were issues where lawyers, mortgage lenders and one or two RICS members were engaged in collusive activities. Where you had a combination of a few unscrupulous developers, aided in some cases by the way that mortgage valuations were done, plus the lack of transparency over prices, it caused problems in certain cities with flats being overvalued.

PRIME CENTRAL LONDON: BOOM, BUST – AND BOOM
Knight Frank delineates the prime central London market as comprising Knightsbridge, Mayfair, Kensington and Chelsea, and the City, as well as the South Bank and bits of the leafier inner boroughs. The boom here didn't begin really until mid 2006, when new-build apartment prices passed the £1,000 per square foot mark. Values had doubled over the five years from 1997 to 2002, rising from £425 to £860. But they bumped along at that level until towards the end of 2005. Boom number one then occurred between mid 2006 and November 2007, when prices jumped by fifty percent, from £1,000 to £1,500 per square foot.

In 2006, young developers Nick and Christian Candy persuaded their Qatari backers to buy Chelsea Barracks from the government, and Bowater House in Knightsbridge from Land Securities. Six years later, the 12.8 acres of the barracks site still lay undeveloped at the end of 2012, long after an extraordinary fight between the Candys and the Qataris, sparked by the intervention of Prince Charles. More on that at the end of this chapter. Meanwhile, Bowater House became One Hyde Park and set undreamed-of prices that began at £4,000 per square foot during pre-sales in boom number one, and reached £7,000 in boom number two.

The crash did affect prime central London values. They fell £300 a square foot to £1,200 by early 2009. But along came boom number two: two years on, in early 2011, prices had recovered to the 2007 level of £1,500. By late 2012, they had moved to £1,750. Why so rapid a recovery?

PRIME CENTRAL LONDON PROPERTY VALUES

Though the crash did hit property values in prime central London, with a twenty percent fall in value in the space of two years, prices rapidly recovered then continued to climb

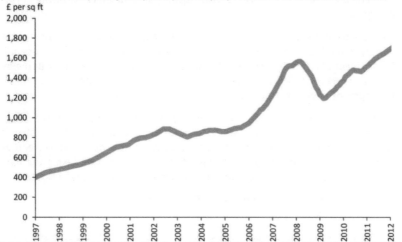

Source: Knight Frank

BOOM NUMBER TWO

The London market became hot again for two reasons: first, the continuing rise in the capital's population, which grew by a million between 2001 and 2011, to reach 8.2 million; second, the surging interest in property among foreign investors. In boom number two, sixty percent of newly built flats were being sold to overseas buyers: a far higher proportion than in boom number one, when the figure was about a third.

Demand from overseas buyers was not a new phenomenon; it helps kick-start development, as Tony Pidgley of the Berkeley Group explains: "It began in about the Nineties, actually – at about the same time that Berkeley moved into London. Since then, we have always had a percentage of what we build going to foreign investors. Every developer likes to forward-sell, to secure cash flow, to create some certainty. But I don't think that anybody foresaw the rise in values we have experienced. The planning regime we enjoy and the lack of supply has pushed prices up in areas of high demand."

How to capture the heady mood of what was building up into this second boom? In 2011 and 2012, the huge rise in foreign buyers and thus prices became a story hard to ignore. Here are seven extracts from my Friday columns in the City pages of the *Evening Standard*. The first tale is written after the summer riots of 2011. I took the train to Woolwich and walked past scorched shops and offices to reach a site behind the main square where Tesco was building homes over a superstore.

Tesco Bids to Tempt Chinese into Living over the Shop
9th September 2011

Between November 2 and 6, James Talbot of Savills will be selling Tesco own-make homes under construction in Woolwich to Chinese buyers in Shanghai. The flats in question sit over a megastore being built by the supermarket giant, just behind the newly refurbished town square, around which sit newly burnt-out shops.

The riots are not likely to feature in the sales pitch. What will is the 28-minute journey to Bank on the newish DLR line; six trains an hour to Charing Cross and the prospect of a Crossrail station, thanks to a £100 million pledge by Berkeley Homes to pay for a concrete box to house a future station on its 3700-home development at nearby Royal Arsenal.

Completed Berkeley flats are on offer at roughly £450 and £550 per sq ft. They will be undercut by Tesco, whose more spacious units will be sold off-plan at £400 a sq ft in China, where the supermarket giant now has 94 stores and at least 4.5 million clubcard holders to target. "We would not be taking the flats to China if it was not for Tesco's strong brand in the country," says Talbot.

Carlyle Prepares to Unveil Giant South Bank Complex
4th November 2011

Carlyle, the American private-equity giant, is working up secret plans for a massive £2 billion development on the south bank of the Thames, close to a newly enlarged Blackfriars Station, it can be revealed today.

Office blocks on either side of the track will be torn down, and replaced with 1.5 million square feet of flats, offices and shops.... The one million square feet of apartments could be worth a total of £1.5 billion, given nearly £1500 per square foot is being paid at nearby Neo Bankside, just behind Tate Modern.

Burns Unit That Put on the Ritz Makes a Packet
4th May 2012

Joe Burns, 38, his wife, Sharon, 37, and the anonymous backer of their plan to turn offices opposite The Ritz into five luxury flats have struck gold. Knight Frank has sold the penthouse atop the former home of Sir Robert Walpole for £20 million. That works out at a record £4500 per square foot for St James's....

Joe Burns says the total value of the five flats at 3-5 Arlington Street is £70 million and converting them from offices cost £22 million. What he won't say is how much his anonymous backer paid for the freehold in April 2009, at the nadir of the crash.

The seller was a property fund run by General Electric which had, in 2005, paid £11.5 million in a joint venture with developer, Nigel Kempner.

Supply Grows as Demand Falls... How Suburban
15th June 2012

Forget central London sales hype, the price of new homes in the outer boroughs fell 8% in 2011. No wonder: work began on 23,000 new homes last year, mostly in the suburbs. More than 16,000 remained unsold in January.

The statistics are six months old. But London Residential Research makes 6000 site visits a year to peer behind the sales boards at the real picture. It takes it a while to tot up the stats for its annual Red Book, out this month. This contains an even scarier number: 236,363. That's the number of units planned or with planning permission.

Within that number lies the scariest figure of all: 50,000 — how many units are planned within a mile of so of the Olympic park. Demand is weak. Yet supply goes from strength to strength. Be afraid.

Duke Sells So Qataris Can Go Native
20th July 2012

Yet another flood of Qatari money is set to gush into the London residential property market. The ruling family of the oil-rich state has signed a deal to take a 45% stake in luxury flat developer, Native Land. The agreement requires the Qataris to provide between £375 million and £400 million over two years as part of a £1 billion expansion plan to build 500 flats in central London.

The deal signed last Friday after a year of talks will make millions for the Duke of Buccleuch, who has sold all but 10% of his 50% share in Native Land to the Qataris. The new venture is said to be "within a hair's breadth" of paying around £100 million for 30 Old Burlington Street, near Piccadilly, with a view to converting the 83,000-square-foot commercial block into flats.

"We are confident that over two years we will buy enough sites, " said Alasdair Nicholls, who co-founded Native Land in 2003. The former Taylor Woodrow executive said the Qatari cash plus between £100 million and £125 million from the "current investor pool" will pay for sites where each flat will cost roughly £1 million. Then £500 million of debt will be raised and spent on construction.

"We are looking from Spitalfields in the East to Kensington & Chelsea in the West," says Nicholls. "We are interested in sites that have consent. But only if they are capable of improvement."

... But the Bubble of Foreign Money Could Soon Burst
20th July 2012

Overseas buyers have caused the London housing market to become "distorted and dysfunctional" warns a Labour-leaning think tank in a report to be published tomorrow. The Smith Institute says "the huge rise in overseas investment in expensive properties risks creating a bubble".

The 52-page analysis, London for Sale, written in conjunction with policy body Future of London, reveals that 60% of new homes in the capital are purchased by foreigners. Overseas buyers are now spending £5 billion a year on London property, with many of them being kept empty, says the report.

Paul Hackett, director of the Smith Institute, said: "If the Mayor of London wants to provide assistance to first-time buyers, then attention must be devoted to the dynamics of the private housing market. The most urgent task is to develop a strategy in relation to overseas investment."

Battersea Lights Up at Last – Now All It Needs Are Buyers
7th September 2012

There is scepticism the Malaysian developers of Battersea Power Station will be able to keep a promise made on Wednesday to sell 800 flats off-plan by next September. But at least the new owners of the 39-acre site are going to build the first huge linear block of apartments after closing the £400 million purchase this week. Yes, believe it or not, diggers are about to begin scuttling round the iconic power station after 27 years of inactivity.... The target price for the 730,000 square feet of sellable space is £1000 a square foot. So flats worth a total of £730 million need to be sold. Can it be done?

Er... yes, it was almost done by Christmas. The Malaysians sold six hundred flats in Asia by the turn of the year, making a mockery of what I had written in my *EG* column on 15th September 2012. The sentiment (below) was perhaps overly influenced by the Malaysians' seemingly rash promise in early September to sell all those flats in Battersea...

Will the Flow Continue?

OH MY GOD! THE SOUTH BANK RESIDENTIAL MARKET HAS PEAKED. SELL! SELL! SELL! A conclusion easily reached. Take a riverboat from Tower Bridge to Battersea Bridge. Gape at the ranks of riverside projects underway. Take a taxi along the tangle of roads at the rear. Gawk at the hoardings guarding cleared sites. Click on EGi and browse through the prospective developments. Imagine how they must all be predicated on strong, continuing demand.

Capital values have risen 43.5% since the first quarter of 2007 in this area, said Knight Frank. How many more danger signs do you need? Will the market collapse? Of course: One day. When? No idea. Because South Bank prices are entirely supported by a strong and continuing flow of foreign buyers.

THE MAN WHO RODE BOTH BOOMS: TONY PIDGLEY

I went to see Tony Pidgley down in Chobham in February 2012. The Berkeley Group chairman was canny, kindly and helpful. On his bare, computer-free desk lay an inch-thick plastic folder. "In 'ere", he said, in an accent unmodi-fied by wealth, "is everything I need to know. Every site, every plot, every sale, everything, brought up to date every week."

Tony Pidgley's CV is well-known: born to a single mother in 1947 and taken in by Barnardo's, he was then adopted by travellers and lived in a rail-way carriage. As a boy, he worked cutting trees into logs, then left home at fifteen in 1962, founding a haulage business soon after. After selling the business to Crest Nicholson in 1968, Pidgley worked for the house builder until 1976, when he set up Berkeley. Twenty-eight years later, in 2004, the Chobham-based PLC dominated the central London flats market and was flourishing in the Home Counties.

But Berkeley stopped buying land in 2004 and promised to return some £1.4 billion to shareholders, including £24 million to a certain T Pidg-ley. Operations outside London were wound down. At the time, many ques-tioned Pidgley's sanity – until they saw just how well Berkeley rode the 2007–2009 crash. "I'm not saying we didn't have a difficult time," he says. "Our sales came down by over fifty percent. But the market did then pick up fairly quickly. I think we're lucky enough to operate in a city where, if you want a second home, you come to London."

"How come you have so little competition?" I asked Pidgley. He laughed, before explaining: "The model we run is complex and difficult to set up. It takes a long time to develop in London. When you commit to building twenty-storey or thirty-storey towers, it's very different. You have to think about every aspect. We made our mistakes before the business became even more sophisticated. The other thing we have done is stick to our knitting. We've always stuck to residential."

Pidgley says success is down to caution and attention to detail. "Find a backstop. Everybody talks about finding a backstop. Everybody will tell you they've got a backstop. But we really do sit down and look at what happens if we call it wrong. Will we lose our shirt? We look at what happens if values fall by twenty percent, thirty percent or forty percent.

"Then we look at what we can do – what we call 'added value'. How can we make it better? What can we do to make you want to live there? Our teams pre-plan. And when they've done it once, they'll do it again. We chal-lenge a lot: why is it going to sell at that price; how many a week can we sell; why do we believe the site works? We go round and round, then round again.

"We question customers. Did they enjoy the experience; where did we get it wrong? There's no formula. It's the biggest investment anybody makes, so you've got to keep it personal. The minute you standardise it, you become like any other business – and people don't want that. The truth of the matter is, it's about caring and being an owner-driver – not being a pro-fessional manager.

"I've done this since I was twenty years old. We've made our mis-takes. But it seems to me that there were some fairly crazy deals done before it all went pop in 2008." And what to watch out for should it start to go wrong again? Here's some advice on the subject from a man well-qualified to give it...

TONY PIDGLEY, FOUNDER AND CHAIRMAN OF BERKELEY GROUP:

If you see prices move away – land prices, I'm talking about – and your margins are getting slimmer and slimmer, just apply common sense and the brakes. Everything we do is a percentage of the sum total of the selling price. If the land is ten percent of the sum total, you've got a chance. If it becomes fifty or sixty percent, as it does at the top of a boom, you've got no chance. So when a land stack falls on my desk, I go straight to what the price is as a percentage of the gross development value.

If I'm paying sixty percent to start the game, I then have to build it, sell it, finance it and make a profit. Not easy. You get told: "Oh, but we can triple the volume of sales if we buy this site." Well, you can't. Experience and history have told me it's not possible to increase the volumes that fast. Then there are those who start to factor in house price increases into the price they are prepared to pay for land. You shouldn't run a business built on inflation.

If you start doing that, then you might as well go to the roulette table and throw your money down. When the market gets to this point, you have to pull back. You have to find ways of buying your land where hopefully you've got enough skill-led value – but you can't compete in the market for land.

In 2005–2006, the banks would lend anybody money. I remember three young men who had worked for us for six to nine months coming in to see me. They said, "It has been lovely working for you, Tony. Thank you very much. You're the best teacher in the business. But now we are going out on our own." I said, "You're only young men. How are you going out on your own?" "Oh, we just borrowed X from the bank."

Well, they went bankrupt. I could have told them that on the day they left. You've got to use common sense. When land gets up to fifty or sixty percent of your gross development value, you've got forty percent left. And it's not enough.

On 4th June 2012, Berkeley announced that it would be returning £1.7 billion to shareholders over the coming decade. Managing director Rob Perrins said the move to pass money back to shareholders reflected Berkeley's comfort with its size. "We don't want to grow the business from here. We are at an optimum size. If you gave us another £1 billion in capital, we would not be able to make the best use of it."

THE SUPER-BRAND BROTHERS: NICK AND CHRISTIAN CANDY

IAN MARCUS, BANKER:

We worked very closely with Nick and Christian Candy on a num-
ber of schemes. We were very disappointed not to actually finance
One Hyde Park. They were visionaries in their own way. If I said to
you, "Name a brand in the real estate industry," you'd struggle
beyond Regus. But the brothers created a brand. For them it didn't
matter whether it was a boat or an apartment; they tried to create
this brand around the Candy & Candy name.

I had to look up what a Maybach was when, in 2003, I was told that
Nick and Christian Candy were being chauffeured around in one. (The car
turned out to be a super-posh Mercedes.) I had to ask the *EG* journalist concerned, Adam Coffer, why this merited a diary story. "Because they are the
hot new developers; haven't you heard of them?" Actually... no. I subsequently watched Nick and Christian become the best-known and most controversial residential developers in Britain.

The young brothers were making a name for themselves at the time
by developing high-end apartments for the very rich. Not many. But they had
an exceptional talent for sales, marketing and interior design. I invited them
to an *EG* conference at Claridge's in June 2006 to present their view on the
prime central London market. The brothers were nervous, but well prepared.
One PowerPoint slide from the presentation sticks in the mind. It forecast
that values would rise from £1,500 per square foot to a seemingly preposter-
ous £4,000 by 2010.

This was the pitch: *Lots of rich foreigners want to live in London.*
There are no apartments being built to meet their exacting standards. We
are going to build them. They will pay £4,000 a square foot. A month later
came the purchase of Bowater House in Knightsbridge from Land Securities;
the Qatari royal family backed the deal. The vision for eighty-odd hyper-
luxury flats came from Nick and Christian Candy. Half the apartments were
sold off-plan for around £4,000 per square foot. By the time the project was
complete in 2011, prices of £5,000, £6,000 and £7,000 were being achieved.

The One Hyde Park vision enabled the Candy brothers to persuade
their Qatari backers to pay the Ministry of Defence £976 million in 2006 for
the 12.8 acre Chelsea Barracks site. Selling agent Drivers Jonas had previously estimated that bids would come in around the £250 million mark. The
£726 million difference between the two figures provides an indication of
how values were soaring in the mid Noughties.

But the Candys' plans for six hundred and thirty-eight modern flats
designed by Lord Richard Rogers fell foul of the Prince of Wales. The story
became a *cause célèbre*. The Qataris' development company, Qatari Diar,
took over and redesigned the scheme – basically to suit the Prince of Wales,
who had complained to the Emir of Qatar – and the Candy brothers were
told that their services were no longer required. The brothers then sued the
Qataris for loss of fees.

At this point you have to ask yourself: who else would dare sue the Qatari ruling family, especially as they were still the client at One Hyde Park? The Candys did. I played a bit part in proceedings after being invited down to Monaco on 25th November 2009 to meet Christian Candy. I'd been quoted as saying it would take three to four years to sell the One Hyde Park apartments and was seen as "not on-side", according to former Guards officer Christopher Joll, the public relations man who accompanied me on the trip.

But he promised a story and a chance to spend the day with Christian Candy. Why not? So it was business class from Heathrow to Nice, followed by a glide along the coast to Monaco in a black Rolls-Royce, then into the marbled foyer of an unpromising modern office block and up in a private lift with the C&C logo engraved on the threshold, finally stepping into an apartment of eighteen thousand square feet overlooking the harbour.

The thirty-room duplex was beyond stunning. The flat was sold the following year for a reported €200 million. The brothers had bought and refurbished Monaco's best flat as a demonstration of their talents. Christian Candy mentioned that the refurbishment had cost €29 million.

The place was a *World of Interiors* advertisement for what money and exuberant taste can buy: a double-height library complete with gleaming piano and custom-made Monopoly set; a his-and-his wood-panelled office; bedrooms with saucy photographs and chinchilla fur bed throws; a shaded roof terrace where a hundred or more people could party.

After lunch at the Hotel de Paris, it was a glide to the airport and a flight back to Biggin Hill with the younger Candy and his lapdog, who had accompanied us on the tour. We travelled in a private jet furnished with four large, leather seats embossed with the C&C logo. I wrote the adventure up for my *Evening Standard* column that week, in early December 2009:

Brandy Candy – Limitless Style for Limitless Money

To Monaco for the day to meet Christian Candy, the younger and slightly quieter of the two brothers who have been making headlines all week by blaming Prince Charles for the breakdown of their joint venture with the Qataris to build 638 flats on the 12 empty acres that once held Chelsea Barracks.

The visit took place 48 hours before a multi-million-pound claim became available for public inspection. So he was circumspect on the detailed charges levied by his company, CPC, against Qatari Diar, the development arm of the oil-rich state.

But the leaked news that Christian, 35, and his 36-year-old brother, Nick, were taking Qatari Diar to court made it possible to ask over lunch why they are suing the Qataris on one project while still working with them on another — the construction of 81 hyper-luxury flats in Knightsbridge.

"Because they signed a contract agreeing to pay us once planning permission was granted — and then they caved in to pressure from Prince Charles and didn't even apply," to précis the view of Christian Candy.

The details came out in court on Tuesday, making it easy to see why CPC is su-ing. Qatari Diar agreed to pay tens of millions to break the development agreement on the £3 billion project because the Richard Rogers design faced local opposition and hostility from Prince Charles.

CPC was paid exactly £37,917,806 in April to give up its share of the joint ven-ture. An additional success fee of up to £81 million was agreed for whatever scheme is granted permission. Or, if the Qataris felt inclined, they could pay CPC £68.5 million to just go away.

Christian Candy was indeed circumspect over the charges being lev-ied against Qatari Diar that day in Monaco. That's because the Qataris had yet to acknowledge the claim: until that happened, it remained a private document. The deadline for them to do so was 4.30pm that day, while my own deadline for submitting the article was 10.00am the following morning. And since Christian had mentioned Prince Charles's name, I guessed that HRH would be mentioned in the claim, so I was gleefully imagining a scoop under a "Prince Charles Is Sued" headline.

Somehow, the Qataris managed not to "acknowledge service" until the Friday, so the headlines appeared elsewhere. A full hearing of the case (with no Prince Charles, incidentally) took place the following spring at the Royal Courts of Justice. I attended proceedings occasionally – and came away admiring Christian Candy's intellect and aplomb: and not admiring the witnesses from Qatar, some of whom the judge pretty much accused of fib-bing. This, as lawyers say, is a contemporaneous report, from the *Evening Standard* of 21st May 2010:

Looking Sweet for Christian Candy after Grilling in Legal Row over Royals

Christian Candy came away from his Tuesday morning grilling in Court 57 at the Royal Courts of Justice in a fairly perky mood. Christian is the younger of two brothers who are suing the Qatari royal family after their joint venture to build 638 flats at Chelsea Barracks was "blighted" by Prince Charles.

The slight 35-year-old had just spent two hours being questioned by Joe Smouha, the Qataris' QC, whose rimless glasses and icy demeanour brings to mind Clifford Rose, the actor who played the German commander in the late Seventies TV series, Secret Army.

There was a great deal of "and now Mr Candy, perhaps you would be kind enough to answer the question". Or, when things became a little tenser: "Mr Candy, you have failed to answer the question." Then when Mr Smouha finally gave up after five stabs at the same issue: "Mr Candy, you have clearly failed to answer my question. But we will move on…"

The main question is this: are Christian and his brother Nick entitled to an £81 million success fee denied them when Charles allegedly persuaded the Emir of Qatar to junk the plans for the Qatari-owned site, which were drawn up by the brothers? Beyond that it all gets very complicated.

That's why three weeks have been reserved for this hearing presided over by Mr Justice Voss. He sits in a sixth-floor court, complete with faux atrium, pale wood fittings and lemon yellow walls. Christian Candy addressed him with great deference as "My Lord" when answering counsel's questions.

Our man gave a simple "yes" to some questions. But he did hesitate and think very hard about answering others, especially when he thought his inquisitor might be leading him into a cunning trap that would close with the words "Aha! Mr Candy, so you do admit..." So whatever answer was given was stuck with, however many times Mr Smouha came back with versions of the same question.

For a mere spectator it was hard to judge the subtleties: but judging from the intermittent grin on the face of Candy's junior counsel, his boy done good.

A month later, a confidential settlement was announced that is thought to have cost the Qataris close to £40 million. The price the Candys paid was to apologise "unreservedly" to the Emir of Qatar "for any offence caused by the decision to commence litigation against Qatari Diar and the allegations made by CPC during the course of proceedings".

Prince Charles received a similar apology. Fortunately, I missed the forty-minute slot during proceedings when my trip to Monaco and the resultant article were dragged up as an example of how the Candy brothers manipulated the press. Well, they did a bit. Everyone does. They were just better at it than most.

RODEO RIDE

During the crash, the brothers had to work harder at their image than most. The Chelsea Barracks saga was a firestorm, but they also had to tend bush fires on two other fronts. One was a site on Rodeo Drive in Beverley Hills, bought for $500 million before the crash: their equity partner on the scheme went bust, and the loans went into default. The cast included Mexican Carlos Slim, the world's richest man, whose bank had lent part of the purchase price, as well as partner Kaupthing, which advanced nearly $250 million.

The Icelandic bank, which went bust in 2008, also featured in the other smaller saga: the 2006 purchase and 2008 loss of the old Middlesex Hospital site north of Oxford Street. An advance from Kaupthing allowed the Candys to pay £175 million for the three-acre site. Planning permission was then gained for a residential scheme of nine hundred thousand square feet; by mid 2008 the site was clear and ready for work to start.

But the world was then in economic meltdown – and so of course was Kaupthing. It decided it wanted its money back: by then, interest and costs had taken the amount outstanding to £220 million. After a fair amount of to-ing and fro-ing, Kaupthing finally repossessed it, although by that point the Candys had swapped their stake in the site for a stake in Rodeo Drive. The bank's administrators were going to sell the Middlesex site, but eventually went into partnership with developers Clive Bush and Dan Van Gelder of Exemplar and funder Aviva instead and began work on a revised scheme in the spring of 2012.

Nick and Christian Candy saw before anyone else just how much rich buyers were prepared to pay for hyper-luxury flats in the centre of London. By 2012, the rest of the world knew and everyone was piling in. But back in 2004, hardly anyone except the Candys had seen the potential of this market, and they pursued that vision harder than anyone else.

Nick went further, by achieving mild celebrity status. His courtship of Australian pop singer Holly Valance and their extravagant marriage in Los Angeles in September 2012 moved the more pugnacious of the two brothers into the world of *Hello!* and the tabloid press. Meanwhile, Christian began the recovery of the brothers' property industry reputation with the £34 million purchase in February 2012 of a hundred-and-ten-thousand-square-foot office block in the City at Sugar Quay on the north bank of the Thames: their first big purchase since the Chelsea Barracks debacle. Foster+Partners was commissioned to redesign Sugar Quay in July 2012.

We'll never know what might have happened if there had been no crash. We'll also never know what might have happened if the Candys had settled their differences with the Qataris over Chelsea Barracks quietly, as older heads might well have chosen to do. But the brothers had grown used to winning legal arguments early on. Back in 2004, they had threatened to sue the Land Registry.

Four confidence tricksters had persuaded them to pay £6.7 million for a site of forty-seven acres near Ascot containing a burned-out mansion once owned by the Thai royal family. The quartet did not own the land, despite having Land Registry documents purporting to show they did. The Land Registry quietly paid £8 million over to the Candys for a mistake that they admitted was theirs.

A "wide-ranging review" of procedures followed – and the Land Registry set up a fraud unit. Three of the con men were jailed in March 2009 after a three-year investigation and a six-week trial at Reading Crown Court.

CHAPTER ELEVEN
UNDER THE HAMMER

Large groups of people are smarter than a few experts
James Surowiecki, author of 'The Wisdom of Crowds'

Commercial and residential property has long been auctioned in much the same way as cows, sheep and pigs, but without the smell. Property auctioneers set up their stalls in hotel ballrooms and show only pictures of the stock; otherwise there's little difference. All comers are invited to bid for goods deemed not quite suitable for sale by the snootier purveyors of bricks and mortar. On a freezing day in February 2012, let us thankfully enter the warm, subterranean ballroom of the Park Lane Hotel on Piccadilly.

Here, the UK's leading auction house, Allsop, is diligently banging out a hundred and seven lots of commercial property. These include a nineteen-year lease on a Kwik-Fit garage on the Walworth Road in east London, a shop in a poor quarter of Manchester occupied by the Society of St Vincent de Paul, and the ground rent income on the Buckskin pub in Basingstoke. The auctioneer is Duncan Moir, a somewhat Pickwickian character who sells offices, shops and sheds for prices reaching into the low millions. A half-empty office block in Crawley is knocked down for £1.2 million to a sharp-suited character surrounded by a family group of co-investors all eyeing each other a little nervously.

Moir must gently cajole his reluctant audience. "Come along now, please! What am I bid?" A few hands slowly ascend; then, with barely perceptible nods, the bidding begins. There's a low buzz of chatter from non-bidders at the back of the room; one complains about the poor quality of the lots on offer and the perfidy of bankers refusing to lend.

Alongside Moir are seated two Allsop partners, Patrick Kerr and senior partner Neil Mackilligin, whose role it is today to take telephone bids. Junior Allsop staff sit separately at green baize-covered trestle tables, fingering computers; some are dealing with the paperwork for winning bidders, others updating a website that enables online bids – which are few, as the auction community prefers to bid in the room.

This particular room is three-quarters filled by an audience of two hundred or so, of varied ethnicity – worth mentioning because of the vivid contrast to the largely monocultural nature of the rest of the property world. The typical buyer is nevertheless a white male, often one with every appearance of not having two pennies to rub together – until he sticks up his hand and bids £1.2 million. Three-quarters of the lots are sold in the room that day, raising £37 million; post-sales take the total to £60 million, giving an average sale price per lot of £478,000. Auctions are big business.

The man who keeps count of business done is David Sandeman, a jovial descendant of the eponymous port wine dynasty and founder of the Essential Information Group. The essential information that Sandeman collects is the value of all lots on offer, the percentage sold, and the sale price of each lot. The numbers from each and every auction are totted up, to provide the total raised in the UK by every auctioneer of substance. Not that there are many; you can fit most of them into a single room.

A FREE LUNCH

For years *EG* held an annual Christmas lunch for leading auctioneers in a private dining room on the first floor of a coveted Covent Garden restaurant, the Ivy. The room holds only sixty – sixty people who raised a combined total of £46.8 billion in property sales between 1997 and 2011. Those selling houses and flats brought their hammers down on £26.6 billion; those in commercial property raised £20.2 billion. To repeat: auctions are big business. This list (opposite) of the biggest in the business shows just how big this business had become by 2011.

The reason for dividing the figures into two categories is that the market itself tends to split naturally into a residential and a commercial faction, at the top end at least. Individual auctioneers prefer to specialise in one or the other, and each sector attracts a different type of customer. Professional traders are to the fore at commercial sales, while residential auctions attract more amateurs, hopeful either of living in the property or of making a profit refurbishing a wreck, inspired by endless daytime TV shows.

At Allsop the leading residential auctioneer is the genial Gary Murphy, star joke teller at those *EG* lunches and master cajoler of reluctant amateurs. A week or so after the Allsop commercial auction, Murphy takes to the rostrum in the same hotel basement.

RESIDENTIAL AUCTION SALES 2011

In terms of total amount raised in residential sales, the UK's leading auction house was Allsop, followed by Savills and then Barnard Marcus

Auctioneer	Total raised (£m)	Auctioneer	Total raised (£m)
Allsop Residential	294.21	Agents Property Auction	49.74
Savills	213.38	Pattinson Property Auctions	49.08
Barnard Marcus	138.45	Harman Healy	47.96
Clive Emson	113.70	CP Bigwood	45.97
Andrews & Robertson	107.93	Graham Penny	45.32
Strettons	83.16	McHugh & Co	41.97
Eddisons	66.24	Cottons	37.92
Countrywide Property Auctions	50.50	**Market total***	**2,567.32**

Source: Essential Information Group   ** Firms listed represent fifty-four percent of the market*

COMMERCIAL AUCTION SALES 2011

In the commercial auctions sector too, Allsop leads the table of the UK's top firms in terms of total amount raised, with its closest competitor being Acuitus

Auctioneer	Total raised (£m)	Auctioneer	Total raised (£m)
Allsop Commercial	344.90	CBRE	30.71
Acuitus	144.66	Cushman & Wakefield	28.07
Barnett Ross	71.73	Lambert Smith Hampton	22.49
Pugh	59.12	King Sturge	15.16
Jones Lang LaSalle	44.00	Osborne King	3.11
		Market total	**766.85**

Source: Essential Information Group

The atmosphere is more bullish this time, since house buyers are less reliant on bank loans than are their commercial counterparts. By the end of the day, Murphy has raised £47 million from a mix of traders and intending owner-occupiers, with half of the two hundred and eighty-five lots selling to those living within five miles of the property.

Residential auctions march to a different economic beat. It was the homes side that rocketed during the boom, not the commercial. In 1997, just £370 million worth of houses and flats went under the hammer; by 2007, this figure had soared almost tenfold to £3.6 billion. The number of homes sold increased from nearly nine thousand in 1997 to more than twenty-one thousand ten years later, at the height of the boom. The average lot price soared from £42,000 to £166,000.

The buy-to-let boom that began at the turn of the century fed stock into the auction market as investors started to trade. By 2005, buying off-plan flats unseen in places like Leeds had become almost a fashion statement. Over six hundred thousand flats were sold between 2000 and 2007, mostly bought by buy-to-let landlords. That was to provide fodder for a subsequent wave of repossessions as house prices began to crumble in 2007.

Between 2003 and 2009, repossessions quadrupled to forty-eight thousand a year. This helped keep the number of homes sold at auction steady, hovering around twenty thousand a year between 2007 and 2011. Building societies and banks were anxious to avoid being labelled heartless for putting families on the streets, a charge they'd suffered twenty years earlier. To this end, many owner-occupiers unable to pay their mortgage found themselves placed in the hands of fixed-charge receivers (such as Allsop) under a quiet policy of "forbearance," allowing loans to be slowly paid down.

Residential auctions have always been affected by politics. When council tenants were granted the right to buy their own homes in 1980, this brought hundreds of thousands of homes into the private market. Many of the homes that go under the hammer nowadays are former council houses.

But it was a change in English and Welsh tenancy law at the end of the Eighties that had a bigger impact. Prior to 1989, regulated tenancies were the staple diet at residential auctions. Sitting tenants on these leases have what amounts to tenure for life, so their presence reduces a property's market value – by how much depends on the tenant's age. Regulated tenancy buyers are gambling on how long the tenant will live. Then in January 1989, along came assured shorthold tenancies, which allow the landlord or the tenant to pull out after six months. The new regime effectively ended the era of the regulated tenancy lease. No new ones were created, while those remaining died off along with their tenants, reducing the number of lots at auction and the ensuing income from commissions.

A VISIONARY BUSINESS
Auctions are a confidence barometer for the rest of the property market. The "percentage sold" figure is the mercury. If eighty to ninety percent of lots on offer are selling, then confidence is high. But if this figure falls to between sixty and seventy percent, then it is time to beware, even if the rest of the property market seems confident. The collective wisdom of the auction

How's this for anticipation? When the market was hit by the collapse of the dot-com boom in 2002, no one thought it would recover fast, yet it did. The auction crowd must have collectively known it, though, because about eighty-five percent of the twenty-three thousand lots on offer in 2002 were sold. In the year to June 2008, by contrast, just sixty-three percent of the thirty-one thousand residential and seventy percent of the six thousand, six hundred commercial lots were sold. Meanwhile, many outside the auction rooms were still confidently buying real estate. Fear also produces more sellers. The number of lots rose to a record high of twenty-seven thousand, three hundred in 2007, bringing in a record total sale income of £5.8 billion. The biggest auction Allsop ever held took place post-Lehman, in late 2008, with a catalogue containing over eleven hundred lots.

The "rack rate" quoted for auctioning both commercial and residential property is two percent of the sale price. Regular clients with multiple lots to sell can squeeze that down to one-and-a-half and sometimes one percent. The fees have changed little since the time when selling by auction was mainstream. In the nineteenth century, sale by auction was the first, not last choice. What auctioneers still dismissively call "private treaty" sales – the norm today – were then in the minority.

Even in the early twentieth century, everything from verdant country estates to squalid tenements still went under the hammer, at sales such as those held regularly at London's Tokenhouse Yard, near the Bank of England, which was home to the London Auction Mart from 1867 until 1917, when it was severely damaged by a German air raid. Sales began again in earnest in 1921, when the trade moved to 155 Queen Victoria Street. In 1923 the Mart entered into a deal with *EG* to publish its results. The market moved in 1969 to Fur Trade House in the City, then in 1978 to the Connaught Rooms in Covent Garden; after that it gradually fragmented, and nowadays auction houses prefer to conduct their own sales in hotel function rooms.

In the second half of the nineteenth century, page upon page of *EG* was filled with accounts of auction sales. The magazine's very first edition, published on 1st May 1858, sported a front cover consisting entirely of auction advertisements. Reading through them gives a flavour of the range of properties sold by auction at the time. A two-hundred-acre farm in what later became the Bedfordshire brickfields was on the block, as was the Little Titnest Estate near Ascot, comprising thirty acres in then-hyphenated Sunning-hill, as well as "five-acres, three roods and eight poles of rich Berkshire meadowland" to be sold at the Bear hotel in Wantage. The absence of planning laws and the rise of the monied classes, as captured in Galsworthy's Forsyte sagas, allowed auctioneer J&E Belcher to suggest that "private residences are much required in the neighbourhood and the land provides the opportunity for building, either for occupation or investment".

Since the late twentieth century, Allsop has dominated the auctions business. The limited liability partnership held a forty-five percent market share in commercial auction sales in 2011. The partnership, led by Alan Collett and then Neil Mackilligin, also held the number one spot in the booming residential market, ending 2011 with an 11.4 percent share.

RESIDENTIAL AUCTION RESULTS ANALYSIS 1997–2011

The residential auctions sector grew tenfold in the boom years of 1997–2007; after the fall, the number of lots remained relatively high, thanks to sales of repossessed homes

Year	Lots offered	Total sold	Lots sold (%)	Total raised (£m)	Lot size (£)
1997	11,002	8,704	79	369.8	42,480
1998	15,177	11,692	77	491.4	42,029
1999	18,256	14,752	81	700.4	47,481
2000	18,657	15,068	81	824.4	54,713
2001	18,087	14,585	81	990.0	67,881
2002	18,063	15,372	85	1,379.4	89,733
2003	19,385	15,482	80	1,610.0	104,570
2004	24,509	17,209	70	2,004.7	116,489
2005	24,362	17,158	70	2,273.6	132,507
2006	26,698	20,568	77	3,161.6	153,712
2007	30,604	21,569	70	3,593.1	166,583
2008	31,037	19,677	63	2,553.6	129,774
2009	23,805	17,884	75	2,218.5	124,047
2010	25,059	17,579	70	2,186.1	124,360
2011	26,206	19,447	74	2,268.3	116,640
Total		**246,746**		**26,633.6**	**107,939**

Source: Essential Information Group

"We decided to stick to what we knew during all the takeovers and mergers," says Collett, who went on to be president of the Royal Institution of Chartered Surveyors. "We also decided the business must be fun, so we had to stay in control." Fun brings its rewards. The nineteen equity partners in the two-hundred-and-seventy-strong firm earned on average £391,000 in 2011, although that was a whopping £200,000 less – yes, *less* – than they had taken home the previous year.

Make partner, and it can be a very well-paid trade. But not an easy one; the job is for quick-minded impresarios who can spin multiple plates. For one thing, auctioneers must handle bids coming from four different directions. Some are submitted prior to auction and known only to the auctioneer, then during the sale a few arrive through the internet, and more via the telephone; meanwhile, the auctioneer needs to keep an eye on every bidder – and potential bidder – in the room. But achieving a successful sales rate relies on a more intuitive skill. "You have to get the reserve price right," says Allsop's Gary Murphy. "That is by far the most important thing. It is imperative the auctioneer sets what they believe to be the right price. If not, there is no point in even trying to sell the lot."

Second place in the commercial auction house tables was long held by Jones Lang LaSalle, where the team was run for many years by Richard Auterac and Peter Cunliffe: the former as Mr Eccentric, the latter as Mr Sensible. The pair left the firm after a quarter of a century's service in March 2010, to set up as Acuitus, now the number two firm. Auterac, who is about the best-known auctioneer in the business, describes himself as "highly innovative, humorous and approachable", and all these things are true.

COMMERCIAL AUCTION RESULTS ANALYSIS 1997–2011

The commercial sector also grew rapidly in the boom years. The figure for total amount raised collapsed in 2008, but the percentage of lots sold perked up in 2009

Year	Lots offered	Lots sold	Lots sold (%)	Total raised (£m)	Lot size (£)
1997	4,020	2,947	73	564.0	191,391
1998	3,886	2,857	74	521.4	182,486
1999	4,451	3,410	77	793.2	232,601
2000	4,741	3,725	79	816.5	219,196
2001	4,611	3,831	83	1,059.0	276,409
2002	5,169	4,345	84	1,401.8	322,622
2003	5,728	4,854	85	1,592.6	328,094
2004	6,274	5,226	83	2,011.3	384,861
2005	6,348	5,135	81	2,095.9	408,159
2006	7,131	5,846	82	2,591.8	443,353
2007	7,465	5,704	76	2,238.4	392,430
2008	6,582	4,587	70	1,166.2	254,240
2009	5,637	4,348	77	1,233.0	283,585
2010	6,110	4,427	72	1,080.5	244,065
2011	6,482	4,765	74	1,073.0	225,182
Total		**66,007**		**20,239.0**	**306,611**

Note: Mixed-use lots are classed as commercial if offered by a predominantly commercial auction house such as Allsop Commercial, Jones Lang LaSalle or Colliers; otherwise, classed as residential

Source: Essential Information Group

Richard Auterac and I would meet up from time to time, on occasions that were always great fun – and involved plenty of good French white, I seem to remember. As well as chairing the UK Real Estate Auction Group, the auctioneers' annual conference and the Royal Institution of Chartered Surveyors' annual auctions legal conference, he is also the inventor of ARAS, the Auction Results Analysis Service, which brought together sales data from all the big auction houses in 1992. "What the data showed was that auctions are a credible marketplace," says Auterac.

"It sounds like a trivial thing, but that image of the auctioneer with gavel in hand has been a problem for commercial property auctions in the modern day. It falsely ties the business to the Victorian age, whereas what auctions give you in reality is the most up-to-date, unfettered snapshot of where the market is at any given time. We have a better grip of what's happening in the market than the majority of private treaty investment agents," says Auterac, who sold hundreds of Barclays bank branches between 2006 and 2008 in a sale-and-leaseback programme worth between £600 million and £700 million.

At rival firm Savills, Chris Coleman-Smith plays the auctioneer in much the same way as he plays his single-handicap golf: with patience and precision. This has allowed Savills to remain the number two residential auctioneer, selling over £200 million of homes in 2011 to take an 8.3 percent share of the market.

A final figure worth mentioning on the auction scene is the burly Clive Emson, occasional star on TV's *Homes under the Hammer*. His eponymous Kent auction house rose to become the fourth-largest residential auctioneer by 2011, selling £113 million of property. *EG* readers will be familiar with the Emson catalogue, occasionally wedged like a cuckoo into the nest of the magazine. The sight of its bulk drove many readers crazy (me too).

AMERICAN IDYLL

This rather cosy and traditional market was recently barged in upon by an American firm thinking it knew better – followed by another that actually might. In 2009, adverts began appearing on Sky TV calling upon viewers to flock to auction sales organised by the Real Estate Disposition Corporation, a Californian firm that had blossomed on home repossession sales in the US. But charging buyers a ten percent fee, rather than the one or two percent that UK auctioneers ask of sellers, did not go down well over here.

Then in late 2012, another American firm, one charging lower fees to buyers, appeared on the European scene, opening first in Germany. However, auction.com was not terribly interested in the traditional market. Instead the pitch was to those selling multimillion-pound distressed portfolios and distressed debt, using the internet as the auction room. In America, the service sold commercial properties worth $1.2 billion in 2011. Debt once worth $4.6 billion was traded at an average fifty-four percent discount. If nothing else, auction.com proved that when it comes to transparent pricing you can't beat an auction room, even a virtual one.

CHAPTER TWELVE
THE GREAT ESTATES

Diversification may preserve wealth, but concentration builds wealth
Warren Buffet

THE GREATEST ESTATE

The chief executive of the Crown Estate once inhabited an office in Carlton House Terrace fit for a king. By 2012, its entire headquarters had been transformed into a palace fit for the billionaire Hinduja brothers, but back in July 1999 one grand suite there was still occupied by Sir Christopher Howes. In a high-ceilinged room, flooded with light from deep sash windows framing views of the Mall, the urbane and energetic character sat at a polished antique table to talk though the annual results.

The figures were impressive: profits up for the tenth year in a row, swelling eleven percent to reach £126 million. The value of the estate had risen by ten percent since April 1998 to £3.3 billion. Sir Christopher, who had run this royal realm since 1989, spoke of trebling income on the Regent Street holdings, which stretched almost from Oxford Circus down to Piccadilly. Rental income was then around £25 million a year. That meant the shops and the offices above them were altogether worth £600 million. Plans were unrolled showing how streets would become semi-pedestrianised. Sir Christopher's rental predictions came true, but pedestrianisation proved impossible to implement against the combined opposition of Westminster Council and Transport for London.

In 2000, Sir Christopher gave fuller details of a ten-year redevelopment plan for Regent Street. The target was to raise rents to £75 million and so increase the value of the street to £1.8 billion. Another twelve months later came the final meeting with Sir Christopher, in July 2001. His swan-song accounts showed a rise in profits to £148 million and a doubling of the value of the estate to £4 billion since his appointment in 1989. This one-time surveyor from Aldeburgh with a penchant for red socks retired in October of that year, aged sixty. He went on to hold numerous non-executive posts, including one at the Howard de Walden, another at the Duchy of Lancaster, and yet another at Barclays Capital.

The foundations of the Crown Estate were laid in 1760, when George III assumed the throne. The twenty-two-year-old king was cash-strapped, so he unwisely surrendered revenues from the royal estates to the Treasury in return for an annual stipend. Some of that property can be traced back to Edward the Confessor. But the estate as a whole essentially dates from 1066: after the Norman Conquest, all land in England was deemed to belong to William "in right of The Crown".

Despite centuries of change in law and custom, there is still a "presumption in favour of the Crown" – land belongs to the Crown unless proven to belong to someone else. In 1955, a government committee chaired by Sir Malcolm Trustram Eve recommended that to avoid confusion between government property and Crown land, the latter should be renamed. The Crown Estate Acts of 1956 and 1961 established the Crown Estate as it is today.

The objectives of the Crown Estate Act 1961 were to establish "a new board of trustees, subject to parliamentary control but with a substantial measure of independence" to manage the estate. Parliament established the Crown Estate as "not a government department in the sense of an organ of executive government" but a body at arm's length from government. The modern estate owns not just most of Regent Street and half of St James's, but also over a quarter of a million acres of farmland, and the seabed extending out to twelve miles from the shore all around Britain – a wide and watery ribbon seen as rentable anchorage for wind farms.

Sir Christopher's congenial and capable successor, Roger Bright – who took over in 2001 – predicted in 2010 that income from wind farms would reach hundreds of millions of pounds by around 2025. Bright was a former civil servant, who had gone on in the Nineties to become deputy chief executive of the Housing Corporation and then chief executive of the Personal Investment Authority. Bright's prime task was the same as Sir Christopher's: provide the Treasury with steadily increasing profits and keep the Queen's name out of the papers. (Anything the Crown Estate gets wrong is always linked to the Queen.)

The only negative story of substance under Bright's rule was the 2010 sale of thirteen hundred rented homes in London by the Crown Estate. Banner-waving tenants took to the streets, and halfway through the sale process the Crown Estate acceded to their demands. Would-be purchasers such as property firm Grainger had been planning to push up rents and to sell homes as they became vacant. The Crown then suddenly insisted that the buyer of the thirteen hundred homes should retain for key workers all properties falling vacant. That decision drove away almost all eligible bidders, leaving only one that was big enough and reputable enough to be considered: the Peabody Trust, which paid £140 million – some £75 million less than Grainger had offered. It was not the Crown Estate's finest hour.

Bright had an otherwise blameless eleven-year innings. A man who preferred to listen rather than talk, he kept profits rising – quite an achievement, given that the country's biggest economic downturn since the Thirties happened on his watch. In 2002, the surplus handed to the Treasury was £163.3 million. This figure subsequently increased each year, hardly faltering, to reach £240 million in 2012. The target of £75 million a year in rental income from the Regent Street estate was met in 2007. By then the Crown had transformed the image of the street, with a series of major redevelopments behind the Edwardian facades.

In November 2004, Apple opened a huge store on the street. Dusty department store Dickins & Jones folded just over a year later, with Banana Republic then taking the rebuilt space. Trinket outlets near Piccadilly Circus were replaced by fashionable American brands. In 2006, the Crown Estate moved its offices from Carlton House Terrace into one of the redeveloped blocks near Oxford Circus. Meanwhile, an insalubrious spot north-east of Piccadilly Circus was radically transformed through the £300 million Quadrant redevelopment, completed in 2012.

In January 2011, a partnership was set up between the Crown Estate and the Norwegian state pension fund, Norges. It paid £452 million for a twenty-five percent stake in the Regent Street estate, confirming an overall valuation of £1.8 billion – precisely the figure that Sir Christopher Howes had predicted a dozen years before. The Crown Estate is not allowed to borrow money, and the burden of funding the £300 million Quadrant development at the back of Piccadilly Circus was a heavy one. The £452 million it received from Norges enabled it to fund further developments in Regent Street and St James's, as well as the nascent wind farms business.

But credit for these subsequent developments will go to Bright's bright and engaging successor, Alison Nimmo. She arrived fresh from the Olympic Delivery Authority on 1 January 2012, after a selection process that had trawled for candidates well outside the civil service. Her first year was marked by a renewed determination to proceed with long-laid plans to revitalise St James's by bringing in another outside partner. More importantly, it was a year unmarked by controversy – the litmus test for any Crown Estate chief executive.

Nimmo has been burdened with one more media cross to bear than her predecessors. From 2013, the civil list payments to the royal family are to be replaced by diverting fifteen percent of Crown Estate profits into the royal purse via the Treasury. Since 1989, when Sir Christopher Howes took over, Crown Estate profits have risen each year as reliably as the Queen has risen each morning. If they fall and the royal family suffers, the fuss will be enormous. But it is far more likely they will rise – for that is what they have done for a quarter of a century.

THE FOUR GREAT ESTATES

"Trustees of the great London estates serve one purpose for their beneficiaries," explains the chairman of one such – who had better remain nameless – "to prevent the current generation from squandering the capital in order that the next generation receive the same level of income enjoyed by the current generation." In other words, don't let the jammy so-and-sos fritter away their inheritance. The Grosvenor, Cadogan, Portman and Howard de Walden estates did a lot better than just preserve capital during the first decade-and-a-bit of the new millennium. Not that that's a difficult achievement if your estates cover six hundred acres of prime central London, where the 2007–2009 crash registered only as a shallow indentation on a steadily rising line.

Until 2000 it wasn't easy to estimate the collective wealth of the four "great estates" of London. But in that year, the Grosvenor estate produced detailed accounts for the first time, which helped the forensic-minded *EG* writer Alex Catalano produce a survey of each estate. Grosvenor's three hundred acres of Mayfair and Belgravia were altogether worth £2.2 billion. The ninety-three acres of Chelsea owned by the Cadogan family produced accounts showing a valuation of £1.2 billion. The Portman remained fey about the value of its hundred and ten acres situated above the western end of Oxford Street, but a guess of £300 million was made – a very low guess, it turned out. The same figure was put on the ninety-two acres owned by the Howard de Walden, which centres on Harley Street. Another low guess.

The combined value of the four estates at the turn of the millennium was thus an estimated £4 billion. By 2012 this had grown to £15.1 billion, thanks largely to rising residential values. The Duke of Westminster's wealth rose to £7.5 billion, according to the *EG* rich list; Earl Cadogan meanwhile saw his family's wealth jump to £3.9 billion. Viscount Portman and Baroness Howard de Walden both began to publish accounts in the early Noughties. In 2012, the value of the Portman estate stood at £1.3 billion and the Howard de Walden at £2.4 billion.

Debrett's ranks the Duke of Westminster above Earl Cadogan, in aristocratic terms. He in turn outranks Viscount Portman and Baroness Howard de Walden. This ranking also applies broadly to the value of their respective estates. Those junior to the duke run their estates on broadly similar themes: focusing on preservation of capital, with modest development and collection of rents. But the Grosvenor estate runs a financially transparent property company called simply Grosvenor. This business holds real estate around the globe, for which detailed accounts are published each year.

THE GROSVENOR

Gerald Grosvenor rarely fronts his own cocktail party, which is held annually in the estate's modern offices on Mayfair's Grosvenor Street. The sixth Duke of Westminster greets guests with a diffident handshake and a downward glance. Britain's richest man is not keen on the limelight, despite holding countless charitable and honorary positions. The list of these takes up half a column in *Who's Who*, and the bodies in question range from the Atlantic Salmon Trust to the North of England Zoological Society.

Included also on this list are organisations that support young people, farming and environmental work, as well as charities in aid of those with dyslexia, drug and alcohol problems, or rural stress. But the abiding interest of the duke – who is married, with three daughters and a son – is the army. Having first joined the Territorial Army at the age of twenty, he eventually retired some forty years later as its head, Major General Gerald Grosvenor, in September 2012.

The story of his family's fortune begins on 10th October 1677 in the church of St Clement Danes. Here, Mary Davies, the twelve-year-old heiress to land that is now Mayfair and Belgravia, married the twenty-one-year-old Sir Thomas Grosvenor, whose family seat since the 1440s had been Eaton Hall in Cheshire – today an estate of eleven thousand acres that remains home to the present duke and his family.

Young Mary had previously been engaged to marry Charles Berkeley, the first son of Baron Berkeley of Stratton, but the land that Berkeley was due to donate as part of the marriage contract was never forthcoming. He, of course, went on to give his name to Berkeley Square. Lady Mary and Sir Thomas had three sons: Richard, Thomas and Robert. She was declared insane just after her husband died in 1700, but lived on until 1730. Because of his mother's lunacy, Robert obtained an act of parliament in 1711 preserving the descent of the title to the male line.

Sir Thomas's son Richard started the development of Mayfair in 1720. The first Grosvenor to be elevated to dukedom was Hugh, who inherited in 1845 and died in 1869. His grandson, another Hugh, succeeded him in 1899 and lived until 1953, but left no sons. So William Grosvenor, a grandson of the first duke, Hugh, became duke number three. On his death in 1963, the title passed to Gerald (number four), who was succeeded by his younger brother, Robert (number five), father of the sixth duke – Gerald Grosvenor, who took the title in 1979 and is due to pass it to his son, Hugh, born in 1991.

The sixth duke is chairman of the trustees of the Grosvenor estate. The 2012 *EG* rich list estimated his Mayfair and Belgravia private assets at around £4.5 billion. That year the net assets of Grosvenor stood at £3 billion, taking the duke's wealth to £7.5 billion. A separate company going by the name of Wheatsheaf Investments manages the non-property holdings. It employs more than six hundred staff, of whom five hundred or so work on the duke's Eaton Estate in Cheshire, at a garden centre, or at the Chester Grosvenor hotel and spa. Wheatsheaf is wholly owned by the Grosvenor Trusts, which holds freehold interests in the "Hundred Acres" of Mayfair and the two hundred acres of the Belgravia estate.

"The operating companies plan over a five-year time frame, so Grosvenor does not lose the rigour that applies to any business," says group chief executive Mark Preston. The engaging and energetic Old Etonian took charge in 2008, aged forty, after a nineteen-year apprenticeship. "At the group level we look to a ten-year horizon. The shareholders meet every three years to examine the really long-term future – to see what might affect the estate in fifty years' time."

Grosvenor has three main areas of activity. Firstly, direct investment in property, in the UK, North America and Asia; known as the "direct proprietary assets". Secondly, putting its own money into funds being managed by Grosvenor and other property ventures; the "indirect proprietary assets". Thirdly, operating as a fund tending other people's money; fund management. "This diversification has served us well," says Preston of the strategy formed by his measured predecessor, Jeremy Newsum. In 2012, Grosvenor directly held £3.7 billion of assets, comprising £2.5 billion in the UK with the rest in North America and the Asia Pacific region. Indirect investment totalled £750 million, while funds under management amounted to £4 billion.

Finance director Nick Scarles explains the philosophy: "We are like a private equity house, except we invest in teams, not schemes. They make the on-the-ground investment decisions. You can't do that from London. We do provide lots of support to those teams, unlike the private equity world. But they are monitored. We also constrain their gearing. We buy to keep, not sell. They have an overriding objective to survive any crash." Preston adds: "That philosophy has kept us in North America. Look at how many Brits tried to do it PLC-style in the US. All have withdrawn. We are still there. We believe in letting individuals take responsibility."

The home-base business operates under the "Britain and Ireland" banner, despite doing little in Eire. By the early Noughties, Grosvenor was undertaking a number of retail developments up and down the UK, but, oddly, very little development in Mayfair and Belgravia. That changed halfway through the decade, a reversal influenced by two factors in particular. The first was a huge and embarrassing loss on a shopping centre in Liverpool: the second, the rapidly rising price of luxury flats in Mayfair and Belgravia.

The £1 billion Liverpool One development opened in time for the city that gave birth to the Beatles to celebrate its selection as European City of Culture in 2008. But there was a price to pay. A combination of too ambitious a deadline and a desire to meet the duke's wishes to rejuvenate Liverpool led to rushed planning and the assumption of all the risk by Grosvenor, rather than dividing it with funding partner Hermes. The result was a loss, first declared at £140 million in 2007, before rising to £364 million by 2008.

Jeremy Newsum admitted at the time that "there was a clear failure of the board to make the right decisions, as well as the failures of individuals". Most of these decisions were made at the end of the Nineties and in the early Noughties, as the plans for Liverpool One were being drawn up. This was a time when rivals saw Grosvenor as a bit sleepy, according to critics. "They are far too slow, far too cautious and far too nice" was a familiar refrain. In a 2007 interview, I asked Newsum – who was chief executive from 1989 until 2008 – to respond to this charge of niceness. His response? "Sometimes the word is thrown at us. People say we shouldn't be so polite. But we have a lot of respect for individuals."

One individual who took blame for Liverpool One was the company's Britain and Ireland chief executive, Stephen Musgrave. He left in 2006 to join US developer Hines in London. But his last act before leaving was to persuade a reluctant Grosvenor to enter into a joint venture with Native

Land to build nearly two hundred flats on the South Bank behind Tate Modern. The Neo Bankside scheme turned out to be very profitable, and this became one push factor in Grosvenor's switch away from retail and into London residential. The development appraisal in 2006 priced the flats at £700 per square foot; five years later, they were selling at twice that price. "If it were not for Stephen demanding that the board reverse their decision, Grosvenor would have forgone tens of millions in profit," says a friend.

Mark Preston, who came over from North America in June 2006 to replace Musgrave, used his first day as head of the UK division to announce radical management changes. These in effect gave more emphasis to residential development in London, under former management consultant Peter Vernon. In 2008, Preston was promoted to chief executive of Grosvenor, while Vernon got to run the UK. Large-scale town-centre retail schemes were gradually dropped, and the shift to building flats on the home estate was firmly established.

THE CADOGAN
Charles Gerald John Cadogan, born on 24th March 1937, would not be out of place at a Blandings Castle weekend party. He is every inch the old-school earl, an Old Etonian who became a junior Guards officer and rose to a high rank in the Masons, being appointed president in 1999. The eighth Earl Cadogan is a florid, blatantly un-PC character, one whom PG Woodhouse might have described as a "bluff sort of cove". He was wincingly wonderful to listen to at his biennial party, usually held at the Carlton Tower hotel in Cadogan Square. Views were expressed in public that would have best been kept private, let's just say.

In November 2010, the party was held instead at the Natural History Museum. Attendees gathered round a dinosaur skeleton to hear the earl reluctantly announce his coming retirement, likening himself to the extinct species towering over his guests. Sixteen months later, in March 2012, the earl held another party in the museum. Then aged seventy-five, he was finally handing over day-to-day supervision of the estate's ninety-three acres to Viscount Chelsea, his forty-five-year-old son.

The Cadogan estate has published accounts since the Sixties. Charles Cadogan officially took control in 1997 on the death of his father, the seventh earl, but he was running things for a long time before that. So it is possible to track the fortunes of the Cadogan under the watchful eye of the eighth earl. In 1999, the net assets were £750 million; by 2012 they had grown to reach £3.9 billion. On the way, the family and the Cadogan family charities took more than £150 million in dividends, with another £150 million gained by issuing bonds.

The man responsible for tending the estate from 1986 to 2008 was Stuart Corbyn, a charming character with a puckish sense of humour. He later went on to chair Qatari Diar Delancey, the joint venture that bought over fourteen hundred homes on the Olympic Village for rental to the public, but while at the Cadogan estate the big project under his watch was the redevelopment of the Duke of York's headquarters site, west of Sloane Square.

The scheme to build a mix of shops, offices and restaurants on the ten-and-a-half-acre plot began in earnest in 1999, when the Cadogan paid £90 million to acquire the site from the government. Before passing fully into government ownership during the nineteenth century, the site had in fact originally been leased from the Cadogan itself, for construction in 1800 of the grandly titled Royal Military Asylum for Children of the Regular Army.

The foundations of the Cadogan estate were established eighty-three years before that, in 1717. That was when Charles, the second Baron Cadogan, married Elizabeth Sloane, daughter of Sir Hans Sloane – an eminent physician and collector who had purchased the Manor of Chelsea five years earlier, planning to retire to the manor house of what was then a rural retreat. The house itself accommodated a collection that subsequently formed the basis of the British Museum. In 1737, Sir Hans added to his Chelsea estate with the purchase of Sir Thomas More's former home, Beaufort House, along with ten acres of land. He died in 1753 without male heirs, whereupon his estate was divided between Sloane's two daughters: the second Baron Cadogan's wife, Elizabeth, and her sister.

The first great burst of development at the Cadogan estate began in 1777, when architect Henry Holland was granted a lease for the development of Hans Town on fields between Knightsbridge and the King's Road. Holland created Sloane Street, Hans Place and later Sloane Square, designing the street layout, building houses and selling speculative building rights on the development. In 1821, the whole of the Manor of Chelsea was reunited under Cadogan ownership, the lucky Cadogan family being the closest surviving relatives to the offspring of Sir Hans Sloane's other daughter.

A second flurry of development occurred during the era of the fifth Earl Cadogan (1840–1915), and this is when much of the modern estate was formed: Sloane Square Station was opened in 1868; the riverside embankment was completed in 1874. Many long leases were then expiring on sites ripe for redevelopment, so between 1877 and 1900 much of the rest of the estate was rebuilt too. Development then remained in relative abeyance for the next fifty or sixty years, with one notable exception being the construction in 1936 of the Peter Jones department store on the corner of Sloane Square and the King's Road.

Then the spirit of the Sixties infected an estate that stood at the heart of that era. What the Cadogan itself now admits as a "massive glass and concrete Stalinesque dream" was planned for a huge area to the north of Sloane Square. The square was to be transformed by a shopping precinct and a twenty-six-storey residential block, linked by pedestrian bridges to all sides of the square. Sloane Street was to be filled by concrete-and-glass offices and flats, with pedestrian walkways crisscrossing the entire length of the street. Lower Sloane Street was to host a new residential square boasting a tower thirty-three storeys in height, while Pont Street was to be rebuilt with a further tower block and some small mews houses. The whole scheme would take forty years to complete. "Thankfully, it was rejected by the planning authorities," says the Cadogan.

Indeed it was, but only after a public outcry. Which brings us to the least appetising side of life for those otherwise lucky enough to live on one of the four great London estates: the tooth-and-nail resistance to laws allowing those holding long leases to buy their freehold. To a greater or lesser degree, all four estates detest handing over freeholds. But they are forced to do so under enfranchisement laws first introduced in 1967, then reinforced in the mid Seventies and again in 1996 and 2002. These allow leaseholders to buy the freehold of a property, for an amount relating to the projected value of the property when the lease would have run out – perhaps in eighty years' time – discounted back to current-day prices.

Sounds simple? A book twice as long as this one could be written on the complexities, which bring a steady income for an entire sub-set of the legal profession. Much of these lawyers' income derives from the four great London estates, as they struggle with those determined to buy their freeholds under circumstances not quite foreseen under the acts. Case after case has come to court over the decades. Most are boring. But one that reached the Supreme Court in 2012 is worth a mention.

The Duke of Westminster, Earl Cadogan, Viscount Portman and Baroness Howard de Walden all faced the break-up of their estates if the action was lost. So much was at stake that they quietly bankrolled the affected freeholder. Three former homes owned by Hugo Day and Lady Hilary Day off the Old Brompton Road in west London were leased to Hosebay, a company which had set up a short-lease apartment business in the houses.

The competing arguments in *Day v Hosebay* were roughly as follows. Hosebay: "If it looks like a house and smells like a house, well, sorry, it is a house – even though it might now be in use as an office or hotel. If it is a house, we have the right to buy it forcibly from the freeholder." Day: "It might look like a house and even smell like a house. But it is being used for business purposes. It is therefore not a house. You cannot forcibly buy the freehold. Go away." Hosebay won in the Court of Appeal in 2010, under a judgement reached "with no particular enthusiasm" by the Master of the Rolls, Lord Neuberger, who went on to preside over the Supreme Court.

So there was some worry when the arguments were heard again in the Supreme Court in July 2012: would the seven judges who had examined the case agree with their new boss, or not? At 9.45am on the morning of Wednesday 10th October, representatives of the great estates gathered in court number two to hear the news delivered by Lord Carnwath, a man worth a quick mention. Sir Robert Carnwath (as he was then) was a regular attendee at the *EG* legal advisory board dinners.

A more gracious, intelligent and attentive man would be hard to find. Lord Carnwath delivered good news to the great estates: he and his fellow judges had concluded that if a property is being used for commercial purposes then it "does not constitute a house for the purposes of the 1967 Act". In other words, it might look like a house, even smell like a house. But unless it is being used as a house it is not, in law, a house.

THE PORTMAN

The tenth Viscount Portman is a spare but seemingly genial man, who appears regularly at the annual Portman party held at Hertford House in Manchester Square, home of the Wallace Collection. Here hangs Frans Hals's best-known painting, *The Laughing Cavalier*. Hertford House is one of the few properties in the area not owned by the Portman Estate; the freehold was sold in 1898. Christopher Portman, who was born in 1958, has three sons from two marriages, the heir among these being Luke, born in 1984. Dad confesses to non-aristocratic interests such as molecular nanotechnology and paragliding; at the 2012 party he was sporting non-aristocratic stubble.

Christopher Portman took the viscountcy in 1999 at the age of forty-one, on the death of his clarinet-playing father, Edward, at home on the Caribbean island of Antigua at the age of sixty-five. The tenth viscount radically changed the way the estate was managed. Cluttons had acted as the external management agent from time immemorial, but the job was now brought in-house (and a member of the Clutton family was later brought into the in-house management team too).

The Portman Estate was farmland in 1532 when Sir William Portman, Lord Chief Justice to King Henry VIII, acquired the land. He apparently wanted the farm as a source of goat's milk for his ailing wife. At that time, the estate stretched from Oxford Street as far north as St John's Wood, covering two hundred and seventy acres. In the early eighteenth century, Oxford Street was still the rural Tyburn Road. A building boom followed the Peace of Paris treaty signed in 1763 by Britain, France and Spain after seven years of war. London began to spread northwards from Oxford Street. Sir William's descendant Henry William Portman had already begun to develop his London estate in 1755, and by 1785 Portman Square was completed.

By 1948, when the eighth viscount succeeded, the estate was the second-largest in London, covering a hundred and ninety acres, including four squares: Portman, Manchester, Bryanston and Montagu. The northern part of the estate, around eighty acres, was sold in 1951–1952 by the eighth viscount to meet the £7.6 million death duties on his predecessor's passing. Once the debt was cleared, in 1955, the estate was resettled into a family trust. During the post-war property boom, the Portman joined forces with one of the era's famous developers, Max Rayne. Lord Rayne assisted in the redevelopment of most of the estate's Oxford Street frontage and parts of Portman Square

At the turn of the twenty-first century, the Portman's hundred and ten acres to the north of Oxford Street ran from Marble Arch in the west to Orchard Street and Duke Street in the east, reaching north almost to Crawford Street, just three blocks down from the Marylebone Road. After taking over in 1999, Christopher Portman hired the estate's first ever managing director: Hugh Seaborn, a highly regarded investment agent at Richard Ellis St Quintin. He quietly modernised the way the Portman did business. Around £40 million was spent creating the Portman Village retail scheme just north of Marble Arch Tube Station. Seaborn oversaw a rise in the value of the estate from £300 million to £1.2 billion during his very effective eight-year stewardship. He moved over (and upwards) to run the Cadogan in 2008.

Seaborn's successor at the Portman was Gareth Clutton. This tall and elegant member of the Clutton dynasty was given to wearing yellow braces under chalk-striped suits. He was easily identifiable, striding round the estate in a long, black overcoat and matching fedora. At the Portman party held in the run-up to Christmas 2010 he was on good form, but weeks later was diagnosed with a virulent form of cancer and died shortly afterwards, aged just fifty-one. With his passing on 28th May 2011 went too the last family tie to a firm founded by his forefather, William Clutton, in 1765. Former DTZ chairman Richard Lay was chairman of the Portman when Clutton died. "He had that extraordinary quality of making everyone whom he met the better for the experience," said Lay. Former army general Bill Moore was appointed to the post of chief executive at the end of 2011.

THE HOWARD DE WALDEN

In April 2008, Lady Howard de Walden, along with her three sisters, Susan, Jessica and Camilla, and fifty or so other beneficiaries of the Howard de Walden estate, were paid a £150 million dividend. The 2008 dividend was justified by a £140 million upward property revaluation of just fourteen of the estate's assets. The payout was funded by a loan from RBS and Lloyds. Two years later, the estate raised £100 million by selling twelve, fifteen and twenty-year bonds to pay down those loans and fund future developments.

Well, why not? The four-hundred-year-old estate today holds ninety-two acres of land centred on Marylebone High Street and Harley Street. Much of the uplift came after a decade of investment in Marylebone High Street, turning a dull thoroughfare into a lively shopping street. Credit for that goes to property director Simon Baynham and his boss Andrew Ashenden, who retired in March 2006 at the age of sixty-one after thirteen low-key years in charge.

His successor was Toby Shannon, previously the estate's finance director – also a fairly low-key character, but one who oversaw a rise in rental income from £51 million in 2006 to £80 million in the year to March 2012. A drive to improve the Harley Street holdings and the development of a cancer centre of seventy thousand square feet allowed Shannon to increase rents by twenty-eight percent in the area. Rents on seven hundred flats also rose by twenty-eight percent over those six years. The £29 million rise in rents helped drive up the asset value of the Howard de Walden from £1.5 billion before the 2007–2009 crash to £2.4 billion by 2012. Crash? What crash?

The Howard de Waldens came into their estate through marriage, a century ago. The lineage goes back to the Duke of Newcastle, the Duke of Portland and the Earl of Oxford. It was the latter pair who started developing the land. Most of the streets are named after these families, their titles and estates: Harley, Cavendish, Holles, Portland, Welbeck and Wimpole. When John Holles, Duke of Newcastle, paid £17,500 for the southern part of the estate in 1708, it was still largely unbuilt. This was in the then village of Mary-le-Bourne on the fringe of London proper. Three years later, it passed to Holles' daughter Henrietta, who married the Earl of Oxford, Edward Harley. He embarked on an ambitious development plan.

The architect John Prince was commissioned to draw up plans for fashionable housing. The masterplan placed Cavendish Square as the focal point in a grid of streets, bounded by Oxford Street to the south. But by the time of Harley's death in 1734, relatively little had been built. His daughter Margaret inherited. She had married "the handsomest man in England", the Duke of Portland, and his family went on to hold the estate for five generations. In 1879, the estate passed to Lucy Joan Bentinck, widow of the sixth Baron Howard de Walden, and hence became the Howard de Walden estate.

The ninth Baron Howard de Walden inherited the title and estates in 1946, when he was thirty-four. The historic claim to fame for John Osmael Scott-Ellis, as he was then called, was a car accident: one that could have changed the fate of the world. In 1931, at the age of nineteen, the Eton-educated lad moved to Munich, where he bought a car. On his first day behind the wheel he knocked over a pedestrian called Adolf Hitler, although (a fact as obvious as it is unfortunate) not fatally. He married a countess in 1934, with whom he had the previously mentioned four daughters. Life was given over to breeding horses and the Turf. The ninth baron died in 1999, aged eighty-six. Ownership of the estate is now divided between his four daughters and their families.

Like the other great estates, the Howard de Walden remained almost immune to the 2007–2009 downturn. In the year to March 2012, profit rose by three percent to reach £41 million, and the value of the estate's eight hundred and fifty buildings rose to £2.4 billion from £2.1 billion. The key to those valuation increases is of course the level of rental income, because it is a multiple of that income that determines value. In 2011/12, annual rents rose by ten percent to £80 million. The secret behind the riches of the great estates lies in the ability to increase rental income. This can only be done by continually improving the stock and not selling. Remember what the chairman of one said? The prime purpose is "to prevent the current generation from squandering the capital in order that the next generation receive the same level of income enjoyed by the current generation". All four have successfully managed to do just that.

THE NOT QUITE SO GREAT, BUT ONLY NEW ESTATE

Paul Raymond died in March 2008, aged eighty-two. The Porn King, as he is indelibly labelled, had in the course of forty years built up a private property empire in Soho worth nearly £400 million. In his latter years, Raymond was rarely seen outside his penthouse flat behind the Ritz, and rumours were heard of a long-haired recluse drinking a bottle of brandy a day. No one except his close family really knows about the final years of the only man to build so large a private estate in London for hundreds of years.

What is known for certain, however, is that in the last dozen or so years of his life, Raymond rarely visited the offices of his company, Soho Estates. The business was run by his nephew, Mark Quinn, along with John James, the husband of Raymond's daughter, Debbie. She died in 1992 of a drug overdose. Her daughters, Fawn and India Rose, inherited the estate. Raymond's estranged son, Howard, was eventually gifted twenty percent of the estate's properties after a legal struggle.

John James moved quietly to open up Soho Estates and improve the stock after his father-in-law died in 2008. I first met him in late 2011 at a breakfast at the Ritz organised by the Duke of Edinburgh's Award. He was a bit chary of this ostensibly middle-class charity, whose property industry fund-raising group I chaired. But he wanted to do something for young people in Soho, and the duke's charity offered to help. One year on, the affable and open Northerner was to be seen sitting next to the Earl of Wessex at the Duke of Edinburgh's Award property breakfast in an overheated room at the Dorchester. It was an odd sight as the pair from such different backgrounds chatted politely.

I had a chat with James after that 2012 charity breakfast. He had spent £100 million consolidating Soho Estates' holdings since 2008. There were plans to spend £100 million more on development projects, including a one-acre site centred on Foyle's bookshop. I asked him what defined the strategy of Soho Estates. His answer could have come straight from one of the owners of the original four great estates: "We're not going anywhere, and I am going to concentrate on improving our holdings in Soho."

I once received a letter from Raymond himself. *EG* had suggested that Soho Estates had purchased the leasehold of an office block. "I own the freehold," wrote Raymond in the one-line letter. "Please print a correction." What Raymond did not say was that he had bought the block for cash. Just before he died, Soho Estates had no debts and was sitting on an impressive £35 million in the bank.

Leisure agent David Coffer knew Raymond. He tells the tale of visiting the Raymond penthouse to discuss a deal, then being shown a collection of Thirties art and memorabilia. Part of that collection was a small, hardwood box containing a canteen of solid silver cutlery, in which each knife, fork and spoon was engraved with the initials "A.H.". Coffer was asked to guess what these stood for, and was then told they were the initials of the man Baron Howard de Walden had failed to kill when he knocked him over in his car: Adolf Hitler. The probable fakes were left unsold at auction, after Raymond's venture to set up a war museum had failed, says James.

ENCORE

CHAPTER THIRTEEN
AFTERMATH

Experience is the one thing you can't get for nothing
Oscar Wilde

'IT MUSTN'T HAPPEN AGAIN'

In the first week of April 2013, the deputy governor of the Bank of England, Paul Tucker, confessed that "this country learned the hard way about banking boom and bust.... It mustn't happen again." He said that a whole set of new controls had now been put in place to prevent repetition of the 2007–2009 crash, adding: "No system is perfect, and it will eventually be found wanting.... But I think it's fit for purpose for now."

The discredited Financial Services Authority was scrapped on 1st April 2013. The Bank of England took control of supervision, setting up a Prudential Regulation Authority to watch the big banks, while a Financial Conduct Authority to regulate City behaviour was born from the ashes of the FSA – an organisation that "was not so much a dog that did not bark, as a dog barking up the wrong tree", according to a damning parliamentary banking commission.

The commission, which was led by Conservative MP Andrew Tyrie, produced a report on the HBOS lending debacle in the same week that Tucker uttered his reassurances. The account flayed HBOS, revealing that the bank was forced to write off £45.8 billion of bad debt between 2008 and 2011. Business secretary Vince Cable called for further inquiries into the conduct of former chief executive Sir James Crosby, as well as that of his successor, Andy Hornby, and chairman Lord ("Dennis") Stevenson – all of whom had left by 2008.

The head of corporate lending at HBOS, Peter Cummings, had been fined £500,000 and banned from the City the previous autumn by the Financial Services Authority. Cummings had complained to the banking commission at the time (see chapter three) that "the fact that I am the only individual from HBOS to face investigation defies belief".

The two-volume Tyrie report, entitled *An Accident Waiting to Happen: The Failure of HBOS*, squarely blames risky property lending for the collapse of the bank, saying: "Its losses were on a larger proportionate scale than those incurred by any other major UK bank. This was caused specifically by its distinctive loan book, including concentration in commercial real estate." One distinctive feature of the bank's lending was its entering into deals wherein it provided debt to companies it part-owned – not a good idea, felt the commission.

It concluded: "In addition to the dominance of property-based investment, there were other characteristics of HBOS corporate lending which contributed to its subsequent demise," namely: "a close relationship between its conventional business loans, particularly in the property sector, and the provision of equity and leveraged loans, so customers were offered 'a complete funding package'."

These "total funding packages" added up to £4.9 billion at their peak. Debt and equity deals were done with companies such as McCarthy & Stone, Crest Nicholson, CALA Properties and Thornfield Properties. The Tyrie commission picked out a concern alluded to by Ian Marcus in chapter three: "There is a different skill set required to manage and analyse debt/credit exposure versus equity risk," points out the former head of real estate banking at Credit Suisse.

UNAVOIDABLE CONFLICTS

An RBS banker I spoke to privately in 2008 put the issue in plainer terms, saying of HBOS's methods: "We were never allowed to do that. There is an unavoidable conflict of interest when things go wrong. The side of the bank that lent the money just wants it back, but the guys who took the equity stake want to hang on and hope it gets better." HBOS did more than hang on. "The acceleration of loan growth, in part, caused by... neglect of the storm signals of 2007 and 2008, is likely to have exacerbated the scale of the subsequent losses," says the report.

"The roots of all these mistakes can be traced back to a culture of perilously high risk lending," it concludes, noting that by the end of 2008 HBOS "had a high degree of exposure to property", totalling some £68 billion – or fifty-six percent of the bank's entire loan book. "The picture that emerges is of a corporate bank that found it hard to say no," sums up the commission. Two former senior members of the bank each reached different conclusions, however.

Lord Stevenson, who was part-time chairman between 2001 and 2008, told Tyrie, "You cannot look at those provisions and not be horrified and appalled... but the extent to which they were affected by the closure of wholesale markets and the extent to which there was incompetence is a very real question, which I do not have the ability to measure. But please, please, please, I am not trying to avoid the finger saying that we over-lent in corporate, because we did."

Sir James Crosby, chief executive from 2001 and 2006, was a little less appalled. He conceded to Tyrie that lending practices had been "incompetent", but added: "We always believed and my colleagues in the corporate bank always believed that they had a good understanding of the risks they were taking and we in aggregate as a bank had no evidence to the contrary." But he did in the end show penitence by offering up his knighthood and one-third of his £700,000-a-year pension.

OUT OF A DEEP DARK HOLE...

As the market hit bottom in June 2009, the IPD index of capital values for offices sat at 100 – seven points below where it had stood in 1997. Values did rise by fourteen percent between mid 2009 and December 2010. But they remained languishing at that same level at the end of 2012.

Retail values bounced back by nearly twenty percent by the end of 2010 – then slipped down a little by the end of 2012, to give a fifteen percent rise over those three-and-a-half years. Much the same happened to industrial values, which had risen just seven percent by the end of 2012.

In the spring of 2013, the De Montfort loan survey for the whole of 2012 painted a still grim picture. The level of debt held against assets with loan-to-value ratios of a hundred and one percent or more stood at £45 billion – twenty-three percent of the outstanding UK bank debt of £197.9 billion. Add in debt attributed to Irish "bad bank" NAMA and £38 billion of outstanding commercial mortgage backed securities, and total property debt stood at £268 billion at the end of 2012, said the university.

Rents fell over those forty-two months from June 2009 to December 2012. Retail rents sank most sharply, down seven percent, hit by closure after closure of chain stores. Industrial rents were down five percent, knocked back by a languishing economy. But office rents remained flat, propped up by leases obliging occupiers to pay the same rent for five years or more.

The property crash left the FTSE standing at 3,500 in July 2009; by the end of that year it had jumped back up to 5,500. From then until late 2012, it zigzagged up and down, reaching 5,600 in mid November 2012 before nosing up to 6,000 by the end of the year. By mid April 2013, the index had edged higher, to 6,300.

SLOWLY INTO THE SUNLIGHT?

April 2013 opened cold. The freezing weather of March spilled over an early Easter and into the first two weeks of April. Baroness Thatcher died, aged eighty-seven, on Monday 8th April. The Iron Lady had positively encouraged the development of Canary Wharf when prime minister and had attended the groundbreaking ceremony at the huge Broadgate development in the City on 31st July 1985. "We are drawing back the curtain of the future," had said the then Mrs T (see chapter six).

The remark came in a speech to those gathered in a tent pitched by developers Godfrey Bradman and (now Sir) Stuart Lipton on what was then open ground. Her closing remark in that 1985 speech is also worth remembering, if only as a suitable maxim for property developers everywhere: "That which thy fathers bequeath thee, earn it anew if thou wouldst possess it." Lady Thatcher's funeral took place at St Paul's Cathedral on 17th April 2013. By then the weather was warming, at long last.

A detectable thaw could also by then be felt in the property market. A few weeks earlier, in Cannes at the MIPIM property show, the atmosphere was fairly subdued. But one thing had changed. It was summed up by a fleeting conversation I had with Chris Ireland of Jones Lang LaSalle, the former joint senior partner at King Sturge, and it went something like this: "Last year at MIPIM, developers were chasing lenders. This year, lenders are chasing developers." Agent Cushman & Wakefield produced a survey in March 2013 showing that the number of those willing to lend on projects across Europe had increased by twenty-nine percent in twelve months.

Jane Roberts, editor of *Real Estate Capital,* had sensed it first. In early February, the former deputy editor of *EG* wrote of a "gradually improving picture" in a column for *EG.* I was persuaded by a flurry of lettings in the City to write the first positive property story in the *Evening Standard* for a long while during the first week of April.

One particular letting attracted my attention: PR company FTI had signed a deal that week to rent eighty thousand square feet at 200 Aldersgate, a seventeen-storey monster that sits at the western end of London Wall. The former offices of Clifford Chance had lain mostly empty for a decade, after the solicitors moved to Canary Wharf. A previous attempt to attract clients with an extensive refurbishment had failed, so the banks hired developer Helical Bar and spent another £9 million brightening up the offices.

I was tipped that FTI was going to take two floors in the three-hundred-and-seventy-thousand-square-foot building. Crikey. That meant the oh-so-slowly filling block would be nearly full, three years since refurb number two had finished. I rang the queen of property PR at FTI, Sue Brown. "Can this be true, Sue?" I asked. Sure enough, it was. So I talked to veteran agent Colin Hargreaves, who puts in an appearance in chapter one.

Back in September 1997, Hargreaves, who was then at Healey & Baker, told *EG* that occupiers had begun "fighting for space". It's not quite like that in April 2013, says Hargreaves, now at Gryphon Property Partners, but "there are early signs the City lettings market is picking up. We are approaching a tipping point." I, for one, am not going to predict which way things will tip. Instead, let us end with a series of reflections worth recalling next time the market tips down, in 20xx.

REFLECTIONS

SIR JOHN RITBLAT, FORMER CHAIRMAN OF BRITISH LAND:

The recession came about with the failure of banks to manage their affairs in an orderly way. They were caught with their pants down on a tidal wave of bad lending. But bad lending was not only on commercial real estate; it was on domestic real estate. HBOS did lend a lot of money, granted. But it was mostly on residential or speculative development. Lending money on garden centres, lending money for huge developments that were long-term, long-tail businesses. That's where most of the trouble stemmed from. The crash came about because of the irresponsible lending in the US to people who could not afford to pay back their mortgages. A licence to print money for the commission agents, who raked off huge sums up-front from the house sales and then on the mortgages.

I think most analysts have a lot to answer for, in that their horizon is so short and they are extreme in their short-term views. They do the industry a serious disservice. It means some chief executives and chairmen find themselves being governed by short-term performance. They lack the resoluteness the longer-term player has. Management is often impugned unreasonably and then succumbs to the siren blandishments of analysts asking for short-term performance. I think that has been very damaging. You only make money with long-term investment. That I can tell you; disprove it if you can.

GERALD RONSON, CHIEF EXECUTIVE OF HERON INTERNATIONAL:

The government should take a major responsibility in all this. It was in the government's interest for the banks to be pouring money into the economy, because you have a feelgood factor – and everybody did feel good, because everybody was out there spending. I'm talking now about the man in the street: new plasma-screen TV, new three-piece suite, whatever – spending money. Of course you're going to vote for that government that has given you that ability in terms of buying the things that you like or want because the economy's booming away.

That was the deepest recession the property business has experienced since 1929. I might be old, but I wasn't around then. I was around in 1939; that's when I appeared on the scene. A lot of people are very good at selling themselves. But when it comes to sorting out big, complicated and problematical deals, there are not hundreds of people in the business who are capable of doing that.

I think there are people who have survived. The main thing is not to believe what you read in the rich lists. I know a lot of people that wish they were worth half of what they say they're worth.

FRANCIS SALWAY, FORMER CHIEF EXECUTIVE OF LAND SECURITIES:

I think the lesson to be learned is that if values rise in a short period of time by twenty to thirty percent, that should ring alarm bells. You should then double-test every assumption, even if the forecasters are saying values are going to continue to rise. You have to be prepared to act defensively in the face of critical commentary from others – "What are you doing selling when there's growth around you?" You have to say, "Well, I'm delighted to have had thirty percent capital growth. But I'm now going to manage the business on the basis of a more cautious outlook. After all, I've already had thirty percent upside."

JAMES DARKINS, MD OF GLOBAL PROPERTY AT HENDERSON GLOBAL INVESTORS:

We have one of the best research teams in the business. So the question is how did we get it so wrong, because we were the most accurate of the forecasters during the boom period. We got it wrong because the market was pushing ahead consistently, way beyond our models. What was driving that? Sheer weight of capital: the way research teams are run, using the usual drivers of economic growth, make it very hard to factor in the weight of capital.

NICK THOMLINSON, SENIOR PARTNER AT KNIGHT FRANK 2004–2013:

It always starts with banks. Every fifteen years there's a new set of people in corporate finance who weren't around the last time. By then, the lessons have been forgotten. Even those people who were around are driven by the bonus culture.

ALASTAIR HUGHES, CHIEF EXECUTIVE FOR THE ASIA PACIFIC AT JONES LANG LASALLE:

When do you know when the market is going loopy? For there will be a next time. What are the signals to watch for? If investment agents are drinking champagne and leasing agents are drinking beer, get the hell out because it means the investment market has lost sight of the fundamental truth that property needs occupiers paying the rent. Talk to the investment agents. If they say the market is infused with bankers, talking a language that even smart, well-educated property people don't understand, get out.

ALAN CARTER, INVESTEC:

Companies just surfed all the way up the increasing asset values during the boom. They thought the increasing value of their businesses was down to them. Not true. The market created it. Not all, but the majority of it was artificial, and non-cash – just the value of the properties going up.

Because prices fell so rapidly, CEOs were not able to sell their property. Of course the first cut is the cheapest in those circumstances.

We ended up with some bizarre situations, where companies actually ended up selling assets not just below book value, but also below original cost. Now that is a damning insight.

Most are now focusing on earnings. That's what has changed. Slowly, slowly, these companies are being weaned off the idea of increasing asset values – a strategy which, I hasten to add, has been supported by corporate advisers and bankers and analysts over the years. But investment has to be about income.

With real estate, you have large illiquid assets that you have to remember to sell – and you have to sell before it gets to the top. You have to leave something for the next man. The directors always say they do this, but I would dispute that the evidence will support the claim that they are good sellers. They are not.

IAN COULL, FORMER CHIEF EXECUTIVE OF SEGRO:

I am a devotee of Adam Smith's theory of economics, and no matter how much we promise ourselves we will learn the lessons and not repeat them, the reality is that a new generation comes along very quickly with lots of ideas, lots of ways of making money, and we get back into the same cycle once again. Whether it's a five, ten or fifteen year cycle I don't know, but there will undoubtedly be a crash in property values again at some point over that next fifteen years. Don't ever put yourself in a position where you think it is just going to go up all the way, otherwise...

INDEX

Y

Z